CRAFT AND THE KINGLY IDEAL

Craft and the Kingly Ideal

ART, TRADE, AND POWER

Mary W. Helms

UNIVERSITY OF TEXAS PRESS   AUSTIN

Requests for permission to reproduce material from this work should be sent to
Permissions, University of Texas Press, Box 7819, Austin, TX 78713-7819.

∞ The paper used in this publication meets the minimum requirements of American
National Standard for Information Sciences—Permanence of Paper for Printed
Library Materials, ANSI Z39.48-1984.

Library of Congress Cataloging-in-Publication Data

Helms, Mary W.
    Craft and the kingly ideal : art, trade, and power / Mary W. Helms. — 1st ed.
      p. cm.
    Includes bibliographical references and index.
    ISBN: 978-0-292-73078-6

    1. Political anthropology. 2. Commerce—History. 3. Workmanship.
4. Exchange. 5. Quality of products I. Title.
GN492.2.H46 1993
306.3—dc20   92-26296

. . . the world
Goes round in the climates of the mind
And bears its floraisons of imagery.

—WALLACE STEVENS

"The Sail of Ulysses" (*Opus Posthumous*,
ed. Samuel French Morse [New York:
Alfred A. Knopf, 1957], p. 102)

Contents

Preface

Within the context of my own research, *Craft and the Kingly Ideal* continues a line of thought that was raised but not pursued in a previous work, *Ulysses' Sail.* In that volume I examined concepts and interpretations accorded to geographical distance and distant locales in the political and ideological worlds of non-industrial societies. In *Craft and the Kingly Ideal* I focus on the political and ideological symbolism accorded to tangible things acquired from such "outside" places.

In pursuing this theme I suggest that acquisition of valued goods from afar is comparable in intent and practice to various expressions of skilled artistry. Both types of endeavors are transformational activities directed to effecting energizing links between society and a broader cosmological realm "out there." As such, these activities are also of fundamental concern to political leaders. Considerable discussion is accorded, therefore, to links among the pursuit of political legitimacy, skilled crafting, and long-distance contacts and acquisition.

Like its predecessor, this volume is based on library research and is broadly cross-cultural in scope. I fully realize that to focus (again) on something identified simply as "traditional society" is to cast a very broad net, indeed. I hope that the frequent use of more specific ethnographical and ethnohistorical materials indicative of the data base on which the broader analysis rests will provide some sense of the diversity underlying interpretive generalities.

It has been said that bright ideas are rather like young St. Bernards in that they get into everything, their size and energy are spectacular, and they tend to run off with their handlers. Several colleagues in particular helped me curb the beasts by offering guidance and advice. Thanks are due particularly to Jane Schneider and Richard Anderson, both of whom read an earlier draft of a rather lengthy manuscript and offered sound and very helpful critiques. I greatly appreciate their generosity. I am grateful, too, to the reviewers for the University of Texas Press both for their judicious and level-headed suggestions and for their appreciation of what I am trying to accomplish in these pages. I also wish to acknowledge the research leave-of-absence granted to me by the University of North Carolina at Greensboro for the fall semester of 1989, during which time the manuscript was written. Special thanks are due to the always helpful and courteous staff of the Interlibrary Loan Division of Jackson Library who literally brought the ethnographic world to my finger tips.

Finally, a work of this sort rests entirely on the rich corpus of anthropological observations that has accumulated over the last century. Consequently, my greatest debt of thanks is due to the many researchers and authors whose intriguing accounts not only offered engrossing reading but also provided the basic data and numerous insights for this study.

CRAFT AND THE KINGLY IDEAL

1   *Introduction to the Problem*

Prelude

In the beginning, after the great creator deity, Enlil, had separated earth from heaven and fashioned plants and animals and humans, he benevolently ruled the world, from the Tigris in the East to the Euphrates in the West, from his throne in the splendid temple at Nippur. Enlil then appointed a god of wisdom, Enki, to superintend the great land of Sumer through which gold and silver were to flow in ships to his temple at Nippur. Great, too, were the deeds of Enki and many also were his gifts to man, for he taught agriculture and herding, and built granaries and filled them with grains and fruits. He also molded square bricks from the clay of the rivers and taught craftsmen how to construct walls and lofty cities adorned with precious cedarwood and lapis lazuli.

The greatest city of Sumer was Uruk, long famed for the deeds of its great king, Gilgamesh, mighty hunter of lions and wild bulls, peerless wrestler, and dauntless leader in war. "When the gods created Gilgamesh they gave him a perfect body. Shamash the glorious sun endowed him with beauty, Adad the god of the storm endowed him with courage, the great gods made his beauty perfect, surpassing all others. Two thirds they made him god and one third man. In Uruk he built walls, a great rampart, and the

temple of blessed Eanna for the god of the firmament
Anu, and for Ishtar the goddess of love. Look at it still
today: the outer wall where the cornice runs, it shines
with the brilliance of copper; and the inner wall, it has no
equal. . . ." (Sandars 1964:59).

Eventually Gilgamesh turned his thoughts to his own
destiny, and, realizing that he was partly mortal, wished to
perform a great deed so that his name might be remembered. He determined to undertake a long journey to the
Land of Cedars, an immense forest at the rim of the world
belonging to the sun god, Shamash, but guarded by a fero-
cious giant. Going to his smiths, Gilgamesh ordered his artisans to fashion axes and great swords, bows and quivers.

Accompanied by his close companion, Enkidu, Gilgamesh then journeyed to the gate of the forest, beautifully
crafted of cedar by craftsmen from the holy city of Nippur—so beautiful, in fact, that Enkidu did not try to destroy it with his axe but only opened it to pass through.
Once within they gazed at the mountain of cedars, the
dwelling-place of the gods and the throne of Ishtar. Aided
by Shamash, the sun god, Gilgamesh began to fell the
trees, cutting and binding the fragrant branches and laying
them at the foot of the mountain. Seven times he felled a
cedar, and each time the giant, the guardian of the forest,
attacked him but was repulsed, and, eventually, killed. Gilgamesh was then free to cut timbers for the temples of
Uruk, and at length returned to the city (Sandars 1964:
68–82; Goodrich 1960:9–19).

The Activities of Gilgamesh

It is appropriate for a study which will include (among other things) consideration of kings and culture heroes, and the significance of acts of
skilled crafting and of acquisition, to begin with a portion of the Epic of
Gilgamesh because this adventure conjoins a series of thematic associations that I propose to pursue in more detail in the following chapters
using ethnographic rather than mythic data. As revealed in the Epic, these
include (in order of their appearance in the portion of the myth summarized) skills of craftsmanship taught to artisans by a divine and wise

culture hero, kingship associated with hunting, beauty, and perfection (aesthetics); kingship associated with smithing and other skilled crafts; kingship associated with distant power-filled sacred places that carry ancestral or godly connotations; and the acquisition, from this outside world, of valued resources beneficial for society at home and that will also enhance kingly fame, glory, and authority.

Stated in such a random fashion these diverse themes appear rather unrelated. Yet it is the purpose of this essay to argue that an associational logic does interweave these themes into a coherent and meaningful pattern, whose elucidation may be anthropologically significant. To introduce the basic design I shall begin with the acquisition, by elites of traditional, non-industrial societies, of valuable resources from distant or "outside" locales, for that is the pattern segment which is least understood within the context I wish to apply and which ultimately lies at the heart of this study.

In professional literature, the peaceful acquisition of valuable resources from regions outside a home society generally has been referred to as long-distance trade or as a type of exchange. Although many of the mechanisms and conditions underlying such trade are well understood, several critical components of the overall context within which long-distance activities have been conducted in traditional settings have been largely ignored. One of these components involves the political and ideological symbolism attributed to geographically distant peoples, places, and things in non-Western native cosmologies. As I have argued at length in a previous work (Helms 1988), members of traditional societies do not interpret geographical distance in neutral terms. Instead they accord a range of symbolically charged meanings to distance-related phenomena, generally viewing them as inherently superior or inferior, dangerous, or superlatively beneficial to the home society. Another extremely important, indeed vital, component of long-distance trade directly related to, and contained within, the first that has not been considered in much depth, either, involves the symbolism and ideology associated with the material goods derived from geographically distant places by various mechanisms of long-distance trade (Hodder 1982:205, 206–209; Earle 1982:82). It is this topic that I wish to address in this study. I do so by exploring several related issues which appear to be comparable to and associated with the acquisition of long-distance goods from afar.

Acquisition of long-distance goods generally falls either directly or indirectly under the auspices of specific individuals, usually of exceptional personal prestige and political influence, whom I will simply label as persons of influence or "elites." (It should be noted that the latter term will be used in a very relative manner since I include illustrative material from non-centralized and non-hierarchically organized societies as well as from centralized and hierarchically organized ones.) By obtaining such goods from afar, persons of influence, or elites, are involved in symbolically charged acts of both acquisition and transformation by which resources originating from locales outside society are obtained and brought inside society where they may be materially altered and/or symbolically reinterpreted or transformed to meet particular political-ideological requirements.

It is my contention that acts of acquisition and transformation of such trade goods are comparable in general context and cultural meaning to acts and arts of skilled crafting (considered for the moment in general terms) which in traditional societies are also frequently associated with influential elites or prestigious public positions. To be sure, scholarly recognition of the association of both craft specialization and involvement in long-distance trade with politically influential persons is hardly new. Generally, emphasis has been placed on elite sponsorship or control over craft production of prestige goods and over foreign commerce or exchange. Not infrequently, crafted prestige goods are used as a means to enhance such exchange, the ultimate goal being the manipulation and distribution of wealth so as to integrate and enhance political power (Brumfiel and Earle 1987:3–4, 8). Basically, I am working within this "political model" of specialization and exchange (ibid.), but from a different perspective.

I wish to shift emphasis from the material things crafted or exchanged to the symbolism behind the production and the acquisition of such tangible goods. I seek the elite association with crafting and long-distance trade not in materialistic or utilitarian terms but in terms of qualities or values (Giddens 1984:258–262). In addition, I see parallels between the qualities, values, or symbolic meanings attributed to acts of skilled crafting and those attributed to long-distance acquisition. I view both areas of endeavor as acts of skilled practitioners, who are themselves accorded certain qualities and statuses for their capabilities. I further assert that the values or symbolic meanings attributed independently to each of these types of activity are fundamentally the same, and that it is this equivalence in qualities and symbolic significance that associates political leadership with crafting and with long-distance acquisition, either individually or in combination.

It is also important to note that I employ the category of "craft" very broadly so as to include not only production of material goods (including such as might be useful in trade) by carving, painting, sculpting, weaving, smithing, and masonry but also a number of other skilled abilities, including singing and instrumental musicianship, oratory and the activities of bards and poets, and dance, as well as hunting and navigation. I argue that, like long-distance acquisition, all these diverse types of skilled crafting involve the initial acquisition of some form of materials from realms geographically or symbolically outside society or "civilization," followed by their transformation into socially significant goods or public services that, again like long-distance goods, are frequently associated with elite activities. (This argument would also hold for raids, warfare, and the booty derived therefrom, but I chose, somewhat arbitrarily, to omit warfare from this study.)

I will explore the premise that skilled crafting and acquisition of long-distance goods constitute a "package" of comparable activities with comparable meanings, qualities, or values attributed to them, their products, and their practitioners. I am curious as to why these *particular* activities may be identified ethnographically as areas conferring influence or prestige as, for example, among the Mekranoti of Brazil, where "hunting, handicrafts, body painting [which I am considering a type of craft], warfare, trade with outsiders" as well as shamanism confer prestige and political influence (Werner 1981 : 364–365).[1] I also wish to go beyond the usual and obvious explanations that these activities produce symbolically and politically valued material wealth. I believe this exercise may be particularly helpful in focusing not only on the qualities associated with elites as acquirers of foreign goods but also on the types of inter-societal (or at least inter-elite) relationships expressed in long-distance trade, as well as on the meaning of the goods obtained. With respect to the latter point, understanding what qualities and values may be generally associated with the concept of skilled crafting may facilitate our appreciation of the significance of both crafted and uncrafted goods obtained from distant places. By extension, it may be expected that the relationship between polities involved in long-distance trade will be differentially expressed by their importation of crafted as opposed to natural goods, or vice versa.

It is within this broad setting that the activities of Gilgamesh, the perfectly formed leader and hunter, builder of temples and city, traveler to distant sacred places, and acquirer of precious foreign goods may be more fully understood, and that the comparable activities of real-life leaders of traditional societies, world-wide, may be further appreciated.

Professional Perspectives

In contrasting skilled crafting with long-distance trade I am juxtaposing data that have commonly been dispersed among diverse analytical categories, including aesthetics, symbolism, and economics, as well as political ideology and political economy. In particular, aesthetics and symbolism on the one hand and economics on the other not only are usually set well apart but also are frequently considered antithetical, perhaps reflecting the prejudice noted by Titus Burckhardt whereby "modern" scholars place art and science into radically different domains because the former is perceived as individualistic, psychological, or sentimental rather than as dealing with physically verifiable facts interpreted with a particular type of reasoning (1987:13–15).

To be sure, making things, crafting, either as a universal cultural characteristic or human capability or as a reflection of increased societal division of labor, may seem inherently "economic." In this study, however, I join with those who consider crafting in a different context, one that is cosmological in orientation. In addition, I am concerned not with crafting writ large but with crafting expressed as specialized skills that generally serve non-utilitarian purposes, are imbued *by definition* with qualities of aesthetics, and are closely associated with political-ideological activities and symbolism (Goldman 1970:477). I am proposing that the same descriptive definition of *non-utilitarian purposes, imbued with qualities of aesthetics, and close association with political-ideology* would also fit acts of long-distance acquisition within the essentially cosmological context I wish to explore.

The common ground I seek between acts of skilled crafting and acts of long-distance acquisition requires, first of all, that categories such as art, symbolism, economics, and politics be eschewed in favor of a different set of analytical classifications—a set that recognizes universal cosmological and sociological principles not only linking every society with a world, a cosmos, beyond itself but also differentiating between a world or worlds "outside" ordered society and the world "inside" ordered society. As numerous ethnographies make clear, this dichotomy can be described with any of a large number of contrastive characteristics and qualities, all of which are shaped by fundamental assertions that the social world within involves that which is immediate—here and now or everyday—in spatial/temporal contexts, is known and understood and in that sense is ordinary and mundane or common, and is morally and politically more or less controlled or ordered, "cultured" or "civilized." Conversely, the world outside society is that which is distant—farther away in time/space, less known and therefore extraordinary and exotic, less controlled or uncontrolled (chaotic, wild, uncivilized), and unordered or ordered in a different fashion (e.g., as the world of ancestors or of evil spirits). Yet "outside" and "inside" are closely interrelated in that native cosmologies regularly assert that realms outside are the ultimate source of the basic raw materials, intangible "energies," original knowledge, and original ancestral creators and culture heroes that ultimately allow for the production of human life and social living inside and without which the world inside could not continue.

In traditional cosmologies, "outside" may be conceived in many ways. A sense of fixed boundaries is not necessarily implied. Rather, the "outside" may be perceived as a series of zones or as a generalized "field" reaching beyond a center. It may be focused on particular sacred places (caves, waterfalls, mountain tops, the ocean), directions (sunrise-sunset, upriver-downriver), or axes (vertical or above/below, horizontal or geographical). Generally, outside is where, when things are normal and society is functioning properly, bad things are banished to and good things are acquired from. I wish to deal with particular types of the latter. I also wish to focus heavily on physically and geographically (horizontally) situated axes, directions, or places "out there," though the qualities that define these more tangible or material outside realms usually are qualities directly related or comparable to those of intangible and non-material distant realms. This correspondence rests essentially on the hypothesis that geographical distance is frequently thought to correspond with supernatural distance, such that as one moves away from the social center geographically one moves toward places and people that are increasingly "different" and, therefore, regarded as increasingly supernatural, mythical, and powerful. More specifically, we will see that consideration of the qualities of things derived from geographically distant places may involve association with qualities and entities such as ancestors or culture heroes, whose more familiar traditional locus "out there" is vertically above (or sometimes below) the center (Helms 1988).

Broadly speaking, I envision a generalized cosmology for traditional societies, regardless of mode of social or political organizational form or complexity, in which the here-and-now of an organized, morally informed, "cultured" social entity at the center is surrounded on *all* sides and *all* dimensions by an outside cosmological realm which is believed to contain all manner of visible, invisible, and exceptional qualities, "energies," beings, and resources, some harmful, some helpful to those at the

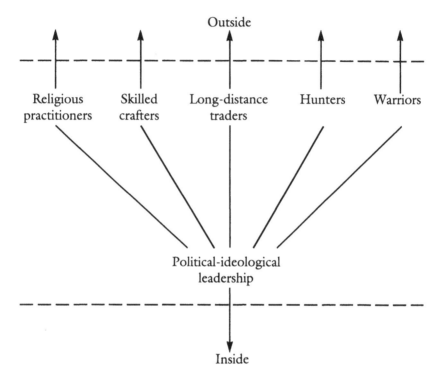

1-1.   Categories of outside specialists.

center. We are well acquainted with characteristics of some of these outside realms as they have been explored, controlled, transformed, and exploited by traditional religious practitioners—shamans, priests, diviners, curers, midwives, etc. I will view skilled crafting and acquisition of long-distance goods as comparable to these activities in the sense, or to the extent, that they also involve contact with some aspect of the outside realm by specialists whose activities mark them, too, as exceptional or liminal individuals by virtue of their involvement with the extraordinary outside world (Figure 1-1).

Commonality is shared further in the sense that, as with traditional religious activities, the results of contacts with the extraordinary, supernatural world by acts of skilled crafting and long-distance trade involve the creation or acquisition of things that are in some manner beneficial either to society at large or to the political-ideological leadership. Much scholarly attention has been given to the manner, mechanisms, and motives by which long-distance "luxury" goods or wealth items or the products produced by skilled craftwork may be distributed or consumed inside society; the consequences of such distributions when applied to the furtherance of personal political ambitions or to the dynamics of various social and political alignments have also been appraised (Brumfiel and Earle 1987). In this study I am not concerned with what is done internally with the things produced or acquired from outside realms. My interest lies primarily in the significance attributed to the types of activities involved in this production and/or acquisition and on the qualities and characteristics associated with the practitioners of these skills. I am less concerned with the particulars of the exercise of relations of power within society and more concerned with certain aspects of the accumulation of "power" that must precede that exercise, particularly with the acquisition of certain accoutrements necessary for the accumulation of this "power."

In order to regard power not as something to be exercised or as a relational condition but as a "thing" or "quality" to be acquired or accumulated, power must be understood not as an analytical term or an abstract concept but as something real and concrete; as something that simply "is," independent of wealth or weaponry or anything else. This perspective has been articulated very clearly by Benedict Anderson with particular reference to Javanese political thought, but his basic points are equally appropriate to the cross-cultural perspective of this study. In Anderson's words, "Power exists, independent of its possible users. It is not a theoretical postulate but an existential reality. Power is that intangible, mysterious, and divine energy which animates the universe. It is manifested in every aspect of the natural world, in stones, trees, clouds, and fire, but is expressed quintessentially in the central mystery of life, the process of generation and regeneration" (1972:7).

In the following chapters I propose that one of the fundamental qualities attributed to and shared by both skilled crafting and long-distance acquisition is the belief that these types of activities provide similar and comparable means to channel and direct this constant energy for human use by creating or acquiring goods that concentrate or preserve this energy in their tangible form. That is, not only do crafted goods and foreign-derived goods encapsulate power from that portion of the universe lying outside society, but the very acts of skilled crafting and of long-distance acquisition are important precisely because they channel and concentrate such energy. Consequently, the individuals who do this crafting or who acquire such goods become associated with, perhaps filled with, this same power, as do those who come to possess such goods and surround themselves with such extraordinary objects (B. Anderson 1972:10, 12).

Crafted goods and foreign goods, acts of skilled crafting and of long-distance acquisition "materialize a way of experiencing, bring a particular cast of mind out into the world of objects" and of actions (Geertz 1983:99). In so doing they also define and make tangible exceptional qualities believed either to be assumed by or to be inherent in those who, by virtue of exceptional abilities, make possible acts of crafting and long-distance acquisition in the first place. Let us identify and explore these qualities and abilities as they are manifested first in acts of skilled crafting and then by acts of long-distance acquisition.

PART I

SKILLED CRAFTING

2   *What Skilled Crafting Means*

> One also understands why the novices make themselves new
> clothes from the fibers of a wild palm growing in the forest, near
> a stream; they are purely and simply reinventing craftsmanship,
> the major expression of culture.   —LUC DE HEUSCH
> *The Drunken King*, p. 120

Qualities of Skilled Crafting

"Humans display the intriguing characteristic of making and using objects. The things with which people interact are not simply tools for survival, or for making survival easier and more comfortable. Things embody
goals, make skills manifest, and shape the identities of their users. Man is
not only *homo sapiens* or *homo ludens,* he is also *homo faber,* the maker and
user of objects, his self to a large extent a reflection of things with which
he interacts" (Csikszentmihalyi and Rochberg-Halton 1981:1).

In the following pages a selection of these goals, identities, and skills
gleaned from the ethnographic record will be discussed in order to illu-
minate the significance of a select category of crafting acts in traditional
societies. Because my ultimate goal is to cast light upon a very particular
type of "craft"—the acquisition of things from far away—the crafts that I
will discuss do not reflect the entire range of human object-making capabilities. Instead I focus on those that, like long-distance acquisition, are
usually reserved for, controlled by, or associated with persons of influence
and that require particular personal crafting skills or are associated with
status identification as artisans.

To distinguish these select activities from the everyday domestic or ordinary production of things I use the term *skilled* crafting in reference to
the former. While fully appreciating that much "ordinary" craft production is also distinguished by exceptional quality, and requires high technical skills and considerable knowledge of the symbolism frequently expressed by design and style, nonetheless I wish to explore aspects of a

more distinctive or specific set of skilled activities: those types of crafting that are noteworthy precisely because they are associated with politically influential individuals and political leaders. "Woodcarvers, potters, and smiths might produce for the palace on special days and recognize that their labour was of a different quality from normal" (Rowlands 1987:61).

Yet, while restricting the arena of relevant craft activities to those associated with a particular context, I wish to broaden the range of relevant craft activities beyond the production of material things referred to in the opening quote from Csikszentmihalyi and Rochberg-Halton. Therefore, I apply the concept of skilled crafting not only to the creation of material things but also to a number of other skilled activities that produce comparable elite-related "states or forms of meaning," including oratory, song, dance, instrumental musicianship, and navigation.

Skilled crafting associated with positions of social and political prominence differs in several important respects from craft associated with more mundane spheres of life. These differences also express basic contrasts between the political and ideological significance of ordinary individuals and that accorded politically and publically prominent persons and people closely associated with them, such as skilled artisans and long-distance traders.

Skilled crafting associated with public political figures is itself public rather than private. Skilled crafting of this sort is also non-utilitarian and non-pragmatic, being ideological in meaning and moral or honorable in quality rather than being strictly materially or economically useful (Gluckman 1965:279–280). Stated another way, skilled crafting is metaphoric and ritualistic in significance rather than literal or inconsequential.[1] Skilled crafting for political-ideological leaders is also grander and more ostentatious than ordinary; it is an explicit and substantial index of the intangible prestige, worth, and valor of the leadership itself (Aijmer 1984a; 1984b). Skilled crafting of this sort helps to *over*-communicate the characteristics of political status and roles as opposed to crafting that has no or little status-related significance.[2]

Finally, skilled crafting, as a value-laden activity expressive of certain emotive qualities in traditional non-industrial societies, is quite distinct from manufacturing, especially as understood in industrial societies. This contrast, which may occur in any society where both valuables and commodities are produced, is based on very different interpretations of what is happening when people make things. In distinguishing between skilled crafting and manufacturing, between the "true" potter and the man who merely works at making pots, I have found Eric Havelock's interpretation of certain aspects of Plato's treatise, the *Republic,* particularly useful. Havelock's discussion focuses particularly on the tenth and last book of the *Republic,* in which Plato offers a scathing examination of the nature of poetry; not just bad poetry or extravagant poetry, but poetry, the bedrock of Greek literature, as a vehicle of communication and especially of the learning that lay at the core of being an effective citizen (1963:27).

Plato argues that the traditional Greek poet produced a view of experience that was dangerously unrealistic, distorted, and truth-concealing. Poetry became a means of creating a world with words, meter, rhythm, and harmony, which concealed reality behind a false, cosmetic outward appearance. For Plato, the poet as creator "with his range, his catholicity, his command of the human emotional register, his intensity and sincerity, and his power to say things only he can say and reveal things in ourselves that only he can reveal" posed a moral and intellectual danger, especially as part of the educational process (ibid.:6; see also Diamond 1960:128–133). Plato condemned a seemingly artificially created reality produced by skilled artisans (in this case artists who work with words), in preference for the absolute recognition of a rational, logical reality that truly exists and whose form is made manifest by being *copied* in material or artifact form by skilled technicians who see themselves as totally separate from and unrelated to what they are working on (Havelock 1963, particularly pp. 25–26, 159).

Plato's discontent with traditional poetry and his preference for a different reality help to clarify certain differences between a more traditional way of interpreting the cosmos and man's place therein and a more industrial or scientific view of the same. The role of Plato's poet and of other artisans skilled in a number of traditional crafts is to act as mediator, transformer, and/or creator standing between two parts of what is viewed as a common whole: on the one hand, the human cultural realm and, on the other, a wider outside realm identified by intangible energetics that must be tapped and transformed via the artisan's various skills into cultural formats that encode qualities identified with whatever is thought to constitute true humanness (for example, the qualities of heroics in Greek traditional poetry). True humanness is then seen to partake of, reach back towards, or link humanity with the dynamics of the wider whole.

In contrast to this perspective stands the industrialized world view in which the cultural world is a separate entity clearly distinct from the world outside, which is rationally understood and embued with physical prop-

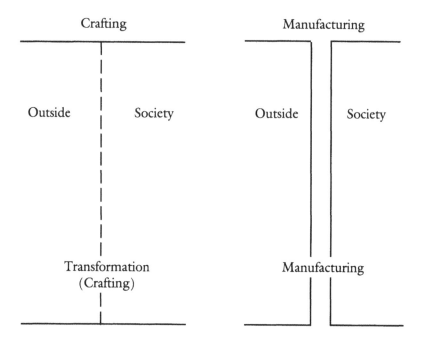

2-1. Relations between society and the outside in crafting and in manufacturing.

erties alone. The latter provides raw materials to be formed into types of cultural goods that are not considered to be connected with the realm without (Figure 2–1). Things manufactured in this way are not viewed as transformations but as wholly new things. They do not relate or connect those who acquire them or those who make them with the original outside realm in any qualitative manner. To the extent they define humanness it is as a state of being totally separate and distinct from the wider realm. As a result, manufacturing is materialistic, technical, routine, impersonal, and oriented toward the continuous production, in series, of goods as end; in a word, it is economic. It is also conducted entirely by application of self-contained and exact mechanical formulas based on physical properties (Havelock 1963:45, 47).

Skilled crafting, in contrast, is political and ideological rather than economic in nature. It is more personalistic and finite, meaning that it is focused on particular individual objects. It is also more event-related, embedded in specific publically significant and value-laden acts or events. It is basically conducted by the ritually defined manipulation of intangible forces aided by application of personal qualities and skills believed to be themselves derived from outside forces or beings. It is oriented toward elucidating, via the tangible qualities of things produced, the intangible qualities of individuals or of interpersonal, inter-group, or inter-realm associations. M. M. Austin and P. Vidal-Naquet, referring to changes occurring in Classical Athens, note that compared with the archaic period, artisans seemed to have lost some of their prestige as "manufacture became separated from magic, but lost in the process something of its value and was demoted to the level of a routine" (1977:108, 162). Or, as Ralph Linton phrased it with reference to Marquesan culture, "A food bowl made without the proper magic ritual would be just a bowl. It would have no real place in the universe and consequently no value" (1939:146; Reina and Hill 1978:236–237).

Given these contrasts, why should Plato (or for that matter we ourselves) attempt to judge Greek poetry in the same manner as science or mathematics or technology? The answer for Plato lay in the importance of poetry as a traditional repository of knowledge, "a sort of encyclopedia of ethics, politics, history and technology" that comprised a citizen's education. The traditional poets, Plato complained, in effect were culture heroes and seers or soothsayers, thought to "possess the know-how of all techniques and all human affairs pertaining to vice and virtue, not to mention divine matters" (Havelock 1963:28, 30). In Plato's view such a Homeric educational manual presented only illusions and therefore was false, but for many native societies, skilled crafting as exemplar, or at least metaphor, for knowledge and as vehicle for moral guidance and understanding of divine affairs is true (see Diamond 1960:134–136).

By extension, skilled artisans and/or the elite patrons for whom they may work also become vehicles or spokespersons not only for technical knowledge but especially for moral qualities and for the supernaturally or ancestrally sanctioned ethics, political-ideology, and myth-history of the polity. Moreover, by their own acts of skilled crafting, artisans and their patrons also actively maintain the vital links believed to connect the polity and its people with the supernatural energetics of the outside world that sustain them. Skilled crafters become present-day transformers and culture hero creators. Their acts of crafting compress the original creations and transformations recorded in myth and legend into still existing actions, maintaining a direct, living connection between the temporal/spatial here-and-now of the cultural setting and the there-and-then of outside dimensions that relate the present to the past by the metaphor of distance.[3]

Crafting as Transformation

Given fundamental processes of crafting in general, it is no surprise to find such activities explicitly associated with concepts of transformation and creation in traditional societies. Transformation is most forcefully or un-avoidably expressed in, and frequently metaphorically associated with, the highly obvious changes in physical state readily observable in certain fab-rication processes. Such changes are unequivocally evidenced when loose fibers are spun into thread and then woven into cloth; when ceramic pieces, shaped from pliable clay, are hardened by firing; and, perhaps most dramatically of all, when raw ores are transformed into molten metal and then reformed and tempered into solid objects. The virtually universal dis-tribution of spinning and weaving, pottery making, or metallurgy may reflect this propensity for dramatic transformational changes in physical state and the symbolism that can then be built upon these changes, as much as it reflects the undeniable utility of the goods produced by such skills (León-Portilla 1963:173; Wellenkamp 1988:324; Klein 1982:1, 11).

Other types of crafting may show more subtle, though no less signifi-cant, changes in state, as when scribes make physically visible with colored ink or paint the words of the ancestors and other learned men on paper, wood, and parchment; when people's movements are converted into the stylized rhythms of dance; when the routine sounds of work-a-day discur-sive speech are transmuted into oratory, chant, and song, and the prag-matic modes of everyday expression transformed into poetic formulae; and when the routine noises of nature are changed into music (León-Portilla 1963:172; Bloch 1974:58–59, 72).

The fundamental transformative and creative nature of crafting is fre-quently expressed in explicit parallels drawn between crafting and human procreation. Warren L. d'Azevedo tells how a Gola woodcarver of western Liberia, who carved masks for use in women's secret societies, expressed a sense of intense fulfillment when he saw his masks "come to life" in cere-mony: "I say, I have made this. How can a man make such a thing? It is a fearfull thing I can do. No other man can do it unless he has the right knowledge. No woman can do it. I feel I have borne children" (1973a:148). In the swampy river world of the Asmat of New Guinea, where trees lit-erally give life by providing food, resources for fire, home building, weap-ons, and means for transportation, and where man and tree are mutually exchangeable concepts, the sculptor who carves ancestral figures from wood is equated with the woman who bears human life and supports that life with sago, the product of trees (Gerbrands 1967:29; Hatcher 1985:215). In the Marquesas, sculptoral creation paralleled human procreation in the sense that finished sculptures were considered to be separate beings, off-spring of artists and their tools (Linton in Elisofon 1958:11).[4]

Before proceeding further it is essential to be very clear about the mean-ing associated with acts of crafting as "creation" in the traditional contexts referred to here and throughout this book. The term is not meant in the familiar Western sense applied to art, when creative artistic skills produce that which is unique or original or unprecedented or highly individualistic or idiosyncratic. Rather, creation as an aspect of traditional crafting refers to elucidating or illuminating the understanding of things, to making manifest things and ideas already existing in another state, or to the ar-ranging and rearranging of traditional patterns and elements into stylisti-cally distinctive but recognizable forms. In other words, creativity in tra-ditional societies refers not to individual artistic uniqueness but to the ordering of nature for cultural purposes. Creation both in crafting and in the wider world of human affairs relates to the transformational process, and refers basically to the sense of moving or communicating between qualitatively different cosmological realms, between an outside or less fully human or cultured state of being and an inside or more fully human or cultured world or state of being (R. Anderson 1990:247–249).

Given this association, some act of crafting or the products of crafting are likely to be a necessary component of any situation involving a concep-tual context of transformation or creation, whether these activities involve members of society in association with Nature pure and simple, as in child-birth or agricultural activities, whether they involve one category of social membership in relation to another, as when the uninitiated become initi-ated, or whether they distinguish one category of human qualities relative to another, as when the ordinary is distinguished from the sublime or "ideal," as discussed in Chapter 4. Acts of crafting, themselves acts of transformation, facilitate these broader transformational contexts by em-phasizing various aspects of that context. By acts of crafting the outside may be activated as a source of things beneficial to society, as a place whence valuables may be derived; by acts of crafting the interface between inside and outside realms may be highlighted; and by acts of crafting the conjoining of inside and outside realms or a cycling between realms may be expressed.

Acts of crafting associated with the outside realm as source of beneficial

things are found wherever (as among Australian Aborigines) painting of
totemic designs and accompanying chants are thought to increase food
accessibility or singing aids the success of the hunt (Mountford 1961:
12–13; see also Forge 1967:82). Since the natural world provides much
more than food, qualities of a different sort have often been identified in
a wide range of inedible things, too. Woods, shells, and precious stones
may be judged rich in various potencies and qualitative attributes, just as
ores are widely believed to contain special powers. Such powers, potencies, and attributes may be encapsulated for human use when implements,
ornaments, or regalia are crafted from these materials (Eliade 1962:27–30;
Addison 1908:78; Childe 1951:93; Duby 1974:52).

The types of things derived from the outside realm and transformed by
crafting into socially beneficial resources need not always involve tangible
objects. "In pre-Islamic Arabia it was thought that the *jinn* and the spirit
world could be called up by music . . . Both the pagan musicians and the
poets, who were also soothsayers 'hummed and chanted their oracles and
verses'" (Anderson 1971:146).[5] Similarly, the natural resource of time is
recognized by Küchler as a vital element in the production of carved wood
Malangan sculptures in New Ireland. Not only does the act of carving
itself involve a reformulation of time as the carver completely changes all
the normal temporal aspects of his being, using daylight and dark in different ways and repatterning periods of wakefulness and sleep while he
works, but, in addition, the image he is carving represents the objectifica-
tion of time as memory, for the patterns and variations of motifs expressed
in Malangan sculptures are "a product of a process of transformation that
occurs in the recall of imagery for reimbodiment in a gift object . . ."
(Küchler 1988:626, 631).

Faced with an outside realm with somewhat different attributes, the
people of the Upper Sepik in New Guinea craft imitations with local materials of valued European material goods (rifles, airplanes, canned goods)
in order to magically acquire the riches and wealth of Europeans (Abramson 1976:264–265). Similarly, a century ago foreign travelers in the country of the Yao in east central Africa noted that Arabic dress and the Swahili
architectural style of coastal trading towns was imitated in Yao communities. In fact, the entire character of several Yao towns was crafted to imitate
the coast: Chief Mataka "moved and built a village at Mloi; there he
planted mangoes from the Coast which grew, sprouted, and flourished.
He was delighted and said, 'Ah! now I have changed Yao so that it resem-
bles the coast, and the sweet fruits of the coast now will I eat in my own
home. . . .'" (Alpers 1969:419). In another town the populace "built dhows

copied from those of the Arabs; also they planted coconuts with the object of making the lake shore resemble the coast" (ibid.).

Of course, another way to obtain distant resources from outside is to craft a means to reach them directly and bring them home. For the island-dwelling Gawa of Papua New Guinea, like many other islanders, access to desirable outside things requires crafting of canoes, itself a skilled act by which natural trees are transformed into useful cultural artifacts. Nancy Munn further relates the materials and procedural steps involved in crafting canoes to qualities associated with various cosmological zones comprising the physical world outside the village. Thus, while the land provides trees for canoes, the final crafting is done on the beach, a trans-formative, medial zone between the land and the sea from which, by means of canoes as supernaturally energized conveyances (see Chapter 4), additional desirable goods are obtained from outside islands (Munn 1977: 41, 51).

This form of mediation has counterparts in a number of other settings where crafting emphasizes the interface between inside and outside cos-mological realms. Particularly interesting are situations where artisans' tools (like Gawa canoes) are accorded special consideration as interfacing artifacts. "Special power dwells in the smith's hammer, as the chief bearer of all the spiritual force of his profession . . ." "[The hammer] bears a high magical charge and is dangerous for all" (Cline 1937: 115, 116 re the Wa-Chagga of east Africa). "The hammer, the bellows and the anvil are re-vealed to be animate miraculous objects. They were regarded as capable of operating by their own magico-religious force, unassisted by the smith" (Eliade 1962: 29).

The same qualities may be attributed to wood carvers' tools that, like the tools of the smith, do not just reflect the crafter's ability but directly help to actualize those skills (Csikszentmihalyi and Rochberg-Halton 1981: 26–27). Adrian A. Gerbrands, speaking of Ivory Coast peoples, sum-marizes an earlier report by Vandenhoute: "In so far as the tools are used for making masks they have a pronounced sacral character. The mask is a supernatural being, and the tools play an important, creative part in its formation. Under these conditions it is natural that a certain potentiality is thought to lie in the tools, capable of greatly influencing not only the success of the work, but the health of the artist. Hence the tools are treated with the greatest care, offerings are brought them, and they may not be shown to women or uninitiated persons . . . , or the work will miscarry, or great evil will come on the unauthorized persons who saw it" (1971: 369; 1957: 70–80).

Polynesian sculptors formalized and virtually apotheosized carvers' tools as "animate, intelligent beings and conscious collaborators in the act of creation" (Linton, quoted in Chipp 1971:153). In so doing they also paralleled the nobility of fine tools with chiefly nobility, an association which we might reverse to relate noble chiefs with fine tools, that is, with the creative power of skilled crafting. Chapter 5 will elaborate further implications behind an equation of the quality of chiefship with the quality of crafting. A sense of that equation in Polynesia is given here: "[Tools] acquired great prestige for fine work in the same way as did the carver himself, and some tribes evolved lengthy genealogies for their favorite tools. This practice was most common in those areas of Polynesia where genealogy was most important to the nobility and the chiefs; indeed, the veneration of fine tools occupied an analogous place in the material culture. . . . the Marquesan carvers often chanted to their tools the line of descent of the distinguished tool ancestors that had produced excellent work" (Chipp 1971:153; cf. Linton in Elisofon 1958:11).[6]

In keeping with a broad definition of crafting, it should be noted that mystically charged crafting tools that form an interface between the outside and home society can take a number of forms. For example, the Abelam not only consider painting to be a sacred and dangerous activity but also regard paint itself as either inherently magical or as a medium by which magical benefit is transmitted to persons. Thus, during boys' initiation ceremonies, the paint from figures and panels representing ancestral spirits is made to rub off onto the bodies of initiates (Forge 1962:16, 13; 1967:75). A comparable initiatory result is obtained with musical instruments by the Barasana of the Vaupes region of Northwest Amazonia, whose interfacing artifacts are flutes and trumpets. These instruments, especially when activated by breath, not only are regarded as living mediators between the human realm of the village and the outside world of spirit life but, when blown, become living ancestors through their sounds. Blowing these instruments over initiates thereby imparts ancestral life-giving breath to the young boys, changing them into strong adults (Hugh-Jones 1979:147, 151, 159).

Singing serves as an interfacing tool, too. Among Altaic shamans songs were sung by assistants during trance to help the shaman journeying in the other world to overcome or transform (control) obstacles: "By the power of songs we cross it" (Rothenberg 1985:491). This example reflects the common belief that the words of a song have considerable creative power since they not only can help or harm but also can create things. This is so because words are the magical formula, the secret, the origins by which things can be made to appear (Eliade 1962:101–102; Rees and Rees 1961:137).

Finally, skilled crafting not only activates outside resources for human benefit and highlights the interface between society and its outside realms but also actively conjoins these inside and outside worlds. This type of transformative activity, though common to many, perhaps all acts of crafting, is perhaps most frequently commented upon with respect to music which, as Seeger reminds us, "in a great many places is said to come from beyond the mind and beyond the body—from the natural order as it is differently conceived by different peoples. This gives music a pre-ordained, transcendent, and often unquestionable reality" (1987:64; see also Hugh-Jones 1979:157–159). This point is well illustrated by Seeger's own investigation of why the Suyá (northern Mato Grosso, Brazil) sing.

> Suyá created space, time, and the person, as well as introduced and controlled the power of transformations through their singing. Song was thus an important way of (re-)establishing the cosmos in its 'correct' order. Singing and ceremonies brought many aspects of the cosmos into direct personal experience. Songs attested to the continued interaction of humans and animals through specialists who heard natural species sing and could teach people their songs. Songs made the events recounted in the myths real to every member of the society. Myths described transformations; in ceremonies people experienced them. (Seeger 1987:132; Rees and Rees 1961:137)

Song and dance, as well as crafted material things, also frequently conjoin the realm of humans with that of ancestors or comparable spirit beings, as Irving Goldman's explanation of the Winter Ceremony of the Kwakiutl aptly illustrates:

> The dance presents the spirit characters in their characteristic motor forms, supplementing the masks which portray physical form. The songs reveal the essential nature of the beings, and the names establish their genre. In addition, there are ornaments and instruments . . . each item is a vital (perhaps a soul) component of the being who is represented. The mission of the human community seems to be to assemble all separate components and thus to create, or rather to reconstitute among themselves, the spirit beings who would otherwise lack a human connection. . . . In the spirit of mutuality of interchange, the human community grants life to the spirit beings who in turn are to grant life-preserving powers to them. (Goldman 1975:116)[7]

Crafting and Creation

Acts of crafting that create visible representations of the conjunction of inside-outside cosmological realms are usually interpreted as acts that re-create the cosmological order originally formed and established by creator gods who, by their formative acts of world and human creation, are often mythologically described as artisans. It is useful to review briefly some of these godly acts of creative craftsmanship not only because they so clearly link crafting with the outside realm but also because of strong associations between creator gods and culture heroes on the one hand and human arti-sans and persons of influence on the other. Some of these associations will be further developed in later chapters and will inform the discussion of both the qualities of skilled crafters and the significance of long-distance activities. Here a summary of creative cosmic crafting by primordial deities can provide an apt conclusion to our overview of crafting as transformation.

Creator gods used a wide variety of skilled crafts to fashion the world and the first humans; virtually all the major categories of skilled craft-ing are represented. At the dawn of time in Laos, the elderly paternal grandfather and paternal grandmother, charged with the task of forming the earth from the primeval waters, "created the world by stamping on the water." Their dance made the land emerge (Aijmer 1979:736, 738). The four Pawnee creator gods used the power of song (the power of dynamic sound), to activate the steps leading to the creation of the material earth (Murie 1981:44, 49). The Fang of Gabon (West Africa) believed that the gods forged the first human from a variety of natural materials as humans now forge iron. Zame, the creator god, made a bellows and a hole in the earth (a smelting pit), and took fire from the sun. He gathered together a ball of earth and shaped it; a drop of blood and a bit of white brain sub-stance ("intellect") were placed in the earthen body. The earth was placed in the fire, the bellows were pumped, and the earth heated red hot. This glowing mass was then taken out of the fire and cracked open to release the first human (Fernandez 1982:328–329).

Woodcarving and drumming created the earth and human life among the Asmat of New Guinea. According to one myth, Fumeripits, a mytho-logical culture hero, drowned in a river and the current carried his body out to sea. Eventually it was washed up on a coastal sandbank where War, the white-tailed eagle, was able to bring the hero back to life by pressing smouldering pieces of wood against various parts of his body. The reborn Fumeripits then constructed a great ceremonial house and carved a large number of wooden figures of men and women. When the house was filled with these figures Fumeripits began to drum, and the wooden figures gradually came to life (Gerbrands 1967:33, 35).

In one of the best described original creation sequences involving the concept of crafting, the primeval Maker and Modeler and the Bearers and Begetters of the original Quiché Maya world, faced with an empty, lifeless earth, began as artisans, as mason and sculptor, to experiment with a variety of possible human forms. According to the well-known story told in the Popol Vuh, their first efforts yielded animals lacking speech and thus unable to praise their creators. Their second try, with earth and mud, yielded clay dolls that could not multiply and didn't last long before they crumbled or turned into mud when they got wet. The next effort, aided by great seers and diviners and master crafters, involved sculpting with wood and yielded manikins that looked and talked and multiplied like humans but had no emotion or intellect and thus no recognition of their creator, "no memory of their mason and builder." Only with their fourth and final effort did these creator-crafters successfully produce fully aware and knowledgeable humans, this time from maize, the true substance of human life (Tedlock 1985:72–86).

Ancient Mesopotamian deities were also skilled in crafting. Ea, whose realm included the waters surrounding the world, was a master artisan, patron of all the arts and crafts, and endowed with exceptional wisdom and intellect. (See Chapter 1; Ea corresponds to the Sumerian Enki.) Ea was also the prototype of the culture hero, Oannes, who (like Enki) taught people the arts of writing and figuring and all other crafts, including how to organize in cities and how to establish temples (Oppenheim 1977: 195, 369).

Crafting associated with such preeminently political and ideological contexts as the creation of urban life and the building of temples epitomizes the concept of crafting-creativity as the creation of form, shape, order, and refinement from that which is formless, shapeless, chaotic, and unrefined. In the mythical worlds of creator deities, creation as achievement of order and civilization is given ultimate expression by the image of the primordial god as Architect of the Universe as is illustrated by Lord Vishvakarma, Hindu God of Creativity and, like the Mesopotamian Ea, patron of all arts, crafts, and creativity (Maduro 1974:314; 1976:232–233; Glacken 1967:44–45, 230–231). In the more immediate here-and-now of existing human life, however, crafting as a mode of transformation that creates cultural order or makes social order manifest can be observed both in the creation of tangible objects and in the ordering of new communities, new social groups, or certain patterns of formal behavior that also assist in the recognition of influential persons as foci for political order.

With respect to tangible objects, to the Eskimo skilled crafting is a "ritual of discovery" by which hidden patterns of nature are revealed. The carver "releases form from the bonds of formlessness; he brings it forth into consciousness. He must reveal form in order to protect against a universe that is formless, and the form he reveals should be beautiful" (Carpenter 1971:165). Thus, the carver "examines [a piece of unworked ivory] to find its hidden form and, if that is not immediately apparent, carves aimlessly until he sees it, humming or chanting as he works. Then he brings it out: Seal, hidden, emerges. It was always there: he didn't create it; he released it; he helped it step forth" (Carpenter 1971:163).

New social groups can be released or aided in their "stepping forth" from chaotic or formless conditions in much the same way. Among the Yoruba ordered towns may be shaped and civilized living achieved in clearings perceived as crafted from the all-enveloping natural forest (Thompson 1974:18). In comparable fashion, creation of a new motif or new patternings of traditional motifs by master carvers and painters among the Ilahita Arapesh signals the creation of a new spirit entity. If political conditions warrant it, the new spirit entity can become a sacred patron supporting the emergence of a new descent group as an autonomous political entity (Tuzin 1978:66).[8]

Skilled crafting expressed by highly formalized speech events can help achieve social order and integration, too. Hendricks describes how, among the Shuar of southeastern Ecuador the ability to speak well indicates personal power and possession of spiritual strength, attributes which increase an individual's prestige and, ultimately, political authority. (Conversely, a person of low prestige is one who "doesn't talk," that is, doesn't know how to use language). This personal ability becomes particularly important in formal ceremonial dialogues in situations where a conflict threatens. The skillful use of language in these circumstances "produce[s] meaning beyond the referential value of the words spoken" by providing opportunity "to display personal power, aggressivity, knowledge, and skill" while simultaneously preventing open conflict and achieving a balance of power by acknowledging the power of one's opponent (Hendricks 1988:223).[9]

In the final expression of crafting as creative transformation celebrating either the achievement or the existence of order we find acts of skilled crafting that celebrate the ultimate order of the cosmos or universe. Sometimes this expression is by way of seeking reassurance, as when Fang artisans, through the reliquary figures they carve, expose the quiet, reflective order and strength that is believed to exist in the unseen world of the ancestors (Fernandez 1973:205–206). Sometimes this expression is by way of viewing a future existence in the there-and-then as the most highly desirable human achievement, one that transforms the dissolution of earthly life by death into the timeless order of immortality, as when the poet's singing of ballads and praise poems transforms heroic deeds and ultimate demise into everlasting honor and fame (Foote and Wilson 1970:430, 432).

Sometimes this expression is by way of associating the exalted order of a high monarch or of the state with the exalted order and harmony of the cosmos by means of elaborate court fêtes. These combinations of separate acts of skilled crafting become, in their entirety, immense expressions of creative art. Such ceremonials transform and create by enacting the "nature of cosmic reality," thereby embodying that reality, including its supernatural powers, and making them actual (Geertz 1980:104). Roy Strong explains the elaborate court spectacles of Renaissance Europe in just such terms: "The court fête could express philosophy, politics and morals through a unique fusion of music, painting, poetry and the dance, all terrestrial manifestations of that overall cosmic harmony which they believed governed the universe and which the art of festival tried so passionately to recreate on earth" (1973:17).

To re-create cosmic harmony and governance, however, was ultimately to strive to control such powers and to apply them to human affairs, that is, to express power conceived as art.

> The world of the court fête is an ideal one in which nature, ordered and controlled, has all dangerous potentialities removed. In the court festival the Renaissance belief in man's ability to control his own destiny and harness the natural resources of the universe find their most extreme assertion. In their astounding [artistic] transformations, which defeat magic, defy time and gravity, evoke and dispel the seasons, banish darkness and summon light, draw down even the very influences of the stars from the heavens, they celebrate man's total comprehension of the laws of nature. The Renaissance court fête in its fullness of artistic creation was a ritual in which society affirmed its wisdom and asserted its control over the world and its destiny. (Strong 1973:76) [10]

3   *Skilled Artisans in Time and Space*

By grace of the Muses some men are poets, as others are kings by
the grace of Zeus.   —HESIOD
Theogony, lines 94–97, quoted in Dodds,
The Greeks and the Irrational, p. 80

Dactylos believed in being foreign wherever he was. It gave him
mystery, which is always useful to technicians.
—MICHAEL AYRTON
The Maze Maker, p. 27

Artisans and the Ancestors

The orderly cosmos created by the gods and celebrated by royal courts
continues to thrive, its purpose maintained by the memory of ancestral
creator-crafters and its powers evidenced in the transformative skills of
contemporary artisans. The awe engendered by such crafting skills, however, reflects not only the exceptional talent of the artist but also the association of those abilities, and the products of those skills, with the ancestors and culture heroes who originally practiced them and introduced
them to mankind. The skilled artisan, in other words, not only is associated with the cosmological outside realm but, more specifically, with cosmological distance in both its temporal and spatial aspects. Judging from
the enthnographic literature, temporal distance frequently is believed to
have provided ancestral role models, inspiration, and even the abilities of
artisans, while spatial distance on occasion may provide all these attributes
plus the physical crafter, too.

The spatial dimension of artisans' activities will eventually provide one
of the most direct linkages between skilled crafting and long-distance trade
or acquisition. However, since spatial distance in general is ultimately associated with temporal elements, especially concepts of ancestors and of
cultural origins, it is necessary to begin this discussion of the association
between skilled crafting and cosmological distance with the temporal
perspective.

It is entirely *a propos* that ancestors and culture heroes, who were originally charged with teaching those cultural activities which are considered

to be ideally definitive of the cultured human condition, should include skilled crafts in their humanizing repertoire, for, as Chapter 4 discusses, skilled craftsmanship is associated with the ultimate expression of humanness in many traditional cultures. Taken overall, these primordial artisans exhibited the full range of specialized crafts. Ancestors and culture heroes (or their animal-spirit assistants) are recognized as the first dancers, first musicians, minstrels, and poets, first potters, painters, and carvers, first tattooers, first ship builders, first weavers, first jewelers and first workers in metal.[1] The general setting for the ancestral origins of humanizing skilled crafts is succinctly described by an excerpt from ancient Balinese tales:

> The first human beings were extremely imperfect creatures. They walked around naked, had no permanent dwellings and slept together like animals. They ate whatever nature happened to offer them. . . .
>
> Consequently various gods were sent to earth to teach men manners and customs and to instruct them in the arts and crafts. God Brahma showed them how to forge weapons and tools and gave the specialists in this field the name *pandé běsi*—ironsmiths. The god Mahadéwa took over the general training of goldsmiths and silversmiths; Sang Citra Gotra gave them special instruction in making jewellery. . . . The god Citra Kāra introduced the art of painting and drawing to man and designated those who had talent for arranging colours with their hands and brushes *sangging,* painters or draughtsmen. Bhagawan Wíswakarmma instructed the carpenters, *undagi,* and the architects and sculptors, *aṣṭakosali;* and the goddess Angga Ratih and her retinue of heavenly nymphs brought the women cotton and weaving tools and showed them how to weave plain cloth. (Ramseyer 1977:60)

Having originated such skills and having taught the first humans or, on occasion, become the first human crafters themselves (Griaule 1965: 42–45), the creator-ancestors left the active expression of skilled crafting to contemporary artisans, who readily proclaimed their affiliation with ancient heroes and evoked their continued assistance.

It is commonplace to find in the ethnographic record direct association between contemporary crafters and their skills and the original ancestral artisans. "Artists all over India, today as in the past, claim descent from, and identification with, Lord Vishvakarma, the primordial creator and supreme patron of all arts, crafts, and creativity. . . . During the ritual of artistic creation, painters say they feel the living presence of the god. . . .

Man does now what the gods did originally" (Maduro 1976:232–233, 234). (See Figure 3–1.) In like spirit, Abelam artists reproduced the power-filled designs and patterns used by the ancestors (Forge 1967:80), while members of the Benin carvers guild felt that "all their work was inspired by their patron deity, Ugbe n'Owerve. The deity appeared in their dreams and gave them ideas for their carving, guiding them at every step" (Ben-Amos 1976:321). The gods also provided the immediate inspiration for poets and minstrels' songs among diverse peoples, including the ancient Greeks and the Kirghiz (Dodds 1951:10, 22–23, 80), for orators' words among the Merina of Madagascar (Bloch 1974:58–59, 78), for dancers' steps among the Ashanti (Thompson 1974:28), and for master drummers' skills among the Yoruba (Bankole et al. 1975:49).

It is important to note, however, that it is not always the skill of the practicing artisan that gives evidence of ancestral ties. Artisans' tools may provide the major point of ancestral connections, just as tools could form the actual transformational interface between the inside (societal) and outside (cosmological) realms. Thus, for the smith, the hammer and forge can evoke the mythological era of ancestors and origins (Balandier 1968:224, 110–114), just as musical instruments (wooden trumpets and flutes, drums, harps) can represent—indeed, can themselves become—first ancestors or can form a connecting tie with the ancestors and gods, especially when played (Hugh-Jones 1979:10, 150; Chernoff 1979:150; Fernandez 1982:441, 537).[2]

The products crafted by virtue of these tools and these crafting skills also attest to an original connection between artisans and the gods. Earthly artists and their tools express the continued life of the beneficient ancestors and the collapsing of temporal distance with the contemporary present, while the crafted products become a contemporary expression of good things derived from outside and afar. By these diverse expressions of the act of crafting, human awareness extends back into ancestral time and human behavior becomes a re-enactment of ancestral behavior and power and of the benefits that are derived therefrom. The particular orating elder becomes the eternal elder, and is "transformed into an ancestor speaking eternal truth" (Bloch 1974:78; Schmitz 1963:73–75). The African dancer steps into a state of timelessness whereby the ancestral presence "diminishes the destroying force of time" and creates an impression of a return to eternal youth (regardless of the dancers' chronological age) for the duration of the dance (Thompson 1974:28, 47). By means of skilled crafting the gods themselves can be re-created and made to be present by virtue of

3-1.   Lord Vishvakarma, god of creativity and patron of all arts and crafts. (From Renaldo Maduro, "Artistic Creativity and Aging in India," *International Journal of Aging and Human Development* 5(4), Fig. 2, p. 313. Copyright © 1975, Baywood Publishing Co. Reprinted with permission from the publisher.)

their images being formed of stone, wood, paint, and precious gems (Lewis 1961:76). The crafting of deities from precious substances and the ritualistic transformation of this lifeless material into the deity itself may express the epitome of the power and significance of skilled crafting, as creating and giving life to the gods returns to them their original acts of crafting and creation of and for man.[3]

In all of this inalienable ancestor-derived crafting skills produce a type of inalienable wealth or benefit (Weiner 1985:210, 212; Küchler 1988: 629–630) such that the there-and-then of temporal distance not only conjoins with the here-and-now of societal life but becomes a crucial dimension shaping and informing contemporary existence.[4] It does so because of the ideological qualities and symbolic significance attributed to the concept of distance and to distant beings, things, and events when distance is temporally defined.

Artisans and Geographical Distance

Distance can have a spatial dimension, too, and qualitative significance may be attributed to the concept of spatial distance and to spatially distant (or distance-related) people, things, and events just as readily as when they are attributed to temporal distance. The qualities and symbolic significances attributed to spatial distance in traditional non-Western society are essentially the same as those attributed to temporal distance (Helms 1988). The proposal that geographical space and spatial distance encompass a sacred or supernaturally charged landscape and realm underlies my argument that the acquisition of goods from geographically distant places is comparable in meaning and significance to the skilled crafting of goods and benefits associated with qualities of temporal distance. In framing these associations it is both appropriate and gratifying also to find that there are a number of circumstances when skilled artisans are associated with spatial distance, too.

Skilled crafters seek, or endure, the reaches of spatial distance to varying degrees and for varying reasons. Their separation from their home setting may be temporary or permanent, voluntary or involuntary, characteristic of a particular stage in their careers or characteristic of their calling in general. Their reasons may be immediately pragmatic or may reflect more esoteric political-ideological ends. Whatever the reasons for or whatever the degree of their involvement with spatial distance, skilled artisans nonetheless are frequently associated with the geographically outside realm, a world which also generally carries supernatural associations of some sort.

Consequently, in a great many traditional societies skilled artisans may be derived from the geographically distant world as permanent immigrant residents, as more temporary visitors, or as itinerant travelers stopping off briefly in the course of their normal peregrinations.[5]

Some types of artisans travel to locales outside the bounds of settled society to obtain natural materials necessary to their work. Certain metal workers are known for this propensity (Herbert 1984:47, Eliade 1962:25; N. Brown 1947:46; Roberts 1970:45), but they are not alone: in the opinion of Dahomeans, the typical wood carver is "always eager to go off into the bush in search of fine wood, and once gone, he may not return for weeks" (Herskovits and Herskovits, quoted in Anderson 1979:203).[6] Travels to exercise one's skill are also common. Generally trips of this sort involve the crafter's attendance at the home of a patron to complete a commission of some sort. The reasons can be pragmatic, at least in part. The Kwakiutl master carver, Willie Seaweed (or Siwid), who was recognized widely for his expertise, usually worked at home, "but if there was a lot of work involved he sometimes moved to the village of the customer, who would put him up for the time it took to complete the carving" (Holm 1983:29). Similarly, in ancient Greece, where marble sculptors (among others) often traveled, they did so either "to carry out the commission, or the size and elaboration of the work were such as to make execution on the spot essential" (Snodgrass 1983:19).

Yet pragmatics are not always the reason for artisans' travels. The rationale underlying travel may also involve the prestige associated with acquiring the services of a famed master crafter (like Willie Seaweed), whose reputation has grown and been further enhanced by the wide geographical range of his or her journeys and the far-flung acclaim accorded his or her work. Among the Abelam, "certain men have reputations as 'master artists' over large areas and are invited to assist and advise in the preparation of ceremonies in many different villages" (Forge 1962:12). Similarly, "some [Maori] carvers and tattoo artists were widely famed and might travel as far as 200 miles to work for their clients" (Hanson and Hanson 1983:110; Buck 1966:299), while in western Liberia "few people can avail themselves of the services of the famous specialist whose name has spread far and wide, who has become associated with legends of remarkable successes, and who is sought after by the wealthy and the great" (d'Azevedo 1973a: 136). These exceptional artisans may live and work in a much more rarefied or esoteric professional environment than other artisans. Thus, in Liberia, "professionalism [aside from a few exceptions] is achieved only by those who appeal to a wider area of demand than that of the local community, or by those who are supported as clients of wealthy patrons. . . . Highly skilled singers, dancers, musicians, and craftsmen may make their services available throughout a region and are frequently solicited from distant chiefdoms of other tribes" (d'Azevedo 1973a: 135–136).

Chiefs' involvement in artisans' affairs warrants separate consideration (see Chapter 5), but it should be noted here that artisans often travel precisely because elites frequently seek and entice skilled crafters from distant locales to grace their courts and enhance their chiefly reputations with their presence and the products of their skills. Benvenuto Cellini records an example of this type of outreach in his autobiography. While living in Florence, Cellini came to the attention of a Florentine sculptor who had resided for many years in England, but had returned to Florence "to enlist as many young men as I can; for I have undertaken to execute a great work for my king, and want some of my own Florentines to help me" (1927: 18–19; Strong 1973: 213). Although Cellini's trip to the court of Henry VII did not materialize, many other skilled artisans have obeyed comparable summons. Moscati notes that a stele from the palace of Nimrud shows that Phoenician artisans from Tyre and Sidon were employed in building the Assyrian palace (Moscati 1968: 16). Thousands of years later, the Oba Oguola of Benin, wishing to introduce brass casting into Benin, is said to have sent to Ife for a skilled brass-smith (Fraser 1972: 261).

Skilled artisans already under chiefly or royal patronage further enhanced the spatial range of both their own and their patrons' reputations when they were lent to the courts of other elites. The Aztecs of central Mexico, for example, "are credited with sending specialists from their own city to add luster to the court of an allied ruler" (Brumfiel 1987: 110), while in traditional Bali, goldsmiths, silversmiths, and specialists skilled in drawing and painting who were in the service of the king were frequently lent to friendly nobles and potentates from other areas (Ramseyer 1977: 60, 65). Master wood carvers of the Yoruba were similarly lent by chiefly patrons to other rulers (Fagg 1969: 54, 55), just as Hiram, king of Tyre, sent carpenters and masons (as well as cedar trees) to build a house of God for David, king of Israel (Holy Bible 2 Samuel 5: 11).

Perhaps the most traveled artisans and those most personally associated with the supernatural qualities of the spatial world beyond or between units of settled life, were those poets, troubadours, carvers, musicians, and smiths whose frequent journeying qualified them as true itinerants. For those whose travels were associated with apprenticeship, the wander years constituted a limited period of time dedicated to acquiring experience in one's craft, as during the European Middle Ages when aspiring artisans of journeymen status were encouraged to travel about to gain experience (Lucie-Smith 1981:146).[7] For others, wandering, or at least periodic relocation from place to place, was more of a permanent life-style. Among the Gola of Liberia, persons of recognized talent made basic decisions concerning the dimensions of their professional lives: "The talented individual has the choice of competing for the limited opportunities that obtain for the exercise of his abilities within the local group, or of creating his own destiny by going out alone into the world. Most full-time specialists have made the latter choice of action" (d'Azevedo 1975:12). For these people itinerancy means that "they must frequently travel long distances to places where their services have been commissioned, and they are often required to reside for long periods away from their own villages" (ibid.:11). Similarly, for Lemba coppersmiths, itinerancy meant staying for a while to make highly prized fine wire bracelets for Sotho host villagers but then moving on to another locale (Herbert 1984:48; Cline 1937:128, 139). In similar fashion, but with a different product, in towns of North Cameroon "small bands of musicians and singers roam the countryside, residing at each and every chief's court" (van Beek 1987:26), much as did "the men of special gifts . . . not only *fili* [poets, genealogists, and seers] but druids, lawyers, doctors, and historians, as well as skilled craftsmen" and, later, Christian ecclesiastics, in early Ireland (Court 1985:10, 16; bracketed phrase in original).

The contemporary expression of these ancient Celtic travelers is found in the lives of roving Irish Tinkers, whose current stock in trade includes many types of craft or trade (Court 1985:3). Artelia Court's description of Tinkerism, explaining why Tinkers are different from settled folk, though perhaps a bit extreme for general application to traveling artisans overall, nonetheless aptly expresses the basic concept underlying this discussion, and is therefore quoted in full.

> Perhaps the most convenient emblem of the difference [between Tinkers and settled peoples] was the Tinkers' alternative name; Travelers. The word *Tinker* was properly an occupational title meaning tinsmith, but in Ireland and Britain the word had long since lost its narrow metallurgical connotation and had come to be applied to all the nomadic Irish outcastes of whom I speak, those who worked tin and those who did not. The apparently less definitive term *Traveler* in fact pointed quite specifically to the more essential, psychological attributes of the Tinker. In common Irish parlance *Traveler* was the counterpoise of *settled,* and the different parts of speech here signified. "Travelers" were never said to be "traveled" folk but

always those who were "Traveling" or who lived the "Traveling life." Perpetual movement was intrinsic to their state of being. "Settled" people and "settled life" had by definition achieved in the past a condition of stability which no amount of superficial change could undo. The terms betrayed not only the two groups' obvious, external distinctions but also their elusive, internal ones; and external and internal usages were, of course, indissoluble." (Court 1985:2)

Given the various opportunities and propensities for travel in spatial domains outside settled society open to skilled artisans, especially the most highly talented (and thus most representative of the very concept of "skilled" crafting), it is quite understandable that skilled artisans are frequently well traveled, in some circumstances are true travelers, and, therefore, in general may be closely associated with outside locales or with foreign places; this association with spatial distance may then form part of the overall identifying character or mystique of truly "skilled crafting" in a number of traditional societies. If we add to this perception the exceptional qualities associated with spatial distance in non-industrial cultures as well as the tendency for persons of exceptional ability to develop far-reaching reputations, it is readily understandable that skilled artisans from outside are highly valued and are often believed to have skills superior to local talents, a concept that may be generalized in the expectation that any people who derive from distant places should have exceptional capabilities.

This point is illustrated in mythological terms by the associations in ancient Greek lore between metallurgy and metal workers and the sea,[8] and, by way of example from the more immediate realm of human existence, in the belief held by the Kerebe of East Africa that skilled drum makers from Buganda were superior to their own and hence were assigned to produce the royal drums (Hartwig 1976:125). Similarly, Ruth Finnegan, speaking generally of oral literature and of poets and praise-singers in Africa, notes that "the power of free-lance poets can be increased if they are regarded as foreign or at any rate set apart from the patrons to whom they address themselves. This can add to the fearsome quality of their words while at the same time making them free from the obligations which are binding on other members of society" (1970:95–96; Ames 1973:137).

That skilled artisans from the outside are considered desirable is also attested to in cases when artisans formed part of the spoils of war (Adamu 1978:114; Nketia 1971:22; Chang 1974:9) as well as in those numerous instances when groups of skilled crafters live more or less permanently as ethnically distinct immigrant groups in host societies. Thus, to note but a few examples, immigrant Korean craftspeople served the Yamato Court of fifth-century Japan as scribes, skilled weavers, horse breeders, gold smiths, and ceramicists (Barnes 1987:87) while comparable groups of master artisans settled in Texcoco and other cities of Aztec Mexico (Bray 1978:388; Soustelle 1961:67–68; Pasztory 1983:269) and settlements of Islamic artisans and smiths formed important sectors of a great many African towns (Adamu 1978:16, 34, 39, 41, 100, 182; Glaze 1981:26–27).

Travelers, Traders, and Artisans

As outsiders, skilled artisans can provide extremely valuable services and benefits other than the products of their crafting skills alone. Peripatetic skilled crafters, for example, can develop wider social ties among culturally or linguistically distinctive groups, as blacksmiths have done among the Senufo (Glaze 1981:27), or may serve as communications experts between widely dispersed communities, as itinerant artists do in India (Maduro 1976:236). In addition, as highly regarded or highly feared (see Chapter 4) "specialists in distance," artisans may be granted safe passage through territories that are dangerous to others. Thus, in early Ireland skilled artisans as well as curers, poets, and others of the literary class, all being persons of special gifts, were the only ones who could pass freely and safely between tribes (Greene 1954:84–85). Similarly, among the Fang of Gabon, in the old days when internecine strife rendered traveling hazardous, the relative freedom with which troubadours could move about made them a valuable source of news and information (Fernandez 1982:59; Finnegan 1970:98; Northrup 1972:231).

Given such protections, it is not surprising to find skilled artisans serving as ambassadors for elite patrons. In this context we find that the expert carver, Olowe, served as messenger of the Yoruba king of Ise (Fagg 1969:54) and that "'Nyamala' smiths travelling through Moslem countries also functioned as mediators and ambassadors; they were inviolable" (Sundström 1974:188). Indeed, the role of supra-communal mediator-ambassador, combined with the ancestral associations, supra-human qualities and capabilities, esoteric knowledge, and supernatural power that have often been attributed to skilled artisans as specialists in transformative and distance-related phenomena, could elevate these professional travelers beyond their immediate roles as skilled crafters into highly influential supra-communal political "entities."

Artelia Court suggests just such a role for early Irish professional travelers, including seers, curers, poets, and other types of skilled artisans, as well as experts in religion and traditional history. Though excluded from full participation in most governmental and social activities of settled life, these persons not only provided essential political and ideological services for the wider cultural whole but also, by subtle use of their skills, wielded considerable influence over highly placed lords and rulers:

> Just as tribal integrity was embodied in king or queen, so an intertribal continuity was embodied in the professional travelers. They preserved literary and religious traditions, assisted in the local interpretation of law or custom, provided genealogical justification for local preeminence. In effect, the needs and strengths of disparate tribes and kings met and were integrated in the person of the professional whose accumulated experience became a polity, modifying the services he rendered. The craftsman made finer spears or ornaments for one king than for another, and the poet's satire was dreaded because it could wither or kill its object. . . .
>
> . . . In the ancient order of things itinerancy was associated with certain occupations that linked scattered and mutually suspicious communities and that thrived by politic use of the secrecy that suspiciousness encouraged. The followers of these occupations, in their freedom of movement and the nature of their works, functioned outside the law of settlement. Or, to put it another way, they were the law, the personification of tradition, and had personal command of some of its superhuman and extrasocial force. (Court 1985:10−11)

In conjunction with the various informational, juridical, and political-ideological functions and powers outlined above, skilled artisans, as professional travelers, frequently have been involved with yet another category of supra-communal or extra-societal activities. As outside specialists and travelers in general, skilled crafters have much in common with long-distance traders who, though they usually do not themselves create skillfully crafted goods, instead convey them from place to place.

Traders and artisans may both be itinerants: "Aside from a lively local trade, the Hausa [of West Africa] are famed for an external trade in which they range over very considerable distances. The itinerant traders have counterparts in many kinds of itinerant musicians . . ." (Ames 1973:131; d'Azevedo 1973b:288; 1975:39). They may both stand somewhat outside direct control by authorities of settled communities, even though their services are highly valued by those same authorities. Indeed, trader/artisans may literally inhabit the spaces between settled communities. For example, Mattison Mines comments with regard to South India that in medieval times certain castes ("right-hand castes") were located in the nu-

cleated agrarian centers dotted throughout the plains areas, while hazardous hill and mountain country separating these agrarian centers and inhab-
ited by "dangerous tribals" were "bridged" by itinerant merchant-artisans
("left-hand castes"), like the Kaikkoolars, who also developed considerable
military and political powers for their own protection (Mines 1984:13,
42–44, 76, 148).

The Kaikkoolars' regional networks functioned to regulate intercom-
munal transactions in a manner not unlike the situation in early Ireland
described by Court (Mines 1984:76–77, 161–162). The parallel is closer
than may be immediately apparent. According to Court, the early Irish
professional travelers, frequently specialists in some aspect of political-
ideology readily recognizable as such to us (poet-diviner-curer-
"historians" and crafters of high status objects), provided rather obvious
juridical and ideological legitimations for Irish rulers. South Indian merchant-artisans were goldsmiths, sculptors, traders, and weavers of fine textiles; they might appear, therefore, to be providing primarily economic
services to South Indian elites. Yet Mines also makes it clear that textiles,
especially fine textiles, have a central ceremonial significance in South Indian society and carry strong political and ideological connotations related
to expressions of dominance or of asymmetrical political relationships.
Thus, as in ancient Ireland, powerholders in South India sought contacts
with trader/artisans not only to gain access to regional networks but also
to obtain ritually and politically important symbols of legitimation and
authority (ibid.:148–149, 161–162).

As "specialists in distance" both traders and skilled artisans may also be
desirable as permanent additions to settled communities; they may be
mentioned collectively in this regard: "The sultan's agents abroad actively
recruited foreigners with valuable commodities *or* skill to come to Sinnar"
(Spaulding 1984:37; my emphasis). Similarly, Andrew Roberts states with
regard to the Nyamwezi of Tanzania, who were famed as energetic travelers and traders during the nineteenth century and who also settled in foreign parts, that "it is clear that several . . . Nyamwezi achieved a special
status as foreign experts in more or less distant countries. Some settled as
traders *and* craftsmen in what is now northeastern Zambia, as well as in
Katanga and Manyema" (Roberts 1970:68; my emphasis). Both the Dyula
and the Hausa of West Africa, skilled in both trade and crafting as well as
in Islamic scholarship, frequently settled as strangers among diverse illit-
erate pagan peoples in much the same way (Launay 1982:2–3; Levtzion
1973:193; Adamu 1978:16, 34, 39, 41, 100, 114). "In almost all cases, whenever Hausa immigrants entered an area for the first time, they tried to

win recognition at the seat of power and cultivated the roles of 'royal' priests, trading agents, artisans, secretaries, advisers, in-laws, etc." (Adamu 1978:182).[9]

Not only are traders and skilled artisans both likely to be mobile and to be associated with outside realms but both types of activities may also be undertaken by the same individuals. "In some areas [of Africa] professional ironworkers made journeys within or outside the tribal territory, thus contributing to the exchange of goods" (Sundström 1974:188; Alpers 1969:406; Northrup 1978:102–3; 1972:231). In Ashanti, the chief's traders included the *asokwafo*—musicians who played the trumpets—and the drummers, who were sent to the coast to buy cloth, beads, and salt (Nketia 1971:21; see also Lord 1960:14–15).

In these instances, as well as in situations where artisans and traders practice their skills separately, it is entirely possible that it is the interest, willingness, and ability to engage in the rigors of travel per se that underlies both long-distance traders' and traveling artisans' mutual associations and activities. Following this line of thought, it may be quite appropriate to view itinerant traders and artisans as travelers first and foremost. Christopher Healey, speaking of the New Guinea Highlands, describes just such a situation as it relates to trade:

> In general, it is the man who travels a lot, for whatever reason, who is given trade goods by distant kinsmen. His mobility fosters confidence in his wide-ranging social relationships and hence his capacity to find other partners to complete a transaction. Thus, while travel is a consequence of heavy involvement in trade, it also generates yet greater trade, for it is the 'big walker' in particular who receives unsolicited overtures to trade as expressions of confidence in his abilities. Several particularly diligent traders remarked how they were continually given new items to trade by distant kinsmen whenever they completed a delayed transaction, and how they eventually refused to accept the proffered goods, complaining that they were worn out by incessant travel. (Healey 1984:56) [10]

Fernandez' description of the derivation of the Fang concept of the *ensama* or purposeful group, a concept used in a number of social situations requiring "corporateness," associates both trade and a type of skilled crafting with qualities of travel in general. At the present time the *ensama* concept applies to certain ceremonial dance teams, but the prototype for the general concept derives from nineteenth-century trading teams that collected rubber and ivory and carried them to the coast for trade. The important point for both trade and dance teams, however, involves skilled travel, both because of practical considerations and because it exemplifies certain social concepts and personal and political qualities, skills and abilities:

> First, the ensama of old knew its way through the forest. Its members were pathfinders and pathfollowers par excellence. Second, as it was an all-male group it was, in principle, celibate as Bwitists [the contemporary Fang cult involving the dance teams] try to be. Third, its members had an essentially positive and profitable relationship with the European coastal merchants with whom they traded. . . . The ensama trading teams were, in short, apt embodiments of composed intention and successful self-sufficiency—qualities desirable in Bwiti 'pathfinding.' . . . The ensama image . . . evokes the Fang passion for journeying about. It was the providing of that psychic benefit, added to the prospect of material gain, that as much as anything confirmed the position of the leaders of both the ensama trading teams of the late nineteenth century and the leaders of the dance exchange teams of the twentieth century. In both these cases there was the plentiful satisfaction of journeying about—from deep upland forest to seacoast in the one case, from village to village, district to district in the other. That journeying about, that pathfinding, both demanded leadership and, in the associated satisfactions, confirmed it. (Fernandez 1982:419).

A basic propensity for travel as a fundamental factor underlying traders' and skilled artisans' mobility reflects certain traditional cosmological and cosmographical concepts and the relationships that are felt to exist between the settled, socialized communal heartland and the wilder, dangerous realms outside. In a manner directly comparable to skilled crafting in general as well as to formal religious activity, experts in travel, be they long-distance traders, entertainers or other artisans, religious scholars, curers, or diviners, are engaged in an activity that involves manipulation and transformation of the resources, powers, or qualities of cosmological spatial/temporal distance for the ultimate benefit of settled society. Not surprisingly, organizers of expeditions, master ship builders, cartographers, and navigators may be expected to have special understanding of outside phenomena, too; they especially comprehend the means to manage, control, or transform these outside factors so as to obtain safe passage through such hazardous realms.

In this context consider, in Greek thought, the explicit parallels in technical skills, cunning intelligence, and resourceful ability (*metis*) attributed to the master ship builder, the navigator, and the charioteer, and especially the concept of the pilot or navigator as exemplative of skillful and inventive human control over the uncertain forces of nature (Detienne and Vernant 1978:224–225, 236–237). Consider, too, the magical smith and builder of Welsh lore who fashions beautiful shoes and magical ships and horses, all of which clearly have to do with travelers' control ("speed") over distance. The colony of foreign Jewish craftsmen in fourteenth-century Majorca who produced astrolabes, quadrants, clocks, and maps of Africa may be one of many examples of real-world travel experts whose skills in controlling space and distance may have seemed almost as magical (Bovill 1970:108–109). So do the skills of master navigators on Lamotrek atoll, considered the most powerful manipulators of the supernatural in Lamotrek society (Alkire 1965:12, 119, 123; Oliver 1974 (I):218–219).

Regarding travel organization and ritual expertise, descriptions of caravan organization in Africa and elsewhere note the special care with which a leader may be selected, perhaps giving preference to sons of former leaders who may be credited with special powers or explicitly requiring ritual leadership along with other organizational and protective abilities (Curtin 1984:55; Edwards 1962:9; Hill 1948:382–385). The use of fetishes and medicines by caravan traders to ensure a successful trip is also widely reported (Sundström 1974:33–34; Alpers 1969:410, 416–417; Helms 1988:80–94).

Management, control, or transformation of outside realms marks the specialist in cosmologically distant phenomena no matter what the medium involved. It creates a commonality of interests, intents, and means among all skilled artisans (who transform natural materials into cultural goods), diverse sorts of religious experts (who tame unruly spirits with ritual and curative herbs or acquire knowledge of distant time and foretell the future), and skilled directors of travel; the latter including professional itinerants who, as individuals, may also engage in long-distance trade and/or crafting and/or formal religious activity and by these means acquire and convey politically and supernaturally potent goods, skills, and knowledge from geographically distant, mystically charged places, and make them available to the members of settled societies.

Travel as a distinctive, ritualized, even sanctified activity comparable to skilled crafting and to religious expression is also suggested in the interpretation of the ancient Popol Vuh given by contemporary Quiché Maya, to whom use of feet in walking and use of hands, as well as use of articulate speech, are seen as interrelated capabilities of truly human beings (D. Tedlock 1985:298). We may consider use of feet also in the sense of traveling, which in turn may be interpreted as another way of knowing and giving form to a portion of the world, just as use of hands shapes, creates, gives form to tangible objects, and speech shapes, creates, and gives form to men and gods by naming and praising.

Traveling, in this context, is a serious matter.[11] In Mayan practice, ancient and modern, human beings as travelers must seek permission and protection from the gods as they cross the landscape, meaning they must proceed in a ritualistically sanctified manner. In addition, travelers must proceed along particular pathways that not only lead to a given destination but in the process also shape and delinate the temporal/spatial landscape.[12] In the Quiché world the significance of these actions are of particular interest because they are identified as uniquely human attributes. As Dennis Tedlock points out, "In Quiché thinking one of the major differences between animals and humans is that humans must ask permission of the gods to go abroad in the world. To pray that nothing bad happen to one in the road is to ask permission to pass; the need for such permission is more acute in the case of visits to powerful shrines or distant towns" (D. Tedlock 1985:260).[13] As Chapter 4 will illustrate, the uniquely human quality accorded acts of human travel by the Quichés corresponds to the uniquely or ideally human qualities accorded skilled crafting in many societies, for skilled crafting is also frequently identified as exemplative of, or metaphor for, the ultimate meaning and nature of true humanness.

Traveling as Skilled Craft

The capacity for successful travel may be seen not only as comparable to but also as manifestation of a form of skilled crafting involving the creation or organization of an orderly, cultured, ritually sanctified social entity (for example, a caravan or a ship's society) which can successfully mediate geographical space/time and can pass between permanent and settled foci of human society and more distant domains of the outside world (see Chapter 7). The capacity to create such travel groups and to negotiate such passages is required of all those who are mobile, and defines them as skilled "artisans" regardless of what other professional expertise they have. In this context, long-distance traders (for the moment strictly defined as means for moving goods through geographical space and distance) are first and foremost skilled crafters of travel.

Stated otherwise, trade, depending on how it is defined, may be viewed as a particular type of long-distance activity which, in its broader or perhaps more fundamental sense, contains elements also associated with skilled crafting in general. In suggesting this perspective, I find the discussion of the nature of trade offered by Karl Polanyi in his essay on "The Economy as Instituted Process" (1957a) to be especially appropriate.

> . . . the organization of trade in early times must differ according to the goods carried, the distance to be travelled, the obstacles to be overcome by the carriers, the political and the ecological conditions of the venture. For this, if for no other reason, all trade is originally specific. The goods and their carriage make it so. There can be, under these conditions, no such thing as trading 'in general.' Unless full weight is given to this fact, no understanding of the early development of trading institutions is possible. The decision to acquire some kinds of goods from a definite distance and place of origin will be taken under circumstances different from those under which other kinds of goods would have to be acquired from somewhere else. Trading ventures are, for this reason, a discontinuous affair. They are restricted to concrete undertakings, which are liquidated one by one and do not tend to develop into a continuous enterprise.
> (1957a : 260–261)

Trade as a basically *acquisitive* enterprise (rather than as an exchange enterprise) is fundamental to Polanyi's interpretation of trade and to my own, and will be considered in more detail in Part II. Polanyi's interpretation of trading ventures as very specific or discontinuous types of activity, however, is relevant here. It may be argued that travel by artisans is equally specific in intent, and in the sense of individual craftsmen traveling for specific purposes and commissions, it is. However, in cases of truly itinerant traders and crafters and in the many situations where the experience of travel itself is valued for its own sake (even though specific trading, crafting, diplomatic, or religious ventures may also be conducted), I suggest that we are seeing a more generalized activity which is far closer in overall characteristics to skilled crafting as basic human activity than to trade (especially in the sense of exchange—see Chapter 6) as basic human activity.

Once again, the reasons for this interpretation rest on the fundamental tenet that in traditional cosmologies geographical distance and space/time are accorded political and ideological qualities virtually identical to those associated with vertical (heavens-underworld) distance and space/time. The qualities, powers, and resources of vertical spatial/temporal distance are tapped, controlled, transformed, and made available for human use by skilled crafting and by diverse activities defined as religious in character rather than by trade (when trade is viewed as economic exchange). Therefore, as I shall illustrate in more detail in Parts II and III, the means by which the qualities, powers, and resources of the realm of geographical spatial/temporal distance are identified, transformed, and made available for human use can also be appropriately understood as ideological in character and as including acts of skilled crafting involving the acquisition and transformation of desired resources, rather than as acts of economic exchange.

It can be readily contended that it would be equally logical to reverse this argument; to see skilled crafting emerging from a type of exchange relationship between the physical qualities of natural resources and human technological ability, and (as is often done) to interpret involvement with the powers of the vertical realm as a comparable type of relationship in which human recognition and appreciation of the deities is exchanged for blessings and benefits from those gods. However, when additional concepts associated with skilled crafting, particularly the quality of aesthetics, are further developed (see Chapter 4), when the nature of trade with the outside is seen as acquisition rather than as exchange (Chapter 6), and when the role of elites as skilled traders/artisans is considered, I believe it is both intellectually appropriate (meaning closer to what is really going on) and heuristically useful to interpret the overall situation as exemplative of crafting in general rather than of exchange in general.

Finally, in those situations where goods and artisans travel together, it is by no means always clear which activity, trading or crafting, is viewed as primary or as the more important. For example, the Siassis of the Vitiaz Straits (New Guinea) are famed as voyagers and traders, and skilled dancers and singers; their services are particularly valued when big-men festivals are held. On such occasions "a local big-man planning a festival may invite a group of Siassis to perform the main dance of his festival. The dancers are rewarded with gifts of food and pigs, and normal trading transactions occur at the same time. Even when trade rather than an invitation to dance is the reason for a Siassi visit, it would be a rare occasion if a *singsing* were not held. For the most part, therefore, the exchanges of overseas trade take place in a festive atmosphere" (Harding 1967:143, 142, 124). In addition, "their reputations as storytellers and retailers of gossip are also significant . . ." (ibid.:183).

In his study, Thomas Harding explicitly considers the Siassis to be traders first and foremost, but, judging from the context in which trade occurs, the Siassis appear to be as highly valued as skilled crafters (dancers, singers, storytellers) as for their skills as traders. If we focus primarily on trade and fail to recognize or trivialize skilled crafting (dancing is only entertainment) or consider it only as adjunctive background to trade (dances enhance sociability) we fail to properly understand the full meaning and significance of trade and skilled crafting for both the Siassis and their host communities, and we fail to comprehend the full dimensions and significance of the Siassis as travelers, trader/artisans, and general specialists in distance within the wider orbit of the Vitiaz Straits. Anthony Seeger's comments concerning the importance of craft-related activities among the Suyá of Brazil are especially relevant here. Speaking of the tremendous importance of music in the lives of lowland South American natives and of the many hours spent each day playing flutes or singing, especially during ceremonial periods when it is common to hear singing all day for days, even weeks, on end, he concludes, "Studies of the work habits in this region indicate that subsistence can be assured with between three and four hours of work per day under traditional conditions. . . . Members of many lowland Indian societies play flutes or sing for that number of hours for long periods. Yet we know much more about the socio-economic features of these communities than about the musical ones. Anthropological research priorities rarely start from the natives' views of what is important about their own lives" (Seeger 1987:7–8).

The Authenticity of Distance

Although the cosmographies of traditional societies accord diverse interpretations to geographical distance, all basically contrast such realms with whatever qualities are associated with the heartland. This comparison fundamentally distinguishes between the cultural and the natural or the cultural and the supra-cultural. That is, the safe, civilized, ordered, moral, domesticated life of the home society where people live in the here-and-now is contrasted either with a dangerous, chaotic, immoral or amoral, pre-civilized natural world outside or with the outside as a mystically powerful place of sacred superiority, as paradisiacal source of that which is good, as a place imbued with beneficial qualities of ancestral creativity (Helms 1988: Chapter 2).

Within the perspective of skilled crafting/trading/traveling and the transformative creation or acquisition of good things from afar, the most important cosmological characteristics of geographically distant space/time, whether chaotic and primordial or paradisiacal and beneficially creative, are those involving concepts of cultural origins essentially because concepts of origins ultimately relate to issues of political authenticity and legitimacy. In addition, concepts of origins provide a common conceptual and symbolic link relating realms of geographically distant space/time with realms of vertically distant space/time; concepts of origins conjoin the two

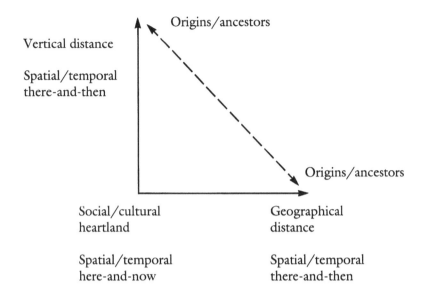

Origins/ancestors

Vertical distance

Spatial/temporal
there-and-then

Origins/ancestors

Social/cultural
heartland

Geographical
distance

Spatial/temporal
here-and-now

Spatial/temporal
there-and-then

3-2.   Origins and the congruence of spatially/temporally distant axes.

axes into a single all-encompassing three-dimensional cosmological outside realm with common sets of supernatural or mystical qualities and
powers, though not with common physical properties.

In addition, cosmographical and cosmogonical locales may meet at
places geographically out there, at or beyond the horizon, where the heavens seem to touch the land or sea or where "world pillars" of various sorts
(piles of rock, waterfalls, giant trees, mountains) are believed to bridge
whatever gaps separate heavenly and earthly planes. At such points direct
contact between the vertical and horizontal axes, that is, between the celestial and earthly realms, is believed both to have previously occurred
some time in the mythical past and to continue still. Not surprisingly, such
locales are regarded as highly charged contact points. They are places
where ancestors or culture heroes may have originally come to earth,
where the dead may ascend/descend to otherworldly abodes, and where
the living, if they journey far enough, may expect to effect contact with
places and conditions of origins or with primordial or ancestral creational
beings that are believed to continue to exist in those distant places at the
edge of the world where the there-and-then of original space/time eternally persists (Helms 1988; Gossen 1974; see Figure 3–2).

In previous pages associations between skilled artisans and ancestors/ culture heroes/creator deities were reviewed in situations where the skills and activities of artisans are associated with the skills and acts of vertically distant creator-crafters and culture heroes, ancestral originators of the knowledge and skills considered to exemplify the most truly human or "civilized" aspects of human existence. If it is accepted, however, that geographical distance can provide cosmologically comparable points of contact or association with origins in some form or another, then it stands to reason that associations between skilled crafting and artisans and concepts of ancestors and origins can also be expressed through contacts between skilled artisans and geographically distant peoples and places. Thus artisans may travel to cosmographically distant locales to enhance their skills or artisans *from* such heralded realms may be sought after and enticed to grace the home premises (particularly the homesteads and courts of the politically powerful or aspiring). If such crafters themselves are unavailable, the elegant or esoteric products of their workmanship may yet be acquired, either by traveling from home to the far away setting or by dealing with foreign travelers who have access to such distant goods and can convey them to the homeland.

In these latter instances it may be assumed that the transformative powers and acts of the original artisans are considered to be "frozen" within the exceptional crafting ability evidenced in a given item. In other words, the crafted piece that has been obtained from afar expresses the general concept of human transformative power and contains within itself, specifically within its craftedness, a portion of that dynamic transformative energy. This is so because such foreign items are considered inalienable objects in exactly the same sense as the goods crafted by skilled artisans at home.

As discussed earlier, objects or activities (such as songs, poems, dances) produced by skilled artisans may be considered inalienable because they are re-expressions or re-creations of original ancestral or creator-deities' acts of creative crafting, now expressed by contemporary artisans who themselves are re-creators of ancestral skills. As such, both the contemporary crafter's skills and the goods produced thereby are inseparable from—and still contain—the original ancestral creative skills and powers; the vertical spatial/temporal past and the present here-and-now are conjoined and kept interrelated by the constant re-expression of this particular type of creative connection. Crafted goods obtained from afar, though now separated geographically from their skilled human creators (whose precise identity may be unknown), nonetheless still contain and retain the qualities inherent in their original production because, by virtue of the work done—the skill expressed—in creating them, they are inseparable from their original skilled creator/crafters. In the cosmography of the receiving society, these distant artisans represent and express the cosmogonical ancestral powers associated with the geographically distant place where they work and whence their finished products are derived. Consequently, the exotic goods obtained from afar conjoin the geographical expression of the spatial/temporal past and the here-and-now of the home society just as goods crafted by skilled persons at the home center conjoin the vertical expression of the spatial/temporal past and the here-and-now of the homeland. In both cases the crafted goods, as inalienable objects, also are believed to maintain a personal relationship with the producer (Gregory 1982:44). Thus skillfully crafted goods are ultimately extensions of the skills of their creators who, in the final measure, are the once and future ancestors themselves, regardless of whether the pathways of their derivation involve the vertical axis or the geographical axis of center-outside relations.[14]

To be sure, not all goods acquired from or by travelers need be crafted products; acquisition of various types of unworked natural goods is also readily attested to ethnographically. Such products, I suggest, are equally expressive of some aspect of cosmological origins associated with their geographical places of origin even though they do not (yet) bear the results of cultural transformation (crafting). In fact, whether a product obtained from afar is crafted or natural may constitute a major statement signifying the type of cosmological interpretations and political-ideological connections accorded by members of the home society to a distant locale and to those who dwell there. Parts II and III consider these points in more detail.

One of the most essential rationales underlying all outside associations, acquisitions, and transformations involves questions of political-ideological legitimation, verification, and authenticity. Those who create and/or acquire goods and benefits from some dimension of the cosmological outside are not only providing goods and benefits per se but also are presenting tangible evidence that they themselves possess or command the unique qualities and ideals generally expected of persons who have ties with distant places of supernatural origins and, therefore, are themselves "second creators." Evidence of inalienable connections with places of cosmological origins thus conveys a certain sacrality which readily translates into political-ideological legitimacy and facilitates successful exercise of power. This, in a nutshell, is why in traditional societies seekers or holders of influential political positions must give evidence of distant outside contacts, be they via the vertical realm, the geographical realm, or both.

Such connections and such sacrality also guarantee the political-ideological significance of acts of skilled crafting and of the things produced, for the symbolic meaning and ideological weight of a craft cannot be questioned if it is associated with concepts of origins: "The texts of songs were said to be entirely fixed, and they were legitimized by extra-human origins." "Not all verbal utterances carried the same authority. Everyday speech was the responsibility of the individual—it carried no more weight than the speaker in the immediate context. Plaza speech carried the authority of tradition and office: the old people used to speak and were listened to; . . . Song, however, has a very different kind of authority: its exact form came from outside society altogether. Songs are beyond question: they simply existed. Any doubt about a song text came up against the impossible: finding and communicating with the original animal or plant performer from which it was learned" (Seeger 1987:44, 49 regarding Suyá songs).

Sometimes, however, the issue of authenticity or genuineness has to be overtly established for the objects in question before any additional authenticating virtues can be forthcoming—a useful reminder that not every item from a distant place may carry the aura of ancestral potency. On the contrary, a considerable degree of cultural selectivity may be expected to operate, as in the case of saints' relics in Carolingian Europe.[15] Since, as Arjun Appadurai notes (1986:46), relics circulated over long periods of time, through many hands, and over large distances, concerns were raised about the nature of their origins. Potential relics were thus subjected to a very public process involving a thorough examination of tombs or reliquaries and any associated authenticating documents or descriptions of burials in hagiographical texts. In addition, there was the custom, in existence by the ninth century, of submitting relics to an ordeal by fire to determine if they were genuine (Geary 1986:178). But the bottom line for determining the authenticity, meaning the continued inalienability, of relics was very pragmatic: if the relics still worked wonders, showing that the saint involved was still actively miraculous, then they were genuine (ibid.).[16]

Speaking of supernatural miracles brings us back to the point that ancestral or origins-associated things from afar are also considered broadly reflective of the capabilities of those who officially create or acquire them to provide benefits for society; in a sense to be "second creators" for the social good and, by extension, to express and reflect the personal attributes associated with culture hero–like creators. Let us turn, then, to consider the particular qualities associated with persons who are skilled at crafting and extended to those who employ them or more indirectly acquire the products of their skills.

4   *Qualities of Skilled Artisans*

The King should not set up or keep in a temple a disproportioned
or broken image; worn out images of the angels, and ruined
temples, are to be carefully restored.

—ANANDA COOMARASWAMY
The Transformation of Nature in Art, p. 116

Flawed Creators or the Epitome of Humanness

Skilled artisans are generally judged to be "different," distinct from ordinary people pursuing the mundane, pragmatic affairs associated with the
immediate needs of daily life. Depending on the ethnographic particulars,
skilled artisans either fail to measure up to everyday standards and requirements, are to be excused from such routine exercises in order to develop
and practice their skills, or are accorded honor and deference that raises
them above the crowd. Thus, skilled artisans may be highly respected and
accorded personal prestige, garner rewards and high esteem, and bring
honor to their families. Alternatively they may be viewed as lazy, guileful,
irresponsible, untrustworthy, overly independent, poor providers, unfit
(polluting) commensal companions, and inappropriate or unwise marriage choices especially for non-crafting families (d'Azevedo 1973a:142;
1975:25; Firth 1925:280; Eliade 1962:91–92; Maurer 1979:135; Ames 1973a:
271, 274; Himmelheber 1963:87; van Beek 1987:4, 30; Herbert 1984:33).

By virtue of their special abilities, artisans may be recognized as community notables and persons of importance, whose words carry special
weight in village councils or, by virtue of those same special abilities, they
may be condemned as perpetual children to sit by the sidelines in community discussions, ignored by the majority of fully adult folk (Gerbrands
1957:69; Eliade 1962:82; van Beek 1987:30; Fernandez 1973:202). If their
skills require manual labor, artisans' work may be considered degrading
within a ranking of societal occupations where work with the hands is
denigrated (Ben-Amos 1975:180; Herbert 1984:33; Bayly 1986:293–294);

as non-farmers in a world of agriculturalists, they may be regarded as close to non-human (Himmelheber 1963:97); if physically less fit due to periods of inactivity required by their craft, they may be despised by those prizing physical strength and perfection (Austin and Vidal-Naquet 1977:169–170); if single-minded in the pursuit of their calling as crafters, they may be scorned for their lack of interest and involvement in the societal goals pursued by the majority (Biebuyck 1969:15, note 6).

Not infrequently, skilled artisans are regarded and treated as social or political outcastes: "The finest type of city will not make an artisan a citizen" (Aristotle in Casson 1984:141; see also Finnegan 1970:97; d'Azevedo 1975:26; Eliade 1962:90–91; Lewis 1970:183). Less harshly, artisans may co-exist with the social majority as ethnically distinctive foreigners (Bayly 1986:293; Maquet 1970:95–96; Herbert 1984:33). At the other end of the social-political spectrum, however, skilled artisans, whether local or foreign in derivation, may enjoy some of the comforts and benefits available to favorites of the privileged and the powerful at the courts and compounds of high elites and kingly rulers, who (as we shall see in Chapter 5), may themselves seek to become skilled in some form of creative expertise and encourage the work of others.

These varied reactions to exceptional crafting abilities reflect the fact that in traditional societies crafting is believed to involve far more than technical expertise; that skilled artisans are in some manner or to some degree inevitably associated with exceptional powers. Since such powers originate and exist in cosmological realms outside settled society, so artisans, like other specialists in extraordinary powers, must be associated with these unsettling outside domains. To the extent that they belong or relate to the outside, they are removed or distanced from exclusive membership in the social center. Underlying this reaction by the social majority is the strong belief that skilled artisans themselves contain, exhibit, and control special powers that may harm as well as help society; that they evidence exceptional knowledge and intelligence and hence may be harmful magicians or adept at the occult and the demonic as well as being helpful bards, diviners, curers, and crafters of beneficial materials and activities (Lucie-Smith 1981:39; Eliade 1962:91, 67, 83; Rees and Rees 1961:127–128; Wright 1989:49–52).

As previous chapters have indicated, skilled artisans' primary outside contact ultimately connects them with creator deities, culture heroes, and ancestors as cultural originators. Consequently, artisans take unto themselves qualities and identities associated with such creators and become creators, too. It is in reaction to artisans as creators that society assigns

4-1.   A twelfth-century scribe at work. (From Julia de Wolf Addison, *Arts and Crafts in the Middle Ages*. Page Publishing Co., 1908.)

them to one or another of two basic liminal categories: artisans may be viewed as essentially flawed creators or as epitomes of the ideal meaning and condition of being human. In other words, either skilled artisans represent the once pristine condition of ancestral creativity marred now by its expression in imperfect human form or skilled artisans (like other ideological specialists) represent the closest to true and ultimate understanding of the orderly working of the created universe that humans may achieve, a comprehension they then express through the philosophy of aesthetics. Since these qualities or characterizations of crafting also commend skilled artisans and their products to political elites, let us consider in somewhat more detail artisans first as flawed creators and then as epitomes of humanness.

My use of the term "flawed creator" derives from C. A. Bayly, who describes the factors underlying the deep ambiguity, the disfiguring flaws and the almost sacred creativity, associated with the weaver in traditional Indian society:

> Most weaving communities hovered uneasily on the line that separated pure castes (best defined in this context as those from whom Brahmins could take water) and impure ones. Yet the cloth the weavers produced was generally considered neutral. According to the Shastras, 'The hand of the artisan is always pure.' The low, sometimes impure status of many weaving communities seems best explained in terms of historical contingencies. First, weaving communities had often differentiated themselves only recently from pickers of wild cotton or producers of plaited leaf baskets, groups of tribal origin on the fringes of Hindu society. Second, manual work was widely regarded as degrading in the Hindu scheme of occupational precedence. Finally, lower village artisans, including poor weavers, were usually in a dependent position in relation to the agricultural castes in that they received grain payments from their hands as payment for work. Since taking gifts depressed status, weavers were ranked below the clean Shudra agriculturalists. . . . At the same time, the act of weaving was itself an act of *creation*, almost an act of worship, and this brought about the ambiguity in the position of the weaver. The notion of creation is central to the caste foundation myths of weaving communities, which themselves embody a claim for high status. According to the legends of the Devangas of Mysore, for instance, in the beginning men went naked and Brahma created Manu to weave clothes for them and hide their shame. When Manu achieved beatitude, he was reincarnated from the eye on Shiva's forehead in the form of Devala. Devala went to fetch the thread

for weaving from the heart of the lotus stems that grew out of the navel of
Vishnu, the protector. . . . The weaver was thus a flawed creator, a status
that bears comparison with the Greek notion that Hephaistos, patron of
artisans, was a divine being, but lame. (Bayly 1986:293–294)

Although Bayly's identification of the Indian weaver as "flawed" refers
to his low or impure socio-religious status, his reference to Hephaistos,
the archetypical flawed creator in traditional Western thought, reflects the
frequent association of exceptional, supernaturally related skills and abilities with physical deformities.[1] In the case of Hephaistos, the smith, the
wise and skillful god's deformities took the shape of curved feet and
twisted limbs (Detienne and Vernant 1978:271–272). Similarly, Ptah, patron of artisans in ancient Egypt, is sometimes depicted as a dwarf (Dasen
1988:263–264), while far to the north, in the mythology of medieval Scandinavia, primordial smiths, as well as the brewers of the mead that made
some people poets, were also portrayed as dwarfs who combined physical
deformity with wisdom and cunning (Foote and Wilson 1970:273,
331–332, 393). Across the sea, in the real world of the Inca state, "cripples,
dwarfs and hunchbacks of both sexes—people less likely to set up family-
type units and engage in agriculture, frequently became very skilled weavers" (Murra 1980:71–72).

The association between physical defect and crafting skills may be interpreted in several ways. As Bayly indicated (see also Casson 1984:141),
physical ugliness may be regarded as comparable to low social status, just
as high status and physical beauty are frequently paired. In addition,
physical deformities which place their bearers outside the category of normal humans and into the category of things that are strange and unnatural,
and thus inherently mystically powerful (Eliade 1958:13), are also tangible
metaphors for other equally unique, strange, and potent but intangible
qualities—like the ability for exceptional performance—that also marks its
bearers as unnatural and places them outside normal human society (Detienne and Vernant 1978:Chapter 9). Physical deformities in association
with exceptional capabilities may also be constant reminders of the sin of
hubris, that human creators, no matter how refined their skills, must not
presume to the absolute perfection that remains the sole possession of the
gods; that humans are, by definition, somewhat flawed.

This point is neatly illustrated by a Dogon myth concerning the creation
of the first humans. The story tells how the first ancestral smith and culture
hero visited heaven and, slipping into the workshop of heaven's smiths,
stole a piece of the sun, an ingot of glowing iron, which he precipitously

carried down a rainbow to earth. At that time the ancestors were not yet fully human in form, for their limbs were flexible, sinuous and snake-like.[2] But, as the smith fled from heaven burdened with his hammer and his anvil, he landed on earth with such a crash that he broke his arms and legs, which is how humankind acquired elbows and knee joints proper to human beings who would henceforth devote themselves to toil (Attenborough 1976:15; Griaule 1965:43–44; Lévi-Strauss 1969:101).

The Dogon myth is only one of many origin tales (including those of the West) indicating that contemporary humans are in some manner flawed in condition, be it physical, social or moral, in comparison with their original creational state.[3] Similarly, if one of the basic characteristics of humans is their general capacity to make things, to be *homo faber* as myths and legends world-wide also assert, then humanity in general represents a state of flawed creativity, and the artisan as flawed creator becomes metaphor for the human condition.

In considering the further implications of this point, however, it is important to remember what the term "flaw" designates. A flaw basically connotes simply a break or crack in a continuum, some deviation from the basic condition. Humans as flawed creators are simply separated from the original state of creation, although to the extent that the original time or state of creation constituted a condition of primordial perfection, the break—the flaw—that created humans also carries a negative connotation in that context. In the same sense, fallible human society is now separated from the wider cosmological continuum and, in turn, separates the deformed or despised artisan from itself, moving him back towards the outside.

However, it has been argued above that all dimensions of the outside are essentially qualitatively equivalent and contrast in equal measure with the social center, which is why, in seeming paradox, artisans of low social status who are socially ostracized and barred from intermarrying within the general population may, in some societies, provide suitable marriage partners for royal clans, whose high status members also are separated from the general population in status and who also deal with outside phenomena (Hartwig 1976:45, 113; see also Chapter 5). In addition, this cosmological configuration, which allows skilled artisans in general to be described either as despised pariahs or as equal in status to princes and connected to the gods, also makes it plausible to associate deformity with beauty, the ugly with the aesthetic. It explains why, even when skilled artisans are social outcastes, their creations, the products of their skills, are still esteemed: "In fact, the very suspicion in which the blacksmith is held as a likely sorcerer strengthens the faith in the quality of his plowpoint, axe, adze, sickle, and other tools" (Messing 1962:392).

This distinction between artisans and their creations is crucial, for it is by acts of crafting that the breaks or flaws that separate deformed (low status) crafters from human society and humans, as flawed creators in general, from ancestral society, may be mended or at least bridged. By their skills and crafted products, low status artisans provide cultural benefits that are gladly accepted by the majority. In a comparable manner, by emphasizing the general development of crafting skills as much as possible, members of society at large may attempt to express the abilities and benefits that were originally derived from ancestral culture heroes. This perspective moves us from artisans as flawed creators to artisans as epitomes of humanness. This concept is represented by general recognition of the importance of crafting abilities per se and by the particular high status and regard accorded master artisans. In this context, the human capacity for crafting becomes an activity that both conceptualizes and strives to achieve or re-establish the true or ultimate conditions and relations of human existence, that reaches for (even if it cannot achieve) ideals and perfections of the universal human experience, that seeks to epitomize the meaning of being human. People "often define themselves through the skills they acquire, and the uses to which they put them" (Lucie-Smith 1981:11).

This interpretation of skilled crafting is found wherever crafting is viewed as a fundamental attribute of socially mature adults; part of what constitutes genuine adulthood, genuine humanness. Ethnographically this characteristic is broadly expressed. Thus the Tiwi of northwestern Australia encourage every individual to participate in the various realms of artistic (crafting) expression, including song, dance, body painting, ceremonial basket-making and the carving and painting of ceremonial spears and poles. "Tiwi feel that the individual develops and matures through his efforts at creating. Both formal and informal methods of cultural transmission involve a grounding in symbol and technique, and children of both sexes are encouraged to learn" (Goodale and Koss 1967:187–188). Similarly, Nancy Williams states, regarding the Yirrkala, "Every man is expected to become proficient in carving and painting ritual objects of wood as well as body painting" (1976:270; see also Morphy 1989:23). Among the Kalapalo, fishermen and agriculturalists of the Upper Xingu Basin (Brazil), almost every man and woman holds at least one recognized position as an *ifi,* a "maker," meaning that he or she knows the contents of lengthy ceremonial songs, can manufacture ceremonial paraphernalia, and knows details of rarely performed ceremonies (Basso 1973:113). In Suriname Maroon society "The performances of a well-known singer or dancer are accorded special attention at any communal event, but *everyone* is expected to sing and dance, these activities are considered part of being an able-bodied human being" (Price and Price 1980:36; see also Guss 1989:70). In West Africa, the Anang "assume that under ordinary circumstances any person can learn to sing, dance, act, weave, carve, play musical instruments, and recite folklore in a manner considered exceptional by unbiased Western aestheticians, and Anang culture rewards in numerous ways the acquisition of these abilities" (Messenger 1973:125–126; Crowley 1972:25). Likewise in Melanesia, "Every initiated Abelam man aspires to be an artist . . ." (Forge 1967:78).

Finally, in the Inca state, where, as in all archaic states, the condition of social worth became translated into the condition of citizenship, a mode of crafting again served as a suitable means for expressing this form of "true humanity" (citizen): "The wool from crown herds was stored in warehouses and distributed among the peasants who were expected to weave it into cloth for themselves and for the state. . . . All citizens were issued wool and all were expected to contribute cloth and this exchange was one of the main bonds and symbols of citizenship" (Murra 1980:55).

The widespread recognition of skilled crafting as a distinctively and uniquely human characteristic rests on the qualities and attributes which it expresses and represents; qualities such as ability to control mystical powers and materials, intelligence and wisdom, and expression and achievement of human ideals. Thus among the Andaman Islanders, one of the many societies where the decoration of utilitarian items (bows, canoes, baskets) and of human bodies (by scarification, painting, weaving ornaments) constitutes the predominant non-utilitarian craft, ornamentation signifies increased social value; hence young people are decorated at coming-of-age rituals to indicate that they are now legitimate adults, ready to assume the authority and responsibility that adulthood requires (Anderson 1979:42; Turner 1971:105; Rosengren 1985/1986:34). In the same sense Samoan body tattooing commemorates human accomplishments. "For a man to die without having achieved even partial tattooing would be for him to leave the world without truly becoming a human being" (Cordwell 1979:55).

With respect to crafting and intellect, "As a craftsman-god . . . Hermes is represented as 'pre-eminently intelligent': the primitive mind . . . regards craftsmanship and mental ability as going hand in hand" (Brown 1947:22).[4] On a more worldly plane, "The smith functions as priest, artist, shaman, magician, initiator precisely because his work demands not merely manual skills but the esoteric knowledge to manipulate the dangerous forces at play in the extraction of ores and in their transformation into finished objects" (Herbert 1984:33; Balandier 1968:110). "The practice of their skills gives [the Abelam artist] general prestige and particularly a reputation for understanding and knowledge of the supernatural which invests their opinions with something of wisdom" (Forge 1967:73).

The social worth and esoteric understanding of the artisan are often expressed in personal moral terms which infuse the products of crafting with inalienable value. "It is refinement and character that distinguish the true potter [in Japan] from the man who merely works at making pots. He must be someone who experiences and recognizes what is good, whether in music, painting, literature or philosophy. By absorbing these into his being he can put strength and character into what he makes out of clay" (Fujiwara, quoted in Lucie-Smith 1981:84; see also R. Anderson 1990:246). "The Abelam expect their artists to be good men, and by and large the artists conform to these expectations" (Forge 1967:74). "The players of the harp and the obaka [bamboo staves] are singled out by their talents, as are the song leaders. But it is important that all of them be pure of heart and body" (Fernandez 1982:416 re the Fang). Similarly, "A morally bad person could not be a good artist" among the Aztec (Pasztory 1983:91).

All of these principles, and more, are encapsulated in the concept of aesthetics, the epitome of artistic expression, which is achieved by those artisans recognized as master artists, themselves epitomes of the capacity for skilled crafting and all that talent implies. "Although most men in . . . an aboriginal Australian society can paint, carve, incise, and so on, there are usually some who are regarded as being better than others, or as having prescriptive rights through age, status, or ritual prestige to practice 'art' or one aspect of it . . ." (Berndt 1971:101; Morphy 1989:23). In Tahiti "Perfect knowledge of [the] poems and sacred chants not only served to elevate the fortunate adept to places of honor among humans, but provided him with sacredness and made him a favorite of the gods" (Oliver 1974:946). Some of the implications of this elevated social recognition and exceptional ability have been discussed by Donald Tuzin with reference to master artists of the Ilahita Arapesh:

> . . . men [of ambition] are attracted to art precisely because it provides
> what no other pursuit can to quite the same degree: the opportunity to
> play among—manipulate, exploit, indeed *create*—the images and ideas

upon which community well-being is thought to depend. Achieving mastery over this realm requires a comparable mastery over oneself. The rigors to which the artist ambitiously submits himself—sexual and dietary avoidances and other purifying regimes which, as one artist put it, enhance and focus his personal 'power'—ostensibly ensure that his hand will be steady and the design exact. But in the process he also attains that complete confidence in himself which is the primary character trait of a New Guinea leader. His evidence is the work of art he produces and the magical potency it is presumed to contain, by virtue of which it is also judged to be aesthetically pleasing. (Tuzin 1980 : 197–198)

Tuzin's point, that the crafting of art, the potency such art contains, and the aesthetics it displays give evidence of capacity for political leadership, will be considered further in Chapter 5. With this in mind, the significance and importance of aesthetics in general in the meaning of artistry in traditional societies should be briefly reviewed.

Aesthetics

Aesthetics, or the aesthetic sense, is "the faculty that enables man to modify the quality of his environment" (Read 1963 : 175) by producing or contributing quality (beauty) to what might otherwise be a rather flat and quotidian existence and by expressing or manifesting quality judged already to exist there. In traditional societies these perspectives are intertwined: the production of quality by creating things, behaviors, and attitudes judged to be pleasing presupposes the prior existence of quality in the producer ("the artist must be a good man") and/or is interpreted as activity that gives tangible expression to quality already inherent in the universe.

More specifically, production of quality, of beauty, expresses the morality and orderliness of the properly functioning cosmos. Which is to say, in traditional societies aesthetics signifies beauty *and* moral goodness. Aesthetics expresses truth in terms of what is proper in thought (philosophy), action (ethics), and design (art); what is considered proper and right, that is, the sanction of beauty or of aesthetics, derives from the principle of order deemed inherent in the nature of the gods or of the universe as well as from the expression of that order in rules or canons of form and design prescribed by tradition and authority (Coomaraswamy 1935 : 16–17; R. Anderson 1990 : 244–247; Taylor and Aragon 1991 : 29–30). When these concepts of aesthetics and morality are expressed in the things and events of everyday life, then not only do things have meaning, but life has meaning, too. Frederick Errington, discussing Minangkabau customs, states the matter as follows:

> If morality is an aspect of reality, social constraint—constraint of persons—is not viewed as arbitrary, as mere constraint or convention, or even simply as socially desirable. Rather, it is viewed as entirely reasonable. If aesthetics is equivalent to ethics, the essentially aesthetic judgment of conduct on which social constraint is based is not experienced as only opinion or as mere preference, but again rings true as entirely reasonable. When morality and reality, aesthetics and ethics are viewed and experienced as being inseparable, then social life itself and the judgments and interpretations on which it is based are viewed and experienced as supremely right and proper. (Errington 1984:38)

The Suyá would agree, for they express the same sentiments through the aesthetic medium of song. "Suyá singing was an essential part of social production and reproduction. It re-established the clarity of spatial domains, temporal durations, and certain forms of human relationships. . . . The Suyá would sing because through song they could both re-establish the good and beautiful in the world and also relate themselves to it. Suyá would sing because through singing they could restore certain kinds of order in their world, and also create new kinds of order in it" (Seeger 1987:128).

If reality as morality and ethics as aesthetics are such essential components of social living, it stands to reason that tangible expression of these principles, such as Suyá singing, would be fundamental to social as well as cosmic order, and that those who can produce aesthetic things would hold distinctive social positions and play crucial roles in social management. Which is to say, the acts and products of skilled crafting are valued in large part because they are aesthetic acts and products, and skilled artisans themselves (or those who command their services) are accorded unique positions in society in no small measure because of the influence they can or might wield as creators or manifestors of proper ethics and moral standards. Indeed, the very concept of *skilled* crafting as opposed to production of utilitarian goods exists in identification of the skilled artisan as one who can create or instill the aesthetically proper design or form and feeling in his work. "The artist of highest rank among the Fang is he whose artistic activity provides aesthetic meanings, which in turn influence the activity of those who contemplate or, as in the case of ritual, participate in them" (Fernandez 1973:216, Messenger 1973:123–124). "Knowing how to

make an object well *includes* knowing how to make it beautiful . . ."
(Crowley 1973:228 regarding the Chokwe).

The attraction of aesthetics—the compelling nature of the beauty of
that which is morally good—also rests on the fact that beauty is not only
instructional and exemplary but also has a dynamic of its own: "The skilful
artist who satisfies his aesthetic sense and produces beauty is rewarded not
for the beauty itself but because the beauty . . . is regarded by the rest as
power," power particularly of the supernatural sort (Forge 1967:83). It is
for this reason that the effectiveness of ornaments involved in divination
may be influenced by aesthetic quality: "The evidence suggests that both
the Senufo diviner and client consider that the degree of expert craftsmanship and artistic merit appreciably enhances the power of the ornament to
fulfill its religious function" (Glaze 1981:73, 76).

The same holds true for hopeful kula participants of Gawa (Oceania),
where the capability of members of a kula expedition to successfully obtain
shells from overseas kula partners is seen to lie largely in the power of
attraction produced by various aesthetic devices. Included among them is
decoration by carving, painting, and other ornamentation of the expedition canoe in order to purify it and to impart vital beauty to it. Kula
participants also decorate their bodies in order to produce an attractiveness that will compel kula partners to give up their shells. In short, as
Munn points out, beautification has kinetic effects for Gawa Islanders:
"Conversely, an unpainted canoe might negatively affect *kula* partners, so
that they would refuse *kula* shells" (Munn 1977:46–51; 1986:101–102,
145–147).

Aesthetics, as expressed in fine crafting, not only contains transformative mystical powers of attraction or of communication, such as divination,
but also effects movement from one realm of human experience to another
in the sense of transforming the ordinary into the extraordinary or the
secular into the sacred or the common into the sublime. The extraordinary,
the sacred, or the sublime in this perspective refers to things and activities
that are more abstract, ritualized, or refined, are judged to be particularly
honorable and of higher status, and as most truly or purely human, in a
word, are judged to be elite as opposed to those things and activities considered non-ritual, lower status, coarse, or common. Stated in terms of
other sets of contrasts that we have related to skilled crafting, we may find
conceptual parallels between aesthetics as bespeaking more refined or elitist contexts of expression and experience and master artisans as representing epitomes of the human condition.[5]

William Davenport (1986), speaking of the Eastern Solomon Islands, provides an excellent example of the power of aesthetics to effect transformation from the ordinary to the sacred or sublime (elite) in his analysis of activities and concepts surrounding a series of two funerals and three commemorative celebrations held for important deceased ancestors on the island of Santa Catalina or Aoriki. Portions of his account are discussed here at some length to illustrate the interrelatedness of a number of themes we have addressed so far. The particular transformations produced by aesthetics occur as the scale, especially the time/space dimensions, of the funerals and commemorative feasts (*-murinas*) expand.

As Davenport relates, immediately following a death in Aoriki a brief period of mourning ensues in which business in and out of the community by land or sea is halted and total silence may be maintained in the village. Distant kin and nonrelations continue daily activities and care for the mourners, while immediate kin are so immobilized. A small feast is given at this time. Several months later another feast of somewhat larger proportions is offered, in which, to increase its value, extra effort may be made to acquire a pig from outside the village, while an artisan is commissioned to carve new wooden bowls for the presentations of food. This artisan may be a local person, but if he or she is brought in from another village the value of the feast is enhanced by the extra effort involved in going abroad to obtain a notable carver. During these two funerals the scale of the observances are roughly commensurate with the social rank of the deceased.

Every few years additional commemorative events are held to honor deceased adults of substantial social rank who have died during the interval following the last commemorative feast. For such a feast a large bowl, newly carved for the occasion, is again required, plus a pig. The scale of the second commemorative feast will be larger than the first, but the number of deceased so honored will be smaller. The third type of commemorative feast is the largest and most ambitious. The entire community undertakes the extravaganza with other communities in attendance. An elaborate structure is built by gifted artisans from many communities, and very large carved bowls are similarly commissioned. An extremely elegant trading canoe or bonito and tuna fishing canoe may be built, too. (Such trading canoes, distinct from ordinary canoes, are regarded not only as economically useful but as tangible representations of the community abroad; bonito and tuna fishing is a sacred endeavor dedicated to major deities). Each canoe, which is regarded as the supreme expression of crafting skill and artistry and which may require experts from other communities for its construction, is dedicated to an important deceased individual (an ancestor of sorts) and becomes a sacred object. The deceased themselves, people who had been notable achievers during their lives, are deified, and join the spirits that protect people from alien spirits and enemies or dangerous foreigners; they will be further honored as deities by periodic boys' initiation rites and by the annual bonito fishing quest.

In discussing these activities, Davenport emphasizes that aesthetics enters into preparations for the great third commemorative celebration all along the way. Foodstuffs are carried from gardens or canoes by processions of young singing women, and are arranged with great care in attractive displays; prepared food, tastefully decorated, is presented in the specially carved vessels; new songs are composed, dance teams practice, and groups of dancers and singers from far away are brought in to participate: "The festivities are infused with the spirit of an arts festival as well as an air of lavish expenditure" (1986:103). Davenport notes that such aesthetic embellishment, which involves expression of the highest social values, transforms ordinary material goods into noneconomic goods, that is, into sacra. He further notes that the construction of trading and bonito canoes requires proficiency at *all* the skills that competent persons should possess; "Possession of all the talents required to build one of these craft is the measure of a master craftsman, an artist, an exceptional person" (1986: 105). In addition, "In every truly great work of art there is a connection with the supernatural" via inspiration and assistance, and "The use of exceptional talent is confined to a limited set of objects for use only in ritualized or sacred contexts."

> For example, people eat every day out of simple but very well-carved wooden bowls, and any man minimally skillful should be able to make one. For sacred meals, however, food is served in bowls that are elegantly carved and inlaid—implements that not every man can make. The elegantly carved bowl sets the religious meals apart from everyday meals. The same difference applies to house posts for a dwelling and for a structure in which ritual presentations of food are displayed; to ordinary fishing canoes and the canoes used exclusively to catch sacred bonito and tuna; to canoes made expressly for trading by individuals and the larger canoes that make more ambitious trading voyages and were once used for raiding. No ordinary commodities are embellished or enhanced with exceptional aesthetic skills. In summary, the utilization of exceptional aesthetic skills is confined to objects used only in sacred and secular rituals. (1986:105–106)

In addition, "No ritual object, no aesthetic object, is made for personal enjoyment. Each object made by a gifted artist is for use in a ritual, and afterward becomes a memento of the event for which it was created. Thus, art objects are not generalized types. Each object is unique for two reasons: it is an individualized creation, and it is a material record of the event for which it was made" (ibid.). In short, "The utilization of exceptional skills, or what we think of as aesthetic expressions, sets certain objects apart from ordinary things and commodities and designates them for use on ritual occasions alone. It decommoditizes them. Put another way, aesthetically embellished objects signal ritual contexts and ritual utilization. It is as if a nonmaterial or spiritual, dimension is added to an object, committing it to a domain in which social and religious values prevail over economic ones" (ibid.: 106–107).

In Davenport's account, aesthetic skills transform ordinary, common materials into objects charged with mystical, spiritual worth, just as funerals and commemoration feasts change ordinary persons into honored ancestral spirits. The scale and range of artistry and commemorative feasts widen in scope and in degree of transformation until the ultimate transformations occur in circumstances that not only honor deceased persons of great worth but deify them; circumstances that are organized by living persons, community leaders, of high esteem; that involve a wide range of artistic abilities and participants, including artisans, from a wide sphere of communities; and that require production of means (skillfully crafted canoes for sacred fishing or distant trade) to tap the sacralized benefits of an even wider oceanic realm. The entire scenario grows, rises, and expands from localized beginnings to increasingly broader dimensions of spatial involvement on land and sea that correlate with the creation, by the highest level of living elite, of the highest level of deified elite. These, in turn, are affiliated again with sacralized and spatially distant acts (bonito and tuna fishing, and, I would venture to guess, with long-distance trade). The tangible activities by which these expanding horizontal and vertical dimensions of space/time are expressed are distinguished by increased quantity and quality of goods. The former is evidenced by sheer amount of food; the latter by aesthetic products of increasing diversity showing increasing crafting skill and produced by artisans from outside the community and/ or by master craftsmen with the greatest talent.

In the end it is the abilities of the craftspeople involved, that is, the aesthetics these exceptional persons produce, that transform the quality of the goods used in the feasts and of the feasts themselves; change the meaning, the social values involved from the ordinary, the personally private, and the secularly everyday to the extraordinary or sacred, the societal, and the ritually periodic; in other words, produce circumstances that fall into the political-ideological domain and basically become the responsibility of men of influence and leadership.

Persons of influence, being concerned with all aspects of power no matter how that elusive term may be defined, are naturally drawn to associate with aesthetics, both as expression or exposure of moral order and in the more dynamic contexts of transformation and imposition of moral order, because beauty itself exercises power, beauty itself has the power to attract (Kuper 1973:620, 622; Chernoff 1979:168). As James Fernandez notes with respect to the Fang, however, these modes of aesthetic expression may vary considerably in their potential for political use. Those artists, such as carvers, "who simply expose aesthetically pleasing harmonies for the delectation of their compatriots, while esteemed, are not highly respected and are of low rank." In contrast, those village judges and skilled orators "who impose harmony upon their compatriots, thereby enhancing the quality of Fang life, are greatly to be respected and are of high rank. For they have done the most difficult of all things. They have acted to make universal harmonies manifest in social life which is in its nature, as far as the Fang are concerned, ever disturbed and endlessly gravitating to a state 'nasty, brutish and mean.' In the case of religious leaders this means the closer approximation of secular disorder to sacred order" (1973:196–197). Again, "We have a tendency to leave the imposition of order to those concerned with crude power—the politicians. It may well be that all the mechanisms of social control of modern life enable man to impose order artlessly. But among the highly egalitarian politically unstructured Fang it is impossible to impose order without art. The leader had to be proficient in expressing himself artistically, creating thereby a moving aesthetic spectacle" (Fernandez 1973:217).

The nature of such spectacles can be quite diverse, for persons of influence can, and have, associated themselves with a considerable variety of types of artistic skills. Regardless of the media used, however, the underlying goal remains basically the same; command of aesthetics connotes command of the moral order, socially and cosmologically, and thus evidences capacity for proper rule:

In many festivals and celebrations in many African cultures, a chief is *required* to dance before his people. . . . What is there for the chief to show off, and what do people wish to see displayed? It is not the vanity of self-expression that some observers have taken to be the source of the dancer's pleasure, nor is the chief merely proving that he is still healthy. In his dance, the chief combines aesthetic command and moral command, and the satisfying beauty of his dance is a visible display of his closeness to the ancestors and his fitness for authority. The chief asserts the community through a dance in which gracefulness implies the tranquility of mature strength, elegance implies the bounty of life, precision implies dedication of purpose, happiness implies the accessibility of compassion, composure implies the discretion of power, and dignity implies destiny." (Chernoff 1979:150–151).

Even in the more static forms of skilled crafting, where beauty may simply expose order and harmony, rather than actively impose it, the arts of leadership contrast notably with those of common folk in terms of aesthetic quality (Fraser and Cole 1972:303–309). Indeed, the arts, meaning the aesthetics and the morality, of leadership ideally should always approximate perfection. As the opening epigraph states, "The King should not set up or keep in a temple a disproportioned or broken image; worn out images of the angels, and ruined temples, are to be carefully restored" (Coomaraswamy 1935:116).[6]

5 Skilled Crafting and Political Authority

I bent my neck for Marduk, my lord; and, girding up the robes of
my royalty, I carried bricks and clay upon my head.

— NABOPOLASSAR
king of Assyria, quoted in Henri Frankfort,
Kingship and the Gods, p. 273

Crafting and Politics in Egalitarian Societies

It is by now anthropologically commonplace to associate royal rulers with
coteries of skilled artisans—jewellers, painters, carvers, metalworkers,
composers and musicians, poets and bards, who frequently live in close
proximity to their patrons' royal courts, and whose expertise surrounds
high lords with a wealth of exquisitely produced "fine art." We have also
come to appreciate some aspects of the political and ideological symbolism
expressed in this association between high rank, power, and authority and
quality things, recognizing that chiefs and kings do not glory simply in
the surface extravagance provided by finely crafted materials and dramatic
courtly pomp and circumstance but that the services and products of
skilled artisans are fundamentally expressive of socially acceptable political
authority and influence and assist in the implementation of that authority
(Fraser and Cole 1972; Lindstrom 1984).

In considering the relationship between skilled crafting and high political authority I wish not only to pursue this association between rulers and
skilled artisans but also to consider persons of influence in conjunction
with the act and qualities of crafting per se; specifically, as skilled crafters
themselves. Ethnographic data make it readily apparent that recognition
as master crafters can significantly contribute to recognition and acceptance as political leaders in non-centralized societies. This allows the logical conclusion that the formal separation of these roles into ruler and court
artisans in centralized and hierarchical polities is in a certain sense merely
a division of specialization rooted in this earlier conjunction. The identi-

fication of skilled crafting with political authority can also be succinctly encapsulated in the many instances when chiefs and kings, though ably served by court personnel, nonetheless still personally pursue a skilled craft of some sort. Recognition of persons of influence as skilled craftsmen then suggests the further conclusion that the qualities and values associated with skilled crafting are fundamental also to the role of political leadership and grants us further justification for considering whether various other craft-like dimensions of political behavior, specifically acquisition of resources from outside realms, may also be considered as manifestations of chiefly skilled crafting writ large.

Let us begin by summarizing pertinent points from several ethnographic examples which very clearly relate positions and abilities of skilled artisans with positions and abilities of political authority in non-centralized societies. Several characteristics of skilled crafting among the Fang of West Equatorial Africa have been noted previously, including Fernandez' insightful observation that performance of certain skilled crafts, such as oratorical arts, are valued because they appear to impose order on a potentially chaotic world, while performance of other skills, such as the carving of reliquary figures, exposes order already inherent in the universe at large. The artful and aesthetic imposition of order by judges of village and inter-village disputes, by council house debators, and sometimes by traveling harpist-troubadors, all skilled as orators, carries high rank and prestige in Fang society because it is their delicate task not only to settle disputes by finding a compromise acceptable to the opposing parties but to do so in such a way that the litigants are persuaded to return to a more harmonious association. It is the acceptance of this reconciliation, this imposition of a new order, that is achieved by high oratorical artistry. An accomplished judge strides back and forth, "interspersing his comment with homilies, aphorisms, and proverbial expressions that here distract and there point the attention of his audience to the essentials of the affair. Now he moralizes; now he is pessimism itself about the relations of man to man. As he talks on, his audience tends to forget the passions of the moment, though not their interest in his final decision." Such an approach is far more than superficial display, for "If judgment is not artfully done it will likely fail. There are no procedural mechanisms which will guarantee its success. Every *palabra* demands its particular embellishment. The *nkik mesang* [judge] must creatively work to shape a new and viable social whole from the raw materials and shattered patterns of behavior brought forth in litigation" (Fernandez 1973:207–208).

The qualitative experience of witnessing a well handled *palabra* is very profound for the Fang. They speak about its subtlety and persuasiveness long after. Men who can accomplish these kinds of judgement have quite high rank. I submit that this is partially a consequence of the fact that they are able to artfully impose order upon their compatriots—an order which the *nkik mesang* aesthetically perceives to be possible in village life and which he artfully calls upon his peers to approximate. (Ibid.: 209)

Fernandez concludes that "Among the highly egalitarian politically unstructured Fang it is impossible to impose order without art" (ibid.: 217). He also tentatively suggests that "It would seem that in disintegrated or loosely integrated systems much greater respect would accrue to the artistic imposition of order than in highly integrated ones where order exists and need not be created. In the integrated system, high rank would accrue to the artist who exposed the order already known to exist, while the imposition of order would be regarded as intrusive and redundant" (ibid.: 217). While this intriguing observation may require a bit of fine tuning, particularly in those highly structured systems where chiefs or kings still personally express the roles of master artisans as nominal builders of cities (see following section), Fernandez' emphasis on the artistic and aesthetic requirements underlying the imposition of order in non-centralized society, where compliance with social directives is so delicately voluntary, is supported by additional evidence from comparable political settings where the authority of master artisans again takes an administrative tone.

The Ilahita Arapesh of New Guinea as described by Tuzin (1978; 1980) provide another case in point. Although artistic excellence is not the only path to political prominence, "It is also true that a disproportionate number of big men are, in fact, master artists" (1978: 62). Tuzin does not regard this as merely coincidental. He explains that persons with political abilities and ambitions may also be attracted to skilled crafting, particularly painting and sculpting, because art is the only pursuit that provides the opportunity to manipulate, exploit, even create the images and ideas on which community well-being is believed to depend. Such art also contains magical potency by virtue of which it is also considered aesthetically pleasing by a population well prepared to judge such matters since, given the spiritual significance of artistic production, all people are expected to participate to some degree in the requisite crafting, a process which also makes them particularly appreciative of the exceptional talent exhibited by the master crafter.

The administrative skills of Ilahita master artists are evidenced in the preparation of large wooden figures and of hundreds of paintings used in initiation ceremonies and executed on smooth sections of the splayed mid-rib of sago-palm fronds. These paintings are believed to be infused with the spirits of the group creating and presenting them, an infusion that occurs in the act of crafting. To assure the requisite artistic-aesthetic form, master artists outline the basic designs but then entrust the work to others of lesser talent, who color in the design according to the instructions and under the watchful eye of a master (Tuzin 1978; 1980:175–178). All these paintings and statues then must be carefully installed in an elaborate men's house, again under the constant direction of master artists.

When all is ready, master artisans direct the very delicate and potentially disruptive issues of social protocol entailed by inter-village gatherings and ceremonials that then take place. In their roles as social and political administrators of artistic-ceremonial activities, master artisans not only acquire a considerable authority base but can influence public policy by either agreeing to contribute to future ceremonies or by threatening to withhold such support (Tuzin 1978:66). In addition (as discussed in Chapter 2), new social groups represented by new spirit entities expressed in new design motifs can also be actively created and led by master artists provided the new motifs (social entities) are judged aesthetically (politically) acceptable by other members of the elite political arena that master artisans compose. Tuzin summarizes the authority held by Arapesh master artists by noting that "If, as is commonly assumed, sacred symbols hypostasize the central values of a culture, then it follows—logically, if not always empirically—that those empowered to create and manipulate these symbols are in a special but equivalent sense larger than life. And it is the ardent study of politicians the world over to become seen as 'larger than life,' for such standing affords those opportunities and immunities in respect of convention which leaders require to mold public opinion" (1978: 61; 1980:194, 200–201).

Phyllis Rabineau presents another example, this time from South America, of the role of the master artisan as recognized political leader in her discussion of the production of feather headdresses in Cashinahua society (eastern Peru). Here again, the pertinent issues focus on social recognition of aesthetics as "analogous to the normative rules of the political process" (1975:90). More specifically, those Cashinahua village headmen (the highest political position in Cashinahua society) who were recognized as effective political leaders were also praised by villagers as being excellent crafters of aesthetically pleasing feather headdresses, while ambitious but unsuccessful men who aspired to headmanship but had not achieved a following were criticized as incompetent headdress craftsmen whose work showed unacceptable aesthetic excesses (too many and the wrong kind of feathers). Rabineau also highlights several other very important characteristics common to both the aesthetics of crafting and the pursuit of political life among the Cashinahua and similar societies. She notes that:

> Political leadership in the tropical forest is truly 'an art.' Social relationships defined through kinship, or established through generosity, and maintained by exemplary behavior, provide the materials, the pragmatic rules of political processes. However, no man may successfully utilize these relationships without obeying the formal, normative aesthetic of leadership. The rules of this aesthetic include placing the needs of the community before personal interests, maintaining unity by encouraging consensus decisions, helping to organize cooperative work parties, avoiding overt competition for political leadership, and avoiding coercion in exercising authority. (1975:99)

More specifically, Rabineau emphasizes art and the "aesthetic of the 'ideal man'":

> Headmen are individuals who successfully use the pragmatic rules of social relations to assemble a following. However, the success of their efforts is largely due to their ability to present themselves as representing the aesthetic of the 'ideal man': interested in community before self, willing to impoverish oneself for the benefit of others, uncoercive, and able to make compromises. The latter trait is demonstrated in verbal artistry. . . . among the traits Indians regard as signifying the 'ideal man' are the wearing of feathers and the ability to make feather headdresses. For example, the Cubeo feel that in order to be considered human one must wear ornaments. . . . In myths of the Kaapor Indians . . . the ability to make headdresses sets the Indian apart from animals and from the white man.
>
> Given these attitudes, it seems likely that the ability to make an acceptable headdress is one of the traits defining the ideal Cashinahua man. It is therefore associated with the headmanship, for in an egalitarian society like the Cashinahua, the headman occupies no specialized status; he is simply an 'ideal man.' It is also likely that people's specific notions of the 'ideal man' can change in time, for instance, be modified to fit the traits embodied by the incumbent headman. Consequently, the particular hat-making abilities of a headman might become the accepted standard for his community. (1975:102–103)

As was the case with painting and sculpture among the Ilahita Arapesh, the skilled crafting of featherworking among the Cashinahua also involves contact with the supernatural outside realm, for feathers appear to be the loci of spirits and are used on all occasions when contact is made with the spirit world. "Conformity to aesthetic rules of featherworking would seem to be a means of propitiating the spirits and thus working for the good of the community; the intent is to ensure that they do not interfere negatively in society's affairs" (Rabineau 1975:105). Members of the community also show their support for the headman by giving him feathers, signaling that he is entrusted with the well-being of the village and visibly legitimating his power (ibid.:106).[1]

Finally, a few words concerning the Shuar of southeast Ecuador, whose particular conjoining of skilled crafting and political influence highlights the importance of mastery over both the technical and the symbolic expressions of knowledge pertinent to the acquisition of power (Hendricks 1988:219–224). The Shuar also provide an excellent example of hunting as skilled craft (see also Chapter 9). Socially influential and powerful men are reputed to have exceptional amounts of a vital force, *kakáran,* which provides the prestige necessary for political influence. Their power is demonstrated by a variety of personal characteristics (physical strength, generosity, knowledge of myth, ritual, and nature) including achievements as orators and as skilled hunters. *Kakáran* is actually acquired, however, through knowledge of both technical skills and the means for symbolic control over important resources:

> Hunting ability is considered important evidence of a man's personal power, for a man must master a great deal of technical and symbolic knowledge to hunt well. To be a good hunter, a man must control a vast amount of knowledge about the jungle and its inhabitants. He must know the habits of all the animals he hunts, where to find them and when, and the calls each of them makes; and he must be accomplished in the use of several weapons. An effective hunter must also be able to construct blinds and traps, track game through dense forest, and stalk the game when found. In addition to the technical knowledge necessary for successful hunting, an effective hunter must control the symbolic knowledge associated with hunting. He must know, for example, how to interpret his dreams so that he knows whether it is an auspicious day for hunting a particular animal. He must have knowledge of the food taboos associated with hunting the animals. Most important, he must know the hunting

songs . . . that attract game to the area and make the animals reveal themselves to the hunter. (Hendricks 1988 : 221)

It is also noteworthy that association with the outside world is again involved in the successful acquisition of hunting power, not only in the sense that the realm of animals lies without but also because the requisite magical hunting songs are frequently acquired from other ethnic groups (ibid. : 221).

Power over Things as Power over People

Each of these ethnographic accounts associating master artisans with an expanded field of socio-political influence has highlighted at least one major characteristic of skilled crafting that has direct relevance to political leadership. Fernandez' interpretation of Fang master artisans suggests the political importance of the artisan's ability for exposition and especially imposition of form as manifestation of the fundamental crafting capacity for outside-inside transformation and creation by which the invisible is given tangible credence and the potentially chaotic is controlled.

Tuzin, discussing the Ilahita Arapesh, has noted the opportunities for administrative expertise which may develop when a master artisan can supervise group craft activities and when only the master artisan, by a talent for aesthetic designing, has the requisite authority to summon up the outside spirits whose presence is requisite for community well-being.

Rabineau's analysis of Cashinahua hatmaking emphasizes the importance of the quality of aesthetics, the tangible expression of the morally good and the true, for identifying those individuals who will be accorded political-artistic influence because they represent and attempt to emulate the epitome, the ideal, of a truly worthy social person in a properly functioning society.

Finally, Janet Hendricks' analysis of skilled hunting as a means to acquire politically significant personal funds of power emphasizes that crafting requires understanding of the supernatural forces of the universe without whose cooperation technical control over the physical properties of natural materials would be intellectually unsatisfactory or insignificant; in non-manufacturing societies even judged to be impossible.

Each of these politically valuable characteristics or qualities of crafting can be found many times over in the ethnographic record in the numerous situations when political leaders personally practice a skilled craft (regardless of whether they also subsidize other artisans acting on their behalf); among the Wantoat of northeast New Guinea, only heads of families and lineages have the right, and the requisite knowledge, to paint designs on bark-cloth canvases worn by dancers during cult ceremonies; designs imbued with the outside power with which cult members seek to establish communion (Schmitz 1963:88).[2]

The point is frequently made in metaphor, too, as rulers are likened to the means or the product of skilled crafting. Thus, the Kabaka of Buganda is "'the charcoal fire of the smith,' who can forge the kingdom as the smith forges iron" (Fallers et al. 1964:68) and the newly accessioned chief of the Bashu, primary mediator between the world of the domestic homestead and the dangerous forces of the bush, when he is "reborn" as chief, is likewise likened to a piece of forged iron because, like the iron, he has undergone a transition from one state to another and he is "hot," meaning ritually dangerous (Packard 1981:37). Political-ideological relationships between chiefship and the miracles of metalworking can also achieve very real political expressions when smiths consolidate political authority and personal power (Glaze 1981:140; Paden 1970:162) and when chiefs or kings are also experts in some form of metalwork.[3]

It is particularly noteworthy within the argument of this book that management of the powers of transformation and control expressed by supernatural-cum-technical knowledge can associate leadership and crafting skills in the context of travel, too. For example, William Alkire explains that on Lamotrek atoll "The corpus of knowledge of a navigator includes not only the mechanics of sailing, but also a whole range of supernatural knowledge. Because of the prestige associated with this individual it is usual for most chiefs to seek training as a *pelu* [navigator] so that their status position will be undisputed in all spheres" (1965:127). Similarly, on Puluwat atoll, where for similar reasons navigators hold the highest prestige and distinction, the formal leadership positions of traditional chiefs or colonially defined island administrators are often held by navigators. In fact, since, in this seafaring society, the most important events are those associated with travel by sea to other islands, navigators automatically control most of the really significant occasions in Puluwat life (Gladwin 1970: 125–126).

Even when political activity is not directly associated with skilled crafting the skills of the artisan may be recognized in its practitioners. In ancient Greek thought, the exceptional cunning intelligence (*metis*) attributed to the skilled blacksmith, carpenter, weaver, hunter, shipbuilder, and navigator was equally recognized in the cleverness not only of the physician and the sophist but also of the politician: "Sickness and argument are forces just as hostile and disturbing as the sea, fire, or molten metal. In dealing with them it is always necessary to foresee when the fleeting opportunity for tricking the polymorphic powers [evidencing *metis*] will arise" (Detienne and Vernant 1978 : 307–308, 310, 313).

Michael Ayrton, in his novel *The Maze Maker,* states the situation well when his hero, Daedalus, the craftsman par excellence skilled in building, carving, painting, and especially metallurgy, comments that "A man can make his own power only by disdaining power over other men . . . he need only fear other men's power if he is no more than another man and . . . he can become more than other men by gaining power over things which are not men, for thus he goes beyond men" (1967 : 20). Yet he who goes beyond other men in fact may not totally disdain power over them but may also reach back to guide and control while maintaining his own more exalted position and his own uniqueness, expressed by an expertise, a particular fund of restricted knowledge, denied to ordinary persons. "The dances and court etiquette of the traditional elites in Ruanda or Hawaii . . . [were] displays of finesse that sealed their boundary and kept them above the arena of competition. It was a demonstration of the immutability of their superiority. . . ." (Spencer 1985 : 24; Kaeppler 1985 : 111, 112). Even if that expertise is not entirely denied the commoner, it yet remains exemplary: "Ordinary people look upon their feudal lords as models of conduct and do not hesitate to imitate them, learning their poetry, dancing, painting, and carving in order to be like them" (Covarrubias 1938 : 162, regarding Bali).[4]

The Kingly Craft of Building

A particularly elegant example of political leadership as skilled crafting, that is, of rulers as transformers and imposers of form and order, is found in Susan Kus' discussion of eighteenth- and early nineteenth-century Imerina (Madagascar) political theory. The Merina reconciled the apparent incompatibility of cosmic permanence and human change by recognizing major social, economic, and technological innovations, such as the introduction of cooked meat and of guns, building of irrigation systems, tax and market reforms and social reforms related to class stratification, as "epiphanies of social order" which were attributed, culture hero–like, to various rulers and served to demonstrate the fitness of the ruler to rule. These acts were then further interpreted as "steps toward actualizing an ideal of peace, prosperity and political unity" (Kus 1986 : 4, 5). A similar spirit of beneficial kingly artisanry is expressed in the traditional Khmer conviction that the monarch was the source of benefits through ordered constructions designed to ensure prosperity, such as the Khmer hydraulic system constructed at Angkor and elsewhere (Hall 1985:146; Duncan 1990:38, 40, 53–54, 78).[5]

Without diminishing appreciation of the improvements realized in Khmer agricultural productivity by a system that could regularize the water supply or of the economic and social benefits to the Merina of guns, market reforms, and the like, I would like to emphasize here the identification, in both cases, of kings as innovators and particularly as builders, for it is as builders, and especially as builders of physical constructions such as temples, palaces, public works, even entire cities, that the concept of political leadership becomes most visibly and dramatically intertwined with concepts of skilled crafting at the highest levels of centralized societies. It is as builders that political elites may be most dramatically or visibly seen to impose ordered form on the social and natural landscape, as establishing access to and controlling and transforming the powers of the cosmological realm outside by symbolic and technical knowledge, as realizing aesthetic ideals associated with both skilled crafting and the proper expression of leadership and government, and as literally associating themselves, as master creator-crafters, with ancestral creative powers as these are expressed in places and actions of origins and of new beginnings (Duncan 1990).[6]

Historically we can trace the origins of kings as actual or nominal builders to the lineage headmen, master artisans, and religious specialists who direct the construction of community dwellings, men's houses, initiation quarters, or communal ceremonial-political centers in tribal and chiefdom societies. Speaking of the Cubeo of northwestern Amazonia, Goldman says, "In the case of the headman who is known only as 'owner of the house' . . . his warrant of office is that it is he who has built the maloca . . . It is as 'owner of the house' that the headman is giver, guide, and keeper of order" (1963:155).[7] Similarly, with respect to the Alkatcho Carrier of British Columbia, "The most important noble of the group was recognized as the potlatch chief for the entire village. He built the central potlatch house, and was the center in inter-village potlatches" (Goldman 1940:348–349). In traditional myth-history the origins of kings as builders can be traced to original creator deities who, as artists-in-chief, gave the universe its architectural origin and form (Mbiti 1969:39) or to kingly culture heroes, such as Kun, father of the Hsia dynasty of early Chinese history (ca. 2205–1766 B.C.), who was credited with the first building of cities (Chang 1974:1; see note 7) or Enki, whose gifts to ancient Mesopotamia included instruction in city-building and whose skills were continued by Gilgamesh (see Chapter 1), heralded as builder of the walls, ramparts, and temples of Uruk.

Obviously kings did not build palaces, temples, public works and cities single-handedly, but ordered specialists and common laborers to do the work (Bernal 1969:76–77). Nevertheless, kings personally assumed ultimate responsibility for an enterprise which, like all traditional forms of skilled crafting, involved sacred or supernatural understandings as much as material or technical knowledge. Coteries of skilled artisans performed the labor, but the kings, as official master artisans, carried the supernatural or transformational responsibility and conducted the necessary rituals to ascertain that this endeavor enjoyed the blessings of the gods. They may also have officially provided evidence of that blessing with the labor of their own hands.

The kingly preparation and creation of the ceremonial first brick in the construction of ancient Mesopotamian temples is illustrative, and Henri Frankfort provides a vivid reconstruction of events. After the gods had sent a preliminary sign that they approved the project and a site had been chosen, great ceremonies of purification were undertaken while a period of civil peace was imposed, oracles were consulted, and precious building materials from foreign lands were brought into the city. If all seemed well so far, the time was set for the molding of the first brick, which had to be well and truly formed and extracted from the mold in perfect condition—the ultimate sign that the gods approved the enterprise (see Figure 5–1; see also Duncan 1990:175). Given the awesome significance of the event, the molding was always carried out by the king in person, a procedure surrounded by kingly purifications, godly communications, processions, incense, and, finally, the mixing and molding of the clay; the period of drying; more incense of aromatic wood and at dawn, the breaking of the mold and the joyful display to the population of a perfect brick. After that the work was expected to proceed without incident since the gods, who had indicated their final approval by way of the brick's aesthetic perfection, were themselves now directly participating in the work, as evidenced by Akkadian cylinder seals that depict deities "mixing mud, carrying mortar up ladders, and throwing bricks up to others who are at work on top of the temple" (Frankfort 1948:269–274).

Regardless of whether gods or humans actually did the work, accepting responsibility for the creation of new cities, palaces, temples, or aqueducts placed kings in the company of creator deities and signalled the period of

5-1.   Ur-Nanshe carrying clay to mold the first brick for a new temple. (From Henri Frankfort, *Kingship and the Gods*. University of Chicago Press, Fig. 46, 1948. Used by permission of Musée du Louvre.)

their reigns as a comparable era of pristine beginnings, a time of origins or at least of propitious continuation. "The Incas, in their own legendary history, claimed responsibility for reforming the land and for recreating the social order. Part of the Inca plan involved creating agricultural works, building towns, and constructing palaces and temples, using stone to engineer a new world. It is not surprising that Viracocha might approach the Incas through their quarries, as it was in such places that their own activity most nearly approached his own" (Niles 1987:186).[8] In traditional China such new worlds could be attained by periodically moving and rebuilding capital cities. The decision to relocate cities in this way may have been influenced by divination and was seen as an act of renewal that perpetuated the favor of the gods. Chang points out that the movement from site to site was at the king's option, and the layout and structuring of the new capital were designed to serve him as the center of attention, specifically, it would seem, as a new creator, a rebuilder (Chang 1974:5).

Inherent in the imposition of a new political-cum-cosmological era through the formal shapes of architecture is the idea that prior to this event chaotic irrationality and amorphousness by definition claimed the world. By acts of skilled crafting, however, as by military might, these disruptions might be tamed, the population settled into civilized domesticity, the countryside ordered by roads and canals, and the rich resources of the outside world be brought home to the greater glory of gods and king. An inscription of Nebuchadnezar not only describes such a scenario but grandly claims the formal credit for the king in terms that identify him as unexcelled artisan, military general, and familiar of the deities:

> With the force of Nabu and Marduk, my lords [deities], I armed my troops for an expedition in Lebanon. I drove out the enemy above and below, I brought happiness to the heart of the earth. The scattered population I gathered and brought back to their home. That which no king had done before, I did: I cleft high mountains, I cut blocks of stone from the mountains, I opened paths, prepared roads for the transport of the cedars. On the canal Avakhtu, as though they were reeds of the river, I floated large cedars, tall and strong, of great beauty, of imposing aspect, rich product of Lebanon, and brought them before Marduk, the king [i.e., to the temple]. (Quoted in Moscati 1968:83)

Such events were the stuff of kingly lives in ancient Mesopotamia (as in succeeding ages), where royal inscriptions regularly recount how "as ever-victorious hero [the king] conducts yearly campaigns, and as pious master-builder he restores temples" (Tadmor 1986:206; Wendell 1971:102–103).

The products of official kingly crafting—the palaces, temples, and cities—clearly speak of associations between polity, king, and deities; that is, to the vertical axis of political ideology and cosmology. These same constructions, however, can also glorify the horizontal axis of political-ideology and cosmology, that which relates the king and his polity to the geographically distant places and people beyond the walls of the city and the boundaries of the kingdom, to the rich products of a distant Lebanon. To the extent that the horizontal and vertical cosmological axes are but variations on a common theme, indeed compose a common cosmological realm, of outside contacts and connections, it is understandable that the exotic riches of geographically distant worlds should grace the temples of the vertically distant gods and enhance the palace and the person of the king who mediates between the gods above as well as with the foreigners without. Contacts with either dimension enhance kingly splendours and engage kingly abilities of acquisition and transformation, for neither the graces of the gods nor the wealth or exoticism of the foreign is automatically available. Both may be attained only by suitable attention to transformational devices and procedures—to prayers and oracular divinations, the burning of incense, purificatory taboos, the visions of shamans and the chants of clergy, to the sending forth (also with proper prayers and purifications and other ritual precautions) of pilgrimages, ships, or caravans, and to hospitality extended to foreign travelers and visitors—artisans, traders, holy people—bearing exceptional skills and knowledge or exceptional goods.

Similarly, when successfully obtained, both the grace of the gods and the wealth of foreign places attest to the ability of transformational kings to provide for their subjects the powers and qualities associated with distant locales, whether in the heavens or beyond the horizon. This ability to provide expresses the qualities of kingship, qualities that distinguish and identify the ruler, as they distinguish and identify other skilled creator-transformers, as awesome and ideal humans who stand above or beyond the common social world. Although the qualities expected of the desirable leader vary considerably cross-culturally, there are a number of basic themes that continually reoccur and are closely comparable to the qualities and characteristics commonly associated with skilled artisans, including those of "flawed creator" and of "epitome" of the human condition (Chapter 4).

Although persons of influence, at least while in positions of legitimate authority, are not ostracized with low social status (though they may be feared or disliked) in some cases their exceptionality, like that of some skilled artisans, may be expressed by concepts not unlike that of "flawed creator" in that they display characteristics that place them beyond (cause a break from) established human norms of appearances or behavior. A lord so regarded may exhibit minor physical anomalies, such as polydactylism or clubfeet (Schele and Miller 1986:66, 74). He may approximate the puissant skilled artisan as potential sorcerer by scorning ordinary proprieties and at times using his power to frighten or harm: "A good chief pardons rarely but chastises frequently. . . . He fears neither fire nor heaven nor the anger of men. . . . A chief spits haughtily, he roars and thunders like the storm. He overturns the government of others and provokes calamities" (Fernandez 1982:60 re the Fang; Balandier 1968:36–37; Tambiah 1976: 522). Rulers as "flawed creators" are also exemplified by those whose efforts to approach and approximate the exemplary ancestors are ultimately limited by recognition that only deceased forebears can achieve total, pure political legitimacy and absolute knowledge, while those still living, even though leaders of great ability and influence, nonetheless remain burdened by the unavoidably limited wisdom of their humanity, by their physical frailty, or by the dual nature inherent in power that has potential to harm as much as to help and therefore must fall short of true godly or ancestral perfection (Kopytoff 1987:65; Rowlands 1987:57; Frankfort 1948:6, 8; Kantorowicz 1957:7–8; Gillespie 1989:216–218).

Alternatively, like skilled master artisans, influential persons are frequently expected to represent and express various ideals associated with proper human existence, ultimately seeking to approximate and emulate the perfections believed inherent in the condition of eliteness or aristocracy in general and of rulership in particular as "epitome" of the human condition. Fundamental to this perspective is the idea, common, for example, in African political-ideology, that "it is 'uncivilized' to be without a ruler" (Mair, quoted in Kopytoff 1987:63); that leadership combined with the necessary complement of supporters equates with recognition of the fundamental need for ordered social relationships if the properties of social living as part of the human condition are to be achieved (see Rabineau quoted above).

Thus the king as ideal individual decrees what is pure and impure, lawful and unlawful, and reiterates the higher ideals of human behavior as they should be for all persons (Duby 1974:107; Rowlands 1987:56). In addition, those who lead must also exemplify and epitomize these same standards—must approach the ideal on which all other human behavior should be modeled, the high standard which anyone can try to approximate but which chiefs should actually attain. In consequence, those who rule cannot be ordinary persons (Kantorowicz 1957:44), for they must be paragons of all virtues and devoid of all weaknesses, especially those common to lower human states or conditions. "Symbolically [the king] is separated and different in quality from other men, but he also partakes of all human features rather than the limited few possessed by ordinary people" (Gilbert 1987:327, 328 regarding Ghanaian royalty; Rees and Rees 1961: 130; van Beek 1987:44).

Underlying all else, the ruler as epitome is charged with achieving a fully aesthetic existence: "The ruler [in contrast to other persons] must possess moral goodness in its full and perfect form, because his function, regarded absolutely and in its full nature, demands a master artificer, and reason is such a master artificer; but all other persons need only possess moral goodness to the extent required of them. . . ." (Aristotle, Politics I, quoted in Austin and Vidal-Naquet 1977:182). The king's moral goodness, that is, his "truth" and his "beauty" (Rees and Rees 1961:129; Stephen 1979:91; Biebuyck 1972:18), and the benefits that derive therefrom may be expressed in the physical perfection (corresponding to moral perfection) frequently required of those who would rule (Gilbert 1987:328; Richards 1960:101, 148, 179, 216)[9] and in the high intelligence, wisdom, and exceptional knowledge, skills and abilities demanded of those who lead (Cochrane 1970:4–5, 11–12; Lindstrom 1984; Price 1981:694, 697). The Tsimshian (Northwest

Coast of North America) called such illustrious persons "Real People" and recognized them as their chiefs and as beings who can alter the world. "The notion of 'reality' can be seen as a cline; slaves are outside the cline; commoners are less real than chiefs; chiefs can be ranked from less to more real" (Seguin 1986:484).[10]

Goldman, speaking of the Kwakiutl, further explains that high nobles and chiefs are "real because they are complete; they combine in their person the past and the present. Most important, they are the monopolists of primary power and thus the designated leaders and the only proper hunters of land and sea mammals" (1975:52). As skilled hunters, chiefs are expected to show their aggressiveness and activeness, vital qualities of "real" people in contrast to commoners who are, in principle at least, ritually passive (1975:52–53). As aggressive hunters they are also associated with the acquisition of wealth from outside realms, traditionally expressed in Kwakiutl culture (as in other Northwest Coast groups) in various animal-related forms and things—"mammalian skins or items such as boxes, canoes, or shield-shaped copper plaques ('coppers') that have animal associations" (1975:4). Acquisition of wealth involves such real leaders in other skilled crafts (Holm 1983) or associates them with the products of such crafts, among them wooden chests and boxes, often elaborately (aesthetically) carved, used to hold food and wealth items, and canoes, the means of travel to wealth-producing locales (hunting and fishing sites and other villages for feasts; Seguin 1986:475–476).[11]

As is well known, following the amassing of wealth the Kwakiutl and other Northwest Coast peoples succinctly expressed and encapsulated qualities of rank and chiefship in elaborately orchestrated public ceremonies (the feast or potlatch) that further expressed social, political, and cosmological concepts of acquisition and transformation of outside-derived benefits, both tangible and spiritual, with the dynamics of song and masked dance and by ceremonial distributions of wealth items (see Seguin 1986). All this conjoined the populace with both vertical and horizontal axes of the outside and identified the elite as Ideal humans who stood at the junction of all these connections.

The same concepts, qualities, and conjunctions that identified the elite of Northwest Coast society as energetic, power-filled, acquisitive Real People and that energized the complex formations of potlatches are expressed in other settings in the identification of rulers as master-builders and in the layout and construction of their cities, temples, and palaces. Like potlatches, these constructions are expected to serve as statements and settings or foci for the conjunction of the qualities and resources of the vertical and the horizontal cosmological realms (Wheatley 1971, esp. Chapter 5). Such places serve as points for departure outward toward the far reaches of both the vertically above and the geographically beyond and as centers for return therefrom.

The layout of the medieval Islamic city of Baghdad as described by Charles Wendell (1971) and by Robert Hillenbrand (1988) provides an excellent case in point. Baghdad (founded in A.D. 762 by the Caliph al-Mansur) was constructed at a time of very consciously perceived political origins or new beginnings, when the Umayyad regime was replaced by the 'Abbasid Revolution, a new government geared to a different set of legitimacies. "Moreover, whereas the Umayyad capital of Damascus had been landlocked, Baghdad was on the banks of the Tigris, accessible to ocean-going shipping and thus effectively an inland port whose mercantile horizons embraced the Indian Ocean and the China Sea. Baghdad, then, was the earnest of a new era: a bridge between East and West . . . This momentous political reorientation demanded some symbolic statement worthy of it. Baghdad was that statement" (Hillenbrand 1988:16, 15).

The plan of the city, whose name means "god-given" or possibly, "paradise," was circular, with multiple outer walls and cramped living quarters for the populace located between the outer walls and an inner ring of fortifications. The center of the city, however, was both extensive and empty, containing only the palace and attached mosque and open space. A ninth-century geographer and historian who described Iraq as "the centre of this [Muslim] world, the navel of the earth," identified Baghdad as "the centre of Iraq, the greatest city . . . " (ibid.:20), strongly suggesting that the city was intended as the omphalos of the 'Abbasid world. In addition, the plan of the caliph's palace and mosque, the very center of the city, was laid out at an astrologically-fixed time and the city was built under the sign of Jupiter, the "most fortunate" planet, whose influence was believed to extend over places of worship, the staging-posts of travelers, and residences of teachers (Wendell 1971:122; Hillenbrand 1988:21). Hillenbrand comments that the astrological connection with worship "would fit well with the prominent location of the Friday mosque, while the connection with travel would be especially appropriate in a city which was so obviously intended to represent the wide extent of the Islamic empire. The assembling of craftsmen to the number of a hundred thousand from all over that empire to help build the city can be seen in the same light—a symbolic as well as an actual corvée. These considerations strengthen the case for regarding Baghdad as an Islamic mandala, namely a schematic representation of the whole world . . ." (ibid.:21; Wendell 1971:122).[12]

This "whole world" construction, however, not only engendered a sense of encompassment but also one of access to the vast spatial/temporal reaches that lay beyond, as evidenced by the location and identification of the city gates. The gates of Baghdad were arranged to divide the walls into four equal quadrants and were given names—Sha'm, Khurasan, Basra, Kufa—symbolic of the four major quadrants or spheres of interest composing the 'Abbasid empire. The names also presumably referred to roads leading to particular destinations, though the gates did not face in the cartographically true directions of these destinations. Thus caravans to Iraq, Syria, and Anatolia to the northwest would depart from the Sha'm gate and those to northern Iran, Transoxania and Turkestan would depart from the northeast-oriented Khurasan gate, while the southeast gate, Basra, opened, symbolically, to al-Basra, the emporium near the Persian Gulf for trade with India and China, and the Kufa gate to the southwest would be the departure point for travelers and caravans headed toward al-Kufa, gateway to the Arabian peninsula and to the Hijaz, the Holy Cities (Hillenbrand 1988:22–23; Wendell 1971:116, 117). Presumably, too (though neither Hillenbrand nor Wendell explore this point), these four gates were equally important as points of entry for peoples, products, and information from the holy centers of the Islamic religious heartland, the exotic reaches of India and China, the eastern Iranian world, and the western Mediterranean sphere, all distant realms that had their own political, ideological, and economic significance within the cosmology of the 'Abbasid world that focused its dimensional axes on the center of Baghdad and the absolute power of its caliphal creator.

A city was an emblem of royalty; constructing a city, crafting a city, with all its potent symbolism, brought the king into formal existence in a way nothing else could do. In the words of the successor to Baghdad's founder, who established his own royal center, "Now I know that I am indeed a king, for I have built myself a city and live in it" (Hillenbrand 1988: 26). Yet kingly construction yielded more than a heavy dose of self-justification; it also bespoke official concern for the well-being of the ruled: "I built and completed it, I made it magnificent to the astonishment of the peoples. For life . . . for length of days, for the stability of my reign, for the welfare of my posterity, for the safety of my priestly throne, for the overthrow of my enemies, for the success of the harvest(s) of Assyria, for the welfare of Assyria, I built it" (Esarhaddon, king of Assyria, on the restoration of a temple, quoted in Frankfort 1948:267).

Regardless of whether or not the king is personally skilled in a specific type of material craft and regardless of the extent of his city-building or temple restorations, the very nature of kingship, indeed of rulership in general regardless of the level of structural political complexities, involves the special capabilities and qualities of the master artisan. In innumerable acts associated with rule and government, the king behaves as the skilled creator/artisan that he is expected to be. He transforms, through culture hero–like acts of creativity that constantly create (or impose) socio-political order out of (or on to) the constantly threatening potential chaos of group living. He builds by tapping the resources of the wider world and acquiring or constructing benefits for himself and those he leads. He exemplifies by assuming unto himself aesthetically defined and accepted qualities of the ideal or exceptional human.

He legitimates his use of power and his authority, his transformative, constructive, and exemplative efforts, by invoking liminal associations with the culture hero–crafters who originally initiated these marks of cultured existence. By continually performing these activities anew, the ideal ruler collapses the time/space dimensions that separate the here-and-now from the there-and-then and relates himself to ancestral places and acts of origin on one or the other axis or dimension of the outside realm.

It was a tenet of many traditional political-ideologies that "The king altered the world and promoted the prosperity of his people, not by making them work in harmony and with energy, but by the direct action of his justice upon nature" (Hocart 1969:47).[13] "A ruler's performance of ritual [considered the very hallmark of a civilized people] coupled with correct moral behavior could actually influence the cosmos in a manner beneficial to mankind" (Wechsler 1985:9 regarding T'ang and pre-T'ang China). More specifically, such aesthetic behavior could cause the fish to multiply in the sea and the trees to bend beneath their load of fruit, could regulate the rainfall, the waters of the rivers, and the abundance of crops as well as the health and amiable social living of the populace (see also Seguin 1986:484). Numbered among the benefits and indicative of the prosperity as well as of the cosmos-affecting morality and justice of the king as transformer and as builder would be the successful acquisition of resources, of wealth—goods, skills, and knowledge—from geographically distant outside lands, to which subject we now turn in Part II of this work.

PART II

ACQUISITION

6   *Exchange, Trade, and Acquisition*

> Men are the only animals to set store by discovering, acquiring,
> and displaying materials comparatively rare in nature, frequently
> only to be obtained from distant sources and commonly useless
> for the purposes of daily life. By designating such materials as in
> varying degrees precious they have created symbols of excellence,
> a quality which stems from aesthetic awareness but the striving
> for which lies at the very root of the civilizations created by man.
>
> — GRAHAM CLARK,
> *Symbols of Excellence*, p. 3

Acquisition Defined

The ultimate intent of this volume is to assist our understanding of the
phenomenon frequently referred to by the rubric of long-distance trade by
acknowledging some of the symbolism and qualities associated with geographical distance and addressing the directly related issue of the meaning
attributed to long-distance goods. The basic hypothesis under discussion
asserts that the symbolism or meanings associated with things obtained
from distant places by acts of long-distance trade are comparable to the
symbolic associations that accompany things created by acts of skilled
crafting. The commonality between these two is seen to reside in the fact
that both types of activities involve things that originate in realms or conditions defined as cosmologically outside the bounds of settled, ordered
society and then are transformed in various ways as they are brought into
the socialized world so as to fit within a given cultural milieu. In some
cases this transformation may entail changes in physical state. In all cases
it involves application of meanings and qualities appropriate to the
political-ideology of the society in question. It follows, too, that those
individuals who engage in or take official responsibility for long-distance
trade are considered to be imbued with qualities comparable to those associated with skilled artisans. Part I explored the subject of skilled crafting,
with particular emphasis on the qualities and characteristics associated
with skilled artisans and the cosmological and political-ideological concepts accompanying the acts of transformation they achieve. In Part II the

acquisition of long-distance goods will be discussed in comparable terms, using the contexts associated with skilled crafting as general guide.

The initial task is to consider the notion of *acquisition,* a term and a concept that, when applied to long-distance activities, must also be discussed in conjunction with at least two other terms commonly applied to such affairs: trade and exchange. This is a somewhat daunting task, for trade and exchange are very general terms and widely used. For my purposes the fundamental difficulty with both trade and exchange as they are currently and commonly applied lies in the general emphasis on, or assumption of, some manner or degree of interrelated two-way interaction involving two (or more) separate and distinct social or political units, be they separate polities or divisions of polities or the particular trading partners, bigmen, or chiefs representing such polities. Such interactions generally contain the added implication that this mutual involvement constitutes an ongoing, networking relationship in which the interrelating ties rather than the goods exchanged are of major, even primary, importance.

Acquisition, in contrast, emphasizes essentially one-way activities in which a given social or political unit stands, not in a position of separateness or opposition vis-à-vis another of more-or-less like type, but by itself in a focal position of inclusion within a broader encompassing domain that is defined by the society at hand as cosmological in nature. Although inclusion of this sort does require certain types of associations between the focal heartland and locales outside (see Part III), primary emphasis lies on the significance or qualities associated with the goods obtained and with the type of activities required to get them.

Underlying this emphasis on goods is the fact that acquisition as described here can be understood as a particular type of appropriation in the sense that skilled artisanry can be understood as a particular type of crafting. As uniquely intelligent beings living within a cognized environment, it is an essential part of the human cultural experience that artifacts be made or crafted and, in addition, that some artifacts be further imbued with exceptional qualities and values expressive of the ultimate meaning of being human; this meaning is also tangibly expressed by particular crafting skills that are accorded exceptional qualities and values. In directly comparable manner, it is an equally essential part of the human cultural experience that resources be appropriated from the natural environment and, in addition, that some resources be further embued with exceptional qualities and values expressive of the ultimate meaning of being human. Appropriation of these types of resources may be recognized by a particular type of acquisitive activity that is also accorded exceptional qualities and values (Ingold 1987:2–3, 9–10).[1]

Since both appropriation and acquisition basically focus on the *getting* of *things,* they contrast with exchange in some very fundamental respects. Basic characteristics of acquisition as one-way activity were explicitly recognized by Karl Polanyi, who regarded acquisition as fundamental to certain types of non-market trade. Speaking specifically of administered trade in early Assyrian states he says, "The essential element in the trader's behavior was not a two-sided act resulting in a negotiated contract but a sequence of one-sided declarations of will, to which definite effects were attached. . . . Acquisition of goods from a distance—the criterion of all authentic trade—was the constitutive element. The procurement of useful objects ran in a peaceful way, goods going in both directions. There was a large professional personnel employed in the acquisitional activities and the actual physical carrying of the wares" (Polanyi 1957b:22–23). Elsewhere, speaking generally about trade, he also states, "From the substantive point of view, trade is a relatively peaceful method of acquiring goods which are not available on the spot. It is external to the group, similar to activities which we are used to associating with hunts, slaving expeditions, or piratic raids. In either case the point is acquisition and carrying of goods from a distance" (1957a:257–258).

Polanyi then continues with a point with which there can be little disagreement but from which I will depart in my particular emphasis on acquisition rather than on trade: "What distinguishes trade from the questing for game, booty, plunder, rare woods or exotic animals, is the two-sidedness of the movement, which also ensures its broadly peaceful and fairly regular character" (ibid.:258). Yet another observation is basic: "Emphasis on 'acquisition of goods from a distance' as a constitutive element in trade should bring out the dominant role played by the *import* interest in the early history of trade. In the nineteenth-century export interests loomed large. . . ." (ibid., my emphasis). Other characteristics of early trade recognized by Polanyi were mentioned previously, in Chapter 3, particularly its specificity as necessitated by the constant differences in goods carried, distances traveled, and the political and ecological conditions involved, in other words, its basically discontinuous nature. The point may be further developed here with reference, again, to trade as essentially involving several one-sided types of activities. "The specificity of trade is enhanced in the natural course of things by the necessity of acquiring the imported goods with exported ones. For under nonmarket conditions imports and exports tend to fall under different regimes. The process through which goods are collected for export is mostly separate from, and relatively independent of, that by which the imported goods are repartitioned" (Polanyi 1957a : 261).

Polanyi's emphasis on trade as involving the fundamental goal of acquisition or importing, basically of obtaining goods from a distance, is fundamental to my position. Recognition of the specificity of trade, of the fact that importing and exporting are two separate types of activities, allows attention to focus on one or the other of these enterprises without necessarily involving both. Thus it is totally appropriate that acquisition be considered in and of itself if the investigation lies in that direction. It is also entirely feasible and appropriate to focus exclusively on acquisition when considering long-distance activities involving non-subsistence items in traditional societies since, as Polanyi notes, the demand or import aspect of the wider world of goods was the most fluctuating and determining factor in directing long-distance activities.[2] In contrast to the industrial world, in which the need to constantly increase supply and expand the market (export) predominates, "The [Italian] merchants did not set off for Gaul for the purpose of selling an amphora of wine but in order to bring back a slave" (Tchernia 1983 : 99).[3]

Polanyi's comparison of trade-as-acquisition with other types of appropriational activities also external to the group, such as hunting, raids, and the quest for exotic animals or rare woods, is directly comparable to my association of long-distance acquisition with skilled crafting as an activity that begins in a domain external to the group. I depart from Polanyi's paradigm, however, when he contrasts the one-sided quest for game, rare woods, and exotic animals with the two-sided nature of trade. There can be no argument with the term trade in very general reference to a two-sided situation in the sense that "something must be carried over a distance and that in two opposite directions" for trade to exist (Polanyi 1957a : 258). Yet the more significant factor, as Polanyi recognizes, is that there need be no direct interrelationship between the two sides; that the two-sided nature of trade can be seen as composed of several separate one-sided acquisitional activities ("the essential element in the trader's behavior was not a two-sided act resulting in a negotiated contract but a sequence of one-sided declarations of will"; Polanyi op. cit.). In this sense long-distance acquisition as a category of one-sided external activity is *not* distinguishable from hunting, plunder, the quest for rare woods, or skilled crafting as I have identified it. And it is in that sense as various and diverse one-

sided activities concerned with appropriating goods from outside, combined with the equally important consideration of the qualities associated
with those goods and activities, that I am interested in long-distance
events not as acts of long-distance trade but as acts of long-distance
acquisition.

Eschewing a context of two-sided trade, at least in the long-distance
sense, also implies avoiding concepts of exchange and reciprocity, both of
which also rest upon the fundamental two-sided nature imputed to trade
by emphasizing relationships and negotiations which link the two sides
and tie them together as distinct yet interacting entities; gift exchange and
some types of barter are well known examples of this process. To be sure,
some forms or techniques of exchange can lead to an acquirement of
goods in the related sense of accumulation ("Just as the strip of stuff gets
longer and longer in the process of weaving, and cultivation spreads under
the tool of the cultivator, so cowries ought to circulate" [Griaule 1965:205,
referring to the Dogon]).[4] But exchange as a type of two-sided trade is
fundamentally distinct in character from one-sided acquisition on at least
two other important counts. First, as has been noted, where exchange
primarily emphasizes the nature or qualities of relationships, acquisition
primarily emphasizes the qualities of goods; second, acquisition, specifically long-distance acquisition, as a type of appropriation can reach "beyond" exchange in a cosmographical or cosmological sense. Here again at
least two points of contrast can be noted: first, long-distance acquisition
involves regions geographically beyond society; second, to the extent that
long-distance acquisition involves some type of association or relationship
between provider and acquirer, these relationships will be of a qualitatively
different order from those generally associated with trade and exchange in
the sense or to the extent that they are conditioned ultimately by cosmological rather than sociological principals.[5]

I see the various forms of exchange occurring within the bounds of
ordered, civilized "society," while acquisition occurs between the cultural
heartland inside and the qualitatively contrastive universe outside. To
contain this proposition, however, it is essential to broaden the boundaries
and definition of society to include aggregates of cultural entities, multiple
societies and polities, if they are interrelated by ties of reciprocity or exchange. In other words, we must widen our view of the inside to include,
when appropriate, not just one society but regional networks or interaction spheres composed of several cultural heartlands that may be politically or even ethnically separate and distinct yet related to others by socio-

political alliances *and* by acceptance of mutually understood political ideology. Within such a regional association or, on a higher level of organizational complexity, between one such regional complex and others, various types of two-sided exchanges may occur within what has become in effect an enlarged heartland. This position can be turned around to state that when exchange is found it can be assumed to be operating within, perhaps defining the boundaries of, some level of ordered society.

In contrast, long-distance acquisition occurs not when social space is involved but when cosmological space is involved; when a polity (or a cluster of polities) reaches beyond the recognized boundaries of the ordered social world to deal with the non-social cosmographical distances that lie beyond. Here there is no situation of separate but equal or equivalent, social units. On the contrary, the association between the home society and whatever places and things lie without does not involve two (or more) of the same category or type of social entity at all. Nor can it be considered as being equal or equivalent in any socio-political sense because spatial distance in the domains beyond is accorded (by the home society) cosmological characteristics that by definition contrast with the state of affairs at home and do so not with sociological (relational) criteria but on primarily moral grounds and by focusing on concepts of origins. That is to say, that which is spatially distant is not socially or politically equivalent to but morally either superior or inferior to the home society and, in addition, is identified as associated in some manner with primordial places of origin or with ancestral heroes or original creative events.

Acts of long-distance acquisition associate the cultured, socialized home society not with other units within a known human world but with a different spatial/temporal order of things; with outside places that are regarded as distant from the home society and that are significant because they are accorded a cosmological connotation of one sort or another. Long-distance acquisition associates the home society with the goods and benefits that derive from such places and that are imbued thereby with the inalienable qualities of such locales. Indeed, these goods and benefits can be considered as literally constituting pieces of such places. Such associations do not express relations of exchange embodying separateness and complementary opposition between qualitatively like units inhabiting the same temporal/spatial realm. Rather they express relations of inclusion in which the home society of the here-and-now effects tangible connections with the broader cosmological universe, with the there-and-then that by means of long-distance acquisition as well as by skilled crafting can be made to encompass the here-and-now (Sahlins 1981:38). In such a situation, tangible goods or other types of benefits (knowledge, information) cannot be said to be truly exchanged in two-sided interactions between personnel of qualitatively equal kind but can be acquired (by both sides concurrently yet independently if possible or necessary) by a series of one-sided activities, involving personnel or beings of qualitatively different kind.[6]

We are anthropologically quite familiar with the acquisition of the generally intangible types of resources that may be obtained by long-distance appropriations from the vertical dimension of the cosmological outside; with powers that can cure, bewitch, or foretell the future. We are not so used to thinking about acquisitions that may be obtained by directly comparable long-distance associations with the horizontal, geographical dimension of the outside, acquisitions that need not be only intangible but can readily take material form.[7] To be sure, the notion that differences in the qualitative or moral dimensions of persons or beings inhabiting different zones of geographical space and distance can condition the nature of material exchanges was well expressed by Sahlins in his now-classic paper on the Sociology of Primitive Exchange (1972:185–275), particularly with respect to his formulation of "negative reciprocity," the attempt to turn normally two-sided exchange (reciprocity) into a one-sided attempt "to get something for nothing with impunity" from strangers who live beyond the pale of normal society and therefore cannot be considered fully human (meaning cognizant of or willing to exhibit socially or morally proper behavior) (ibid.:195, 198–199). The very concept of negative reciprocity suggests that positive reciprocity properly takes place within the bounds of properly constituted human society (as generalized reciprocity and balanced reciprocity); that beyond those bounds conditions are different, and thus a different type or category of transaction may be expected to prevail.

In Sahlins' terminology the conditions outside were simply negative of proper exchange relations; hence, negative reciprocity. In my interpretation the conditions that are inappropriate for proper exchange are so because they are of a fundamentally different order requiring not only a negation of reciprocity or exchange but also a completely different way[8] to get something. The critical question thus becomes one of determining what types of conditions do prevail "out there." On this crucial point there is as yet no anthropological agreement. The significance of geographically distant realms very frequently has been interpreted within ecological perspectives that emphasize differences in the naturally occurring distribution and availability of desired material resources. Another approach, not in-compatible with the first, is to view geographically distant realms as simply being without definitive characteristics, as being neutral in quality or meaning for a given home society, or as simply being free of intra-societal ties that condition exchange. In this view strictly commercial (commodity) forms of trade might be expected to prevail, that is, trade in which kinship or other forms of ties informing social relations have no place because they do not exist in a qualitatively neutral setting and therefore do not and cannot condition interactions; a means of buying and selling in which goods may be properly termed commodities, meaning that they are simply what they appear to be without any social loading or features of inalien-ability (Gregory 1982:7–8) and where strictly pragmatic, meaning other-wise unencumbered or unembedded, economic concerns prevail. The dis-tinction made by Godelier (and others) between goods functioning as commodities for commercial exchange when they are moving about out-side society and goods functioning as prestige objects or objects of social exchange when they circulate as gifts or are otherwise distributed within society as part of the process of social life and kinship relations seems pertinent here, particularly since Godelier points out that, of these two possible "functions" for goods, "The second is the dominant one because it takes root and meaning within the requirements of dominant structures in primitive social organization, kinship and power." By implication, then, the first "function" apparently has no meaning within these same struc-tures (Godelier 1977:128–129) and is independent of them (see also Greg-ory 1982:42).

Strictly commercial or economic trade certainly exists in some non-Western or non-industrial circumstances, perhaps most notably under con-ditions of external trade following contact with Western mercantilistic and then industrial societies. But there are also sufficient data (Helms 1988: Chapter 5) to suggest that for traditional societies such long-distance com-mercial trade with the West replaced behavior and attitudes of a funda-mentally different order and/or that Western observers of this traditional activity interpreted it too narrowly within the strongly economic and com-mercial context that they were familiar with, missing the range of non-economic meanings applied to such activities by native societies. These data indicate that natives' dealings with foreigners traditionally involved a ritualized, therefore, sacralized or at least honor-associated atmosphere that bespoke an altogether different contextual interpretation, one involv-ing interactions between humans and recognized other beings rather than between buyers and sellers.[9]

The goods received from such beings are marked by the inalienable qualities associated with their unusual places or sources of origin (Sahlins 1981a: 30–31, 55; see also note 9). This particular locus of value (as defined by the acquiring society), derived from a qualitatively defined distant place, specifically from a cosmographical source, distinguishes such goods from goods defined as neutral commodities, "as objects of economic value" (Appadurai 1986: 3). It also distinguishes them from the view put forth by Appadurai (following Simmel) that sees the value of objects as commodities determined by what must be given up in order to obtain them (Appadurai 1986: 3).

The argument presented here, that the locus of value of long-distance goods lies not in the reciprocity of exchange but in the inalienable qualities derived from association with a qualitatively defined distant place of origins,[10] does not overlook the well-documented fact that acquisition of goods from outside may involve some form of giving. But giving-in-order-to-get in an acquisitional sense does not necessarily mean exchange, simply a means of effecting the desired goal of acquisition. It does not signify "giving something up" so much as "keeping something coming" and thus does not entail the kind of valuative cost-accounting Appadurai describes for commoditized trade.

The point may be made by briefly considering certain types of hospitality, particularly that extended to foreign visitors, a very familiar type of giving in these circumstances. As Munn says of the Gawan Islanders, who use hospitality as a means of creating connections beyond Gawa into the inter-island world and whose overseas trading exploits I regard as largely acquisitional in nature, "Through the transaction of food on Gawa at one particular time, one can produce for oneself the possibility of gaining something beyond that time, and from beyond Gawa itself . . ." (Munn 1986: 11). Hospitality as giving-in-order-to-get within the context of long-distance acquisition is also exemplified by Ingold's description and discussion of the bear ceremonial among circumboreal northern hunters which is in full accordance with long-distance acquisition as interpreted in these pages. The bear, after being killed to provide meat and blood for a communal sacred feast (foods which convey special spiritual strength and identity with the qualities associated with the bear), is then treated as an honoured guest at that same feast, being represented tangibly by its skin (kept attached to the head and shoulders) which is set up in the place of honor.[11] The hospitality issue is expressed in a passage by Ingold describing the end of the festivities: "As all good things must come to an end, the time eventually arrives when the bear has to take its leave of the community and return to its kind. It is given a lavish send-off, laden with gifts, and with exhortations to come again next year. The expectation is that the bear, on reaching home, will tell its friends and relatives about the excellent hospitality it received, so that they may be encouraged to come along too" (Ingold 1987:259).[12]

Even among northern hunters in the modern world the acquisitional context of hospitality, reflecting in turn the special qualities of bear itself (note 11), obviously removes bear meat from any consideration as a neutral economic good or commodity. As Appadurai also notes, speaking of factors that in general decommoditize goods and return them to a different world of values, "[there are] entire zones of activity and production that are devoted to producing objects of value that cannot be commoditized by anybody. The zone of art and ritual in small-scale societies is one such enclaved zone . . ." (1986:22). Again, "It is typical that objects which represent aesthetic elaboration and objects that serve as sacra are, in many societies, not permitted to occupy the commodity state (either temporally, socially, or definitionally) for very long" (1986:23).

This condition, still widespread in spite of several centuries of expanding Westernization, was once far more common in traditional societies. It not only characterized the various products skillfully and aesthetically crafted for ritual occasions of transformation but also characterized the nature of resources acquired from sacralized cosmological realms outside society, that is, characterized a great deal of what we have commonly included in the phrase "long-distance trade." These conditions prevailed during those long millennia when the predominant context for understanding most of what lay beyond the heartland was cosmological and cosmographical and where, consequently, there would be little room for qualitatively neutral commoditized goods.[13]

Acquisition Explored

In spite of the anthropological emphasis on exchange and generosity, ethnographic literature readily reveals that members of traditional societies have an equally widespread interest in acquiring things and make clear distinctions between acquisition of goods and sociologically oriented exchange activities. The Kundagai Maring of Papua New Guinea, for example, recognize two types of activities, *Munggoi rigima* and *Munggoi awom,* for which Healey gives the literal translations of "valuables exchange" and "valuables give" and glosses as "trade" and "prestation," respectively.

Munggoi rigima ("valuables exchange"), which I [Healey] translate as
trade, refers to transactions explicitly concerned with the acquisition and
distribution of goods. As informants explain, the focus of such transactions is on material objects and may occur between people standing in any
relationship. *Munggoi awom* ("valuables give"), or prestations, are applied
to transactions explicitly concerned with the establishment, continuation,
or discharge of social relations, rights, and obligations. Maring exegesis
points to the more restricted nature of *munggoi awom* exchanges: they occur only between particular categories of people in certain circumstances.
(1984 : 43–44, see also p. 45 and 1990: Chapter 4)

Obviously, the two intents are not unrelated,[14] but whereas contemporary
anthropology has carefully considered the ways and means by which
people exchange things, the populations involved have also considered just
as carefully the ways and means by which people acquire things.[15]

The interest in acquisition exists in traditional societies not only because
things may be needed for eventual exchange or distribution but also because the act of acquisition in its own right (as evidenced, for example, in
display) conveys and expresses prestige. Prestige is especially awarded
when things acquired are obtained from outside and thereby contain an
aura of exceptionality. Prestige is also accorded in such circumstances because acquisition of outside things reflects most favorably upon highly
valued and lauded skills and personal characteristics of the acquirer, who
has had to deal in some fashion with a conceptually distinctive foreign
realm qualitatively defined as involving the sanctified, the mystical, or the
power-filled. Acquisitional acts thus become dynamic expressions of the
quality of the acquirer's association with this powerful domain. It is for
this reason that long-distance acquisition, like skilled crafting, characteristically emphasizes or focuses upon the person just as it emphasizes and
focuses upon goods and frequently also is viewed as an activity indicative
of a high moral order or an ideal of humanness (Chapter 8).

Consider, for example, the northwest California tribes (Hupa, Yurok,
Korok), who are famous in literature for their inordinate interest in acquiring certain valuables that derive from locales beyond the bounds of
society, most notably dentalia shell but also white deerskins, redheaded
woodpecker scalps, large flint or obsidian blades, and quivers made of
particular types of furs. These California tribes associated acquisition of
such treasure with notions of personal prestige and honor, proudly displayed them, and used them in various social interactions and transactions (brideprice, shamans' fees, various indemnities). That acquisition in

and of itself was important is suggested, first, by the fact that the circumstances of acquisition were long remembered—each string of dentalia, each woodpecker band or obsidian piece had its own history which made it desirable apart from any other basis of valuation. "Wholly typical . . . is the way particular objects of wealth, and to whom each belonged, and how it had been acquired, are remembered seventy-five years later" (Spott and Kroeber quoted in Bushnell 1977:122, note 4).

In addition, acquisition of dentalia and other goods was "but one part of a more basic and deeply meaningful search for the sacred, the sanctified, and the spiritual aspects of life" (Bushnell 1977:123). This search led directly to realms above and beyond. "Although men yearned and strove for dentalia, sometimes with greater and sometimes with lesser success, it is clear that this most prized of wealth objects ultimately belonged to the gods and partook of their magical, godlike qualities. For the Yurok Kroeber refers to Dentalium Land (also translated Dentalium Home and Money's Home) across the ocean at the north end of the world where the ceremonial dances never cease" (ibid.). "In addition to dentalia, most if not all of the other greatly prized and highly valued objects (especially white deerskins, redheaded woodpecker crests, and obsidians) are intimately linked to the world of the immortals and characteristically emit supernatural power that redounds to the good fortune and health of those who possess them. In myth after myth and legend after legend, gods, heroes, and a panoply of other sacred or magical personages, creatures, and spirits are associated with native treasure which is always symbolic, usually endowed with beauty or splendor, and frequently super-abundant or larger than life" (Bushnell 1977:128).

The Bushnells conclude that the great interest of northwest California peoples in acquiring as many valued goods as possible involved not only social prestige but, more importantly, "their spiritual power and supernaturally-ordained 'luck' in hunting, fishing, gambling, games, and indeed, in the acquisition of even greater sacred treasure" (ibid.:131). In other words, the successful acquisition of such supernaturally charged goods from outside becomes part of the California expression of the widespread native North American sacred quest by which individuals obtain the supernatural power that produces efficacy and success in all manner of endeavors (ibid.:148). What is particularly noteworthy in this California version of the sacred quest, however, is the expressed conjunction of the realms of the above and those of the beyond, that is, dentalia, the ultimate wealth objects and metaphor for treasure, belong to the gods and the world of the immortals (the above) and are also associated with or believed to derive from a land "across the ocean at the north end of the world" (the beyond).[16]

A very similar situation is recorded for the Ojibwa (Vecsey 1983) where a vertically associated wealth-producing activity became re-aligned under conditions of European contact to become a horizontally associated wealth-producing activity while maintaining essentially its original meaning. In this case the traditional use of personal visions as means of establishing contact with powerful outside beings (manitos) who provided worldly benefits by assuring hunting success, healthful cures, and long life was undercut and superseded after European contact by participation in the Midewiwin Society. Members of the Midewiwin (organized on a model derived from missionary contact and Christianity), while continuing to respect revelation by visions, offered means for successful hunting, good health, long life, and a happy afterlife by establishing communication with powerful manitos through initiation into the esoteric lore of the Society, which required payment of high fees with wealth derived from fur trade participation.

The central symbols of Midewiwin were seashells (cowries or megis) provided in large numbers by white traders who obtained them from several factories in New Jersey that collected them. (Hudson's Bay Company stores also distributed shells in return for furs). Seashells were traditionally a part of Ojibwa religious paraphernalia, "representing the frothing waters caused by the underwater manitos" (Vecsey 1983:183). Now the shells were associated with European traders, who were sometimes referred to by nineteenth-century Ojibwas as "messengers from the supernatural" sent by "the great Master of Life" to assist them (ibid.:165), and toward whom the Ojibwas behaved in a manner similar to their behavior toward manitos (that is, by begging and attempting to evoke pity, standard procedure in vision quests [ibid.:135–136]). In fact, "Many Ojibwas treated whites as manitos or as extremely powerful and mysterious beings endowed with the manitos' powers" (Vecsey 1983:136), a very clear and obvious association of traditional vertically located spirits with comparable powerful beings now deriving from a horizontally distant setting replete with sacred shells and other desired wealth, the acquisition of which heretofore had always been associated with traditional spirit powers.[17]

The basic point illustrated by this excerpt, that people and things (wealth items, benefits, access to powers) derived from geographically distant places in the context of what we commonly have called trade can be correlated with closely comparable things and benefits derived from supernaturally vertical locales within a cosmological context that embraces both dimensions, will be further explored in Part III. Here let us return briefly to the California tribes to note the aesthetic qualities accorded dentalia shells, which appear to have been transformed from their natural state into crafted objects: "[dentalia were] frequently skillfully and beautifully incised, decorated with red feathers, fishskins or snakeskins, and occasionally colored with dyes from wild plants or even human blood" (Bushnell 1977:122). Creation of such beauty implies an aesthetic appreciation that, in turn, seems to associate acquisition of things from the outside with the morality and orderliness found in the properly functioning society and cosmos. Christopher Healey touches on similar points in his discussion of acquisitional trade among the Kundagai Maring, in which birds and marsupials from the primary forest are hunted for the feathers and skins which the Maring will send out of their area to the Chimbu Valley in order to acquire a variety of other goods, including pigs, marine shells, and steel tools (1984:46; 1990). Trade involves many people, most of them in an intermediary capacity in which they neither introduce goods into nor extract goods from the flow of trade but do have the opportunity to handle goods. To Healey, this in itself is very important:

> All goods traded are desired at a conscious, articulated level by the Maring because they are critical for the proper conduct of celebration, as decorations, or for use in prestations. I would argue further that to engage in trade is to handle metaphorically, or contact, the symbolic properties of the goods, as these are made manifest and meaningful in other contexts. To trade is to contact and reflect on what these goods mean in the contexts in which they are engaged as signals of social reproduction. There is, for example, a sensuous quality to the way a man may examine a trade plume—running his hands softly over its filaments, waving it gently in the sunlight to catch the gleam of iridescence. Again, shells, axes, knives, and, above all, piglets, are delicately touched, stroked, held, and fondled in a dreamy way as a trader ponders whether to accept them. Trading is thus more than merely provisioning oneself with the means to participate in ceremony or prestation, or the conversion of use values of one kind into use values of another, in that so much trade involves only a transient hold on goods. . . . Even in such ephemeral contact with objects of value, the trader may be brought into contact with their nonmaterial essence and significance. In that sense, trade may be an end in itself, beside the contingent and pragmatic reasons discussed above. (1984:47)

Whatever specific qualities constitute the nonmaterial essence and significance of the acquired goods for the Kundagai (and the discussion in succeeding chapters is directed to suggesting what some of those qualities categorically might be), judging from the "sensuous quality" of the way men touch and examine trade objects it would appear that an appreciation of beauty is involved. Which is to say, again, acquisition of goods from outside, be it from the forest or from the Chimbu Valley, seems to involve the larger issue of aesthetics, meaning the moral goodness and rightness inherent in a beneficent universe that makes iridescent plumes and handsome piglets available to those who lived equally commendable moral social lives.[18]

Long-distance acquisition involves bringing crafted or natural things (see Chapter 9) from some place outside society across some degree of geographical-cum-cosmographical distance to a home locale, crossing a cultural threshold from a more or less unknown or exotic or mystical realm outside to the ordered social heartland inside where instructive qualities and symbolism accrue to the goods procured. Skilled crafting operates in a similar manner, moving unfashioned materials across the same threshold by effecting a transformational change in form that creates objects whose significance closely compares with that accorded goods acquired directly from afar. Skilled artisans have the exceptional talents and the exceptional tools to effect this sometimes hazardous transformation and may also travel some distance in order to apply their skills. Long-distance traveler/ traders have comparable specialized and exceptional talents and tools (conveyances) for the also frequently hazardous task (in traditional settings) of safely crossing distance in order to achieve successful transformations or acquisitions. Both skilled artisans and long-distance acquirers obtain materials from outside and bring them home under circumstances in which the *act* of moving from a locus outside to a cultural setting inside effects a symbolically significant transformation, sometimes of form, always of meaning.

Nonetheless, there do seem to be some very significant differences between the long-distance "trader" and the skilled artisan, though such differences may be more apparent than real. For example, the acts of transformative crafting—the ritualistically enhanced changes in state wrought by fire, hammer, and water at the forge, the ceremonial carving of a mask from a piece of tree limb, the fashioning of a melodious chant from spoken words, or even the artful decorating of a tray of ceremonial food—can be rather dramatic and readily observable, unless, as frequently happens, the crafters secrete themselves away from curious eyes, perhaps by moving to a workshop in the forest or surrounding a forge with potentially damaging spells that keep others at a prudent distance. Acts of long-distance travel,

6-1.   A trading "bevaia" nearing completion, Papua New Guinea. (From
F. E. Williams, "Trading Voyages from the Gulf of Papua," *Oceania* vol. 3 [1932],
p. 167. Used by permission of Oceania Publications.)

in contrast, are less obviously or immediately dramatic. Yet the successful
arrival of a trading party, caravan, or ship engenders a heightened atmosphere of excitement and curiosity, as well as ritual cleansings and formal
ceremonies of social readmission.[19] Similarly, the process of traversing distance, of being out of touch with home and away from society's limiting
strictures, perhaps for some length of time, can appear mysterious and
challenging, both for those who stay at home and for those who travel,
and confers an aura of mystery comparable to that surrounding the skilled
artisan to the traveler, too. Thus acts of long-distance acquisition, like acts
of skilled crafting, can be prestigeful and feared (awesome) undertakings,
because both long-distance traveler/traders and skilled crafters, like religious specialists, are experts at plumbing the unknown and from its mysterious depths, heights, and expanses producing culturally valuable and
beneficial "things" by means of their own exceptional talents and powers.

Long-distance acquisition, like skilled crafting, can be seen as particularistic and event-oriented,[20] as involving goods containing inalienable qualities related to their places or circumstances of origin, as conducted in a ritualized setting (the rituals surrounding travel and travel conveyances), frequently, too, as honorable and honor-related and thereby as involving the elect and the elite, the world of "real" people. Long-distance acquisition, like skilled crafting, is also imbued with the ethos of aesthetics and all that implies. All of these characteristics identify acquisition as a particular kind of appropriation (as skilled crafting is contrasted with crafting in general), and contrast traditional long-distance acquisition very sharply with merchandizing or commercial trade.[21]

Ultimately, as the following chapters illustrate, long-distance acquisition shares a range of very definitive characteristics with skilled crafting, not only in that they are both variations on a common theme of inside-outside contacts and transformations fundamental particularly to the operation of political-ideological interests but also because the two types of activities, though seemingly contrastive in important respects, ultimately work together in complementary fashion to form a larger or more complete whole. The points of contrast are rather obvious. Skilled crafting reveals the transformative powers of a creative universe by achieving very explicit and dynamic changes in material form or character in a way long-distance acquisition cannot do, while long-distance acquisition broadens the dimensional perspective of the outside to include geographically distant peoples, places, and things more directly or more regularly than skilled crafting per se can do. Though skilled artisans definitely reach into the beyond in fundamental ways for the means to effect their transformations and a measure of mystique deriving from geographical distance may enhance their reputed powers, fame, and reputations, they commune primarily with the vertical dimension of the outside and the physical locus of their transformations will probably be in some social setting, either at home or at the home of a patron, or at the liminal edge of the socialized world. In contrast, long-distance acquirers routinely operate directly in the outside theatre, beyond the socialized heartland, focusing specifically on the materials already fully formed (crafted) or naturally contained in that theatre. They are involved primarily with the horizontal or geographical dimension of the outside, though with the ritualistic and spiritual aid of vertically located powers.

What is insufficiently understood from the scholarly perspective, however, is the ultimate cosmological conjunction of geographical and vertical axes not only at the center or heartland but also at distant points of acquisition far from home, and the belief that acts of creation and of skilled crafting have occurred and continue to occur at such points. As we shall see in later chapters, these conjunctions and the qualities associated with these highly charged distant places and products define the symbolic meaning of long-distance goods whether they be natural products shaped by the original-yet-continuing creative/transformative powers of cosmic spirits and deities or whether they be crafted goods shaped by the transformative powers of extraordinarily skilled creator/artisans at recognized political-ideological sacred centers-out-there.

7 Acquisition in Time and Space

> So it kept up all afternoon. The men leaping and prancing wildly,
> ecstatically as great birds; the women, like demure hens, treading
> softly but dancing with their bodies. The grass trod down. Dust
> began to rise . . . shafts of sunlight. . . . And at each pause,
> presents. ———FRANK WATERS,
>
> *The Man Who Killed the Deer*, p. 62

Original Travelers and Original Trade

Lévi-Strauss has stated that "the notion of space evolves by being inserted
in a multidimensional continuum: from being absolute space, now made
indissociable from time, becomes relative. It is no longer to be defined by
the static opposition between the high and the low, but by the dynamic
opposition of the near and the far, which is determined by social, instead
of cosmic, coordinates" (Lévi-Strauss 1978:190).

Geographical space, defined by the "dynamic opposition of the near and
the far," is determined by social rather than cosmological coordinates in
Lévi-Strauss' view in the sense that myth, the context for his analysis, uses
the attributes of relative space as a means to comment on the characteristics and qualities of the relational nearness and farness of the social world
of human communication, kinship, friendship, and enmity as, for example, in the matter of how close or how distant a proper conjunction of
marriage should or should not be to achieve an appropriate sociological
order and balance (Lévi-Strauss 1978:191–192). Yet, when the far and the
near of geographical space and distance are analyzed in sociological (that
is, ethnological) rather than mythical context, the determinants of its
qualities do appear to be essentially cosmological in character, partaking
of the qualities of the vertical axis, the high and the low, in that respect. It
is reasonable to expect, therefore, that activities that take place in geographically distant space will be accorded the same kinds of cosmological
associations as those involving vertical distance. More specifically, travel
through, and acquisition of things from, geographical distance will be re-

lated to cosmic origins and processes, will carry mystical significance, and will be conducted with proper ritual by distinctive specialists. In addition, a common purpose—the desire to acquire good things and benefits from afar—fundamentally underlies the human conceptualization of and approach to both geographical (horizontal) and vertical distance.

On the other hand, the horizontal or geographical cosmological axis allows for direct human involvement with the cosmological outside in a dynamic manner different from that achievable via the vertical axis. Association with the vertical axis poses the intellectual challenge of transmuting the purely spiritual so as to make it available to the tangible, physical world of human existence. The opposite challenge exists for association with the horizontal axis; intellectually transmuting the purely physical world so as to infuse it with the spirituality necessary for its inclusion within the existential world of human being. Those who address the issue of transmuting the spiritual vertical realm must approach that spirituality by attaining sufficient spirituality themselves, for example, by becoming shamans and priests. Those who would address the issue of transmuting the physical (material) horizontal dimension must approach its materialistic features by physically venturing into it as travelers, by hosting or subsidizing those who do, or by learning to transform its physical qualities by acts of skilled crafting.

Travelers directly confront the particular cosmological dynamics of the horizontal dimension by correlating physical passage between here and there with passage through sacred time, meaning that such travels may be seen as re-creations of ancient or ancestral journeys. Because physical travel also permits space to be energetically traversed, and physically and dynamically experienced, it frequently is particularly recommended (especially to traditional elites and other persons of influence) because of the personal challenges involved in successfully traversing geographical distance in the flesh.[1] It is also valued because of the very tangible, durable, and aesthetic material properties of some of the material signifiers geographical distance provides.

The archetypical cosmic travelers in physical space/time are the sun and moon. Consequently, foremost among the readily observable benefits received from geographically distant space/time are the light and warmth provided by these solar bodies, whose attributes have also readily accommodated the constant human need (from earliest times) to intellectualize, specifically to spiritualize, the attributes of the physical world. Not surprisingly, the sun and moon as original and prototypical travelers in the geographical dimensions of space/time, are seen to organize the space/time dimension by moving along specific pathways that run from sunrise to sunset, moonrise to moonset. In addition, the daily and seasonal movements of the celestial bodies are frequently associated with some means of conveyance, such as a canoe (Lévi-Strauss 1978:136, 138, 147, 148), a reed float (Frankfort 1948:155–156), or a bejeweled chariot crafted of gold and silver and drawn by winged horses (Campbell 1949:133, 134).[2] Which is to say, the space/time journeys of the sun and moon by which the most fundamental life-giving order and balance of the human universe is achieved (Campbell 1949:134–136; Lévi-Strauss 1978:191–192), are frequently dependent upon crafted products (transports) if they are to be successfully conducted.[3]

The equally archetypical human traveler is identified in the culture hero, who may also have celestial associations, especially if he has wandered so far that he has reached the ultimate point of geographical distance where sky and earth, the vertical and the horizontal, meet (Campbell 1949:69; Lévi-Strauss 1978:188; Rassers 1959:287–288, 268, 296). Culture heroes have many distinguished and distinguishing features. Their peregrinations to distant geo-cosmic zones effect a time/space connection between ancestral distance and human immediacy. They generally combine a penchant for wandering in exotic places with an obligation to introduce invaluable cultural treasures, such as social institutions, laws and customs, arts and crafts, and other boons, to humans. Not surprisingly, culture heroes (or other forms of legendary ancestors) also may be credited not only with traveling in but also with crafting the first travel conveyances, (Figure 7–1), such as canoes (see Lévi-Strauss 1973:183, 222–223; Horridge 1979:10), or with creating (energizing) the motor that propels ships around the world (Errington and Gewertz 1985:446–447; see also note 3).

Creator-heroes (or other forms of legendary ancestors) may also be linked or credited with the origins of acts of acquisition from afar. The Nunamiut, an inland Eskimo group, have a particularly detailed account of the origins of travel and of acquisitional trade involving a creator-giant and great man, Aiyagomahala, who in the very early times created the Nunamiut themselves and taught them (among other things) how to hunt and to make clothing, tools, and traveling equipment. Aiyagomahala also created a giant white dog to pull the villagers' loaded sleds.[4] The creator-giant then instructed the Nunamiut to collect all kinds of inland animal skins and to prepare dried meat so that they might learn how to acquire, by trade, sea mammal products from the coast (this in conjunction with teaching them how to burn blubber in stone lamps, which introduced heat and light to Nunamiut domestic life). After freeze-up Aiyagomahala ar-

7-1.   Wooden model (Egyptian) of a boat in which sits Meket-Re with his son and a singer. (From James Pritchard, *The Ancient Near East in Pictures*. Princeton University Press, 1954. Photography by Egyptian Expedition, The Metropolitan Museum of Art, New York. All rights reserved, The Metropolitan Museum of Art.)

ranged for the people of Point Barrow, on the coast, to travel inland to the Nunamiut. Aiyagomahala then described and instituted the procedures of trade (Gubser 1965 : 29–31).[5]

If creator-heroes of the time of cultural origins could provide acquisition opportunities, their chiefly human counterparts in the temporal here-and-now may be expected to do the same, frequently also in conjunction with the gods or in a heroic context. The traditional history of the Dagomba of West Africa (Volta Basin) recounts the development of trade on a new long-distance route at the time when their ruler, Na Zangina, had been converted to Islam and, culture hero–like, had made possible thereby the introduction of "a complete civilization," including weavers and Islamic teacher-scholars (malams). Developments in trade, travel, and communication were associated with the ruler's conversion, too: "There were no traders on the main roads to Dagbong. Na Zangina prayed to God, and the roads opened, and many travelled by them. That is why the drummers say that Na Zangina made the world wise" (Levtzion 1968 : 103). In somewhat comparable fashion, members of Nyamwezi (northwest Tanzania) chiefly families who traveled to the east coast of Africa, probably as caravan leaders, and who are credited thereby with the introduction of coveted conus-shells, as well as salt and other goods in the early days (early-to-mid nineteenth century) of coast-interior trade, are remembered and described as "traveller-heroes" (Shorter 1972:188, 233).[6]

Twentieth-century acquisition of desirable goods from afar has continued to associate such undertakings with supernatural intents and assistance. Although the Elema of the Gulf of Papua coast acquire foreign goods by their own travels, they also rely on ancestral assistance. During the 1930s, when trading voyages rapidly expanded (a substitute for defunct ceremonies), ships' captains, individuals who knew the necessary magic, while traveling explicitly and consciously impersonated and thereby became ancestral mythical heroes by the magical use of mythical names, imitative wearing apparel and ornaments, and proper thinking. They did so in order to attain the same success in their trading voyages as the earlier heroes had achieved in theirs (Williams 1932:158; 160–161, 163–164; see also Errington and Gewertz 1986:105–106; Helms 1988:46–47).

The involvement of mythical ancestors and heroes in long-distance travel and acquisition not only in the mythical past but also in the ethnographic present, and the belief that the assistance of such other-than-human beings is beneficial, even crucial, to the contemporary undertaking, strongly suggests that in traditional thought the world of long-distance travel and acquisition is believed still to be imbued with the qualities of the mystical or power-filled domain within which supernatural beings exist and operate. Association of travel and acquisition motifs with the activities of original creators and culture heroes also conjoins the contemporary world of long-distance travel with the supernatural primordial travels that initially introduced beneficial things from afar to the human domain. Such associations between ancestral culture hero/travelers and present day travelers and acquirers also directly parallel associations between ancestral creator/crafters and the skills and abilities of contemporary skilled artisans. To complete the picture, just as the activities and interests of contemporary skilled artisans and traveler/traders may significantly overlap (as we have seen in Chapter 3), so, too, the areas of patronage or the beneficial contributions to humanity attributed to primordial supernatural beings and culture heroes can conjoin travel and skilled crafting. Thus, in European myth, Odysseus, like Athena, is skilled in both the building and the sailing of ships (Detienne and Vernant 1978:235, 236), while Hermes became the god of trade and of craftsmanship (Brown 1947:38) and the Celts of Gaul considered Mercury both the inventor of all arts and the guide on journeys (Rees and Rees 1961:143; see also the multiple roles of Jupiter as mentioned in Chapter 5, note 8).

Epitomizing this combination of craft and travel is the traveler's frequent need for skillfully crafted travel conveyances. Shamanic travelers within the vertical dimension of the cosmological realm have long made use of the skillfully crafted conveyances of ordered rhythm, song, and dance to traverse the heights of the heavens or the depths of the underworld. In the words of Yakut shamans, "The drum is our horse." Similarly the obstacles (frequently portrayed as impassable geographical features and terrain) that often must be encountered and overcome in such journeys are conquered or controlled by the power of shamanic songs (Rothenberg 1985:491).

Due to its different material composition, travel in the equally challenging and dangerous horizontal dimension of the cosmological realm requires crafted vehicles of a different form. Not only is a more tangible mode of conveyance required, but, as Lévi-Strauss has pointed out with respect to canoe travel, moving through geographical space needs to be done in a manner that can become an assertion of orderly, socialized passage through a hazardous and unordered domain. Canoe passengers, for example, take very specific locations at bow, stern, and middle in order to keep the craft balanced and smoothly operative; yet the positions may also accord in myth and in actual practice with status positions or roles in human society (Reichel-Dolmatoff 1978:244; Taylor and Aragon 1991:231, 269). The course of the canoe not only regulates the passage of time through space but also achieves a periodicity of steady, ordered movement as it mediates between near and far. The canoe with its passengers, in effect, becomes a miniature socialized world, a cultural entity, a home (sometimes complete with hearth and cooking fire) moving through an uncultured and unsocialized outside realm and imposing a measure of order upon its potentially chaotic surroundings (Lévi-Strauss 1978:Part III).

The small societies composing the canoe, the caravan, and the sea-going ship (and possibly also the modern organized tour group) reassert for travelers the fundamental propriety of an ordered universe, a cosmic propriety that is also reaffirmed by shamanic "voyages" and reiterated every day and night by the measured passage of the sun and moon.[7] The same cosmic propriety was also expressed in some societies by mythical creator/ancestors' travels through cosmographical space/time, peregrinations that contemporary travelers recreate as they, too, pass through the same landscape (see Chapter 3, note 12). "Just as each mythic being, moving down its original track, left a part of its creative essence at successive points along it, so its living descendants, following the same route, perform an integrative movement, putting the parts together in the construction of their own being. Through such movement, paths in the terrain are caught up in the continuous process of social life, projecting an ancestral past into an unborn future" (Ingold 1987:153).

Talking of paths and of travel conveyances also highlights the fundamental characteristic of acts of acquisition as movements effecting a change in location of goods. This basic feature of long-distance acquisition is comparable to the physical changes of state and form that characterize skilled crafting. Both change of location from far to near and change of physical state from uncrafted to crafted express transformations achieved by exceptional human expertise whereby potentially beneficial and desirable things from outside society are brought into human society. These transformations are achieved by skilled artisans through a conjunction of technical skills and supernaturally assisted knowledge concerning the formation or creation of things. Comparable transformations are achieved by long-distance travelers through a similar conjunction of technical skills and supernaturally assisted knowledge concerning the acquisition and transportation of things.

The latter point is illustrated in the combination of ritual and technical expertise needed at every step, from the felling of the first tree to final launching, by skilled master shipwrights to prepare the wooden sailing ships long used in Indonesian seas. The day for laying the keel is fixed by divination, the work proceeds with incense and with the aid of spells and spirits. "In the mortice hole [cut at each end of the keel for the tenon of the keel extension] the punggawa [shipwright] places a number of objects that symbolize the hopes for the future prahu [ship]. He puts there a grain of gold, a piece of iron, a piece of copper, some rice, some cooked rice, a little piece of coconut, and a leaf of the first tree to be felled . . . These things are wrapped in a piece of white cloth and tucked into the mortice before the tenon of the keel extension is fitted in. . . . The objects placed in the mortice are symbols of the expected returns from the working life of a prahu: gold for profits and safety, iron for strength, rice for sustenance and prosperity" (Horridge 1979:12–13).

As Indonesian master shipwrights know, travel conveyances not only have practical value but may appear as acquisitional "tools" charged with their own mystical acquisitional power, just as the tools of skilled artisans may be believed to inherently contain a creative power of their own. Indeed, mystically charged conveyances become metaphors for the entire concept of travel; magical canoes, flying carpets, and winged shoes may signify the organized, energetic, and intellectualized movement through cosmographical space/time, frequently with intent to successfully acquire and transport desired goods and benefits.

Craft and the Conduct of Acquisition

In traditional societies it is commonplace to believe that no truly meaning-ful human activity can be accomplished without the involvement of higher powers; the examples set by creator deities, ancestors, and primordial cul-ture heroes act both as models of and models for this fundamental tenet. Indeed, it is the identification with such higher interests that marks an activity as truly human, cultural, or civilized and, therefore, as honorable and worthy of prestige in its achievement. Long-distance travel and acqui-sition of goods are very definitively cultural, civilized, and honorable ac-tivities in this sense, since it is physical travel and the acquisition of goods from afar that tangibly expresses the reality of cosmological distance, at least in its geographical context. Consequently, it is also to be expected that travel and acquisition will be thoroughly imbued with rituals since "rituals and related concepts of supernatural powers establish the capacity of a people to acquire valuable properties from outside sources" (Goldman 1975 : 17, 43).

Goldman elaborates upon this point with respect to the Kwakiutl, but his observations may be taken to apply broadly to the vast majority of traditional peoples and to include all manner of outside activities, includ-ing long-distance travel and acquisition from the realm of geographical distance:

> To say of the Kwakiutl that they were deeply religious is to say no more than what is true of all American Indians and probably of all primitive peoples, for whom religion means involvement in a consubstantial nature. Scientific materialism postulates the consubstantiality of matter, primitive religions that of life and the powers of life. In their ritual setting the Kwakiutl are in daily touch with forms of life and with sources of power to which they should respond if they are prudent and energetic. There are rivers and ponds whose waters are the 'water of life,' of which they should drink. They need the good will of all animals upon whom they feed. They ask permission of trees for their planks, of the sun for its general help. They will not hunt or fish without preparing themselves ritually for the encounter. From a materialistic point of view that recognizes only the utility of killing, the ritual of hunting and fishing preparations is for suc-

cess. From the Indians' point of view, the ritual serves to prepare men to enter the foreign realm of the animals by making them acceptable to the animals (1975:22).

In the particular context of long-distance acquisition, ritual sometimes is conducted to seek permission from outside powers for traveler/traders to enter their domain; sometimes to provide protection for traveler/traders against harmful conditions of disorder and chaos encountered in the outside; sometimes it expresses the "real," honorable, moral, or aesthetic qualities of long-distance acquisition; and sometimes it celebrates and assists the transformational character of acquisitional trade when tangible materials and intangible powers are moved between qualitatively different realms.

With respect to seeking permission and providing protection, for those traveling by water, ritual protection of canoes or ships and propitiation of the powers controlling rivers or seas is always prudent; the monarchs of the state of Śrīvijaya in the Malay peninsula, who enjoyed royal associations with deities of the "Waters of the Sea" as well as with those of the mountains, are alleged to have performed daily propitiation rites over the sea and the estuaries (whence so much of the wealth of the kingdom derived via long-distance activities) by throwing gold bricks into the water and to have bewitched the crocodiles of the rivers to allow safe navigation to the sea (Hall 1985:85, 79–81). Elsewhere, baleful crocodiles could be turned to protective use as magical animal agents. In the central Zaire basin, a trader could ritually induce a crocodile to work on his behalf by swimming alongside his canoe or, at night, hovering in the shallow water just offshore, "using his magical power to protect his master. If the master had enemies, the crocodile could lie in ambush until they came to bathe in the evening and carry them away. The master never actually saw his crocodile, but he had confidence that it was helping him" (Harms 1981:202).[8] Traveler/traders in the Zaire basin also relied heavily on charms. "Nobody would undertake a trip without adequate assurance of magical protection. One informant stated, 'You must have charms, if not, you can't go on a trip and return safely.' Charms and trade were inseparable" (Harms 1981: 206). Seafarers in Melanesia feel the same way: "Without invoking the help of the spirits no canoe is built; without submitting it to the will of the Gods no sea voyage is undertaken" (Mander, quoted in Cochrane 1970:70).[9]

Comparable dictates apply to land travel, too, where human intrusion into a qualitatively distinct outside realm involving "the magical art of dealing with strangers" (Brown 1947:35) requires that the enterprise be thoroughly imbued with the distinctive behavior and mindset necessary to achieve safe entry into a unique realm, safe passage through it, and an eventual safe return therefrom. Thus preparations for a departing expedition might involve "fasting for luck, getting a shaman to foretell the future, and holding a feast and dance several days before departure," as well as face painting (Oberg 1973:109–110). While traveling, various ceremonies must be observed (Jablow 1966:69; Campbell 1989:76) and protective fetishes and oracles may be carried along with medicines to render any hostile natives encountered weak and powerless (Sundström 1974:33–34) or to ensure that the hospitality received by designated hosts is truly safe and reliable (Northrup 1978:97).

The ethnographic literature is also filled with descriptions of the ritual and ceremony or other expressions of sacrality associated with the acquisitional trade that transpires at markets and fairs, especially those where travelers or visitors from diverse regions or settlements converge. Norman Brown, speaking of the trade (and other types of activities) that occurred in lands outside the boundaries of settled communities in early Greece, notes that "Trade on the boundary was deeply impregnated with magical notions" and that such trade was "itself a ritual act." Brown finds the "most primitive" example in the ancient, pre-Classical Greek world in so-called "silent" trade (where acquisition occurs without the parties in the trade directly meeting) in which "The exchange generally takes place at one of those points which are sacred to Hermes—a boundary point, such as a mountain top, a river bank, a conspicuous stone, or a road junction. The object so mysteriously acquired is regarded as the gift of a supernatural being who inhabits the place, and who therefore is venerated as a magician and culture hero" (Brown 1947:41).[10]

Brown's proposal of a very ancient belief in the supernatural source of trade goods acquired by silent trade has a parallel in every myth in which celestial beings or culture heroes are sources of foreign goods and in every ethnographic instance where ancestors or other forms of deities are believed to be instrumental in the successful conduct of long-distance acquisition. It also is in accord with one of the major themes of this volume, which argues that the objects acquired by long-distance activities in traditional societies are obtained from a cosmologically charged outside realm that is by definition accorded mystical or sacred properties and powers that imbue the goods derived therefrom with inalienable qualities ultimately associated with concepts of supernatural origins (see Part III). Brown's further identification of the sacred character of the ancient meeting places where acquirers obtained supernaturally provided "gifts" also identifies the traditional market, which maintains its sacral nature not merely as background to trade but as a fundamental attribute of market activities.

Descriptions of traditional markets frequently identify the market locale not only as politically neutral ground but also as ideologically hallowed ground or as proximate to a holy place—a pilgrimage center, the tomb of a holy man, or a place favored by spirits.[11] Markets, like the temples that may be built in their midst or around which they develop, may be inaugurated with religious ceremony, divination, and sacrifice to gain the essential assurance that the gods are in agreement with the project. Similarly, the authorities charged with the day-to-day management of market affairs are frequently associated with sacred affairs as holy people or religious leaders (Benet 1957:200; Perinbam 1973:430; Skinner 1962:255–256; Shaw 1979:111–113).

In scholarly literature the presence of supernaturals or the extra-ordinary aura of the market setting is generally interpreted as conducive to maintaining the peace of the trade, which seems valid. But this benefit derives from a more basic identification of the market as a very tense or highly charged locale, as a sacred site or liminal point where qualitatively distinct realms meet, meaning a place where spiritual forces of the vertical outside realm and unknown strangers and exotic products of the horizontal (geographical) outside realm may engage the peoples and products of the safely civilized world within (Benet 1957:198–199, 204; Brown 1947:34–35).[12] The market thus becomes a place where the basic concept as well as the imposition of social order is highlighted not just as secular judicial undertakings or to assure peaceful movement of goods—though these benefits are realized—but as an expression of the fundamental propriety of cosmically ordained order, as a morally responsible act in circumstances that are inherently or potentially chaotic and unruly. In other words, maintaining the peace of the market is also a cosmologically significant act.

Similarly, the breakdown of order in the market—as at the death of a king among the Mossi (Western Sudan) when symbolic raids may be staged on the markets (Skinner 1962:274–275) or if a murder or other serious assault should actually occur (Benet 1957:205)—is not only a matter of local social disruption but a cosmologically unsettling event which may require that dissatisfied market spirits be pacified or that the market be closed for a period of time until it can be properly purified or cosmologically realigned (Benet 1957:205; Skinner 1962:267–268). "The place where all kinds of merchandise accumulate and where strangers come is a place charged with forces. In time, these forces build up to such a point within the precincts of the market that some purifications are necessary to liberate them. To omit making them would expose the participants to excitements leading to brawls and compromising the place of the transactions" (Zahan, quoted in Skinner 1962:268).

Ultimately the peace of the market and the religiosity of the market are the result of the intense morality of the market. It is this morality, this concentration of those aesthetic qualities of the true, the right, and the good, that guards against the impropriety (immorality) of unfair dealings, that designates the market as the proper setting for political asylum and diverse other judicial activities, and that identifies or qualifies establishment and maintenance of a market as the responsibility of political-ideological elites, who, in addition, are thereby granted access to its material benefits, too (Balandier 1968:135; Ottenberg 1962:126; Henderson 1972:271; Bhila 1982:75; Shaw 1979:112—113; Feldman 1985:20; Wilks 1975:287). When considered in this light it is not surprising that the market may also be the setting for so-called entertainment, that is, for the public performance of music, song, dance, or theatrical presentations, in other words, for skilled crafting. Both the political significance of certain public expressions of skilled crafting as imposition of form and the moral significance of the aesthetic generally inherent in skilled crafting would make such activities entirely appropriate for market life and make the market an entirely appropriate setting for their performance.

The point is made by considering the importance of dance for Hausa (Nigeria) markets. Briefly, the viability of a Hausa market depended on the presence of *Bori* spirits, generally beneficent and protective beings that nonetheless had a capricious streak as well as a passion for dancing. Each market town had a *Bori* cult primarily in the hands of "adepts" who manifested the presence of the spirits by vigorous dancing, "attracting a crowd of onlookers and sustaining the reputation of the market. The higher the reputation of an adept, the larger the number of the spirits who might on different occasions possess her (or him), and the more versatile the range of performance."[13] "To attract *Bori* spirits to a local market gathering, drummers would beat out their characteristic rhythms, tempting the spirits to possess the adepts. If on some occasion the adepts did not successfully respond, then this was interpreted as reluctance on the part of the spirits to leave their abodes, or they may have been attracted to some other town by a rival dance, reflecting the rivalry between markets. For the Hausa, it was the benign presence of the *Bori* spirits, made manifest in the continuous dancing, that determined the community spirit and the success of the market" (Spencer 1985:18–19).

Spencer explains that failure to attract the *Bori* signaled a failure on the part of the community to "generate the right atmosphere" and was symptomatic of a "certain apathy and lack of morale" that was occasioned by wrongdoing but could be redressed by exposing deceit and renewing confidence and credibility in the viability of the market. In other words, *Bori* dancing expressed not only morale but morality, and openly asserted and guaranteed the credibility of the market as a center or focal point where cultural order and morally proper affairs obtained. The Hausa make the same point by identifying the spirits as inherently somewhat out of control (capricious), like the socially/morally marginalized performers they possess (see note 13), but as kept under control by the structured, ordered movements of an accomplished and aesthetic craft.

The same qualities of skilled crafting that conjoin dancing and market activities among the Hausa condition the directly comparable associations of acquisitional trade and ceremonial activities in settings where formal, more-or-less permanent markets do not exist but where people periodically gather to indulge in a combination of trade and festivities involving song, dance, and other expressions of crafting skills. The experiences of European traders to the Northwest Coast (North America) are illustrative, all the more so in that they clearly express the contrast between strictly economic Western expectations of trading behavior and the distinctly noneconomic context insisted upon by native peoples. As Erna Gunther explains, with respect to the Haida, "They sang and danced before they traded, a custom that irked the later fur traders because they were so anxious to proceed with business" (1972:11). Likewise the Nootka: "After the dance and the singing, a typical welcome to the [European] ships included an oration lasting an hour or so. When, after traveling halfway around the world, fur traders at last saw the people who had the precious pelts they wanted, then had to stand by and listen to such an oration in an unintelligible language, their patience was sorely tried" (ibid.:22). Again concerning the Haida, "When a party came to trade, they wore ceremonial clothing and sang songs which were introduced by the chief. He wore, among other things, a large coat of tanned elkskin decorated with dried berries and beaks of birds, which rattled when he moved" (ibid.:122, 163, 167, 177; see also Krause 1956:169).

The Indians of the Great Plains behaved in a comparable manner. Following mutual demonstrations of the art of "superlative horsemanship" between parties of Crow and Hidatsa-Gros Ventres, an "exchange of trading civilities took place dancing; when the dancing was over, the presents were distributed among the individuals in proportion to the value of the articles respectively furnished; this dance therefore is a rule of traffic" (Mackenzie, quoted in Jablow 1966:47). The Kundagai of New Guinea would feel at home in such a setting. "The most fruitful occasions for trade are gatherings where men decorate themselves and dance; . . . thus, at the close of ceremonies the danceground becomes a gathering of traders, where men exchange their decorations [plumes and marsupial skins] for pigs, shells, steel tools, and money brought by other visitors with the intent to trade" (Healey 1984:47, 48, parenthetical comment mine; also Healey 1990:322–323).[14]

In all these examples skilled crafting and acquisitional trade are found operating together because they are basically the same type of activity. In addition to whatever other benefits song, dance, and oratory may provide as entertainment or as means to enhance sociability, the transformational and "civilizing" qualities of ordered speech, dance, and music, in which natural physical movements and noises are transformed into controlled, structured movements, rhythms, and tones, accompanies and conditions the acquisitional process whereby goods also deriving from a distinctive outside realm are received into an organized cultural world where they, too, will be further transformed, by the contexts of their use, into culturally meaningful artifacts.[15]

This point may be usefully pursued a bit further. Since tangible goods generally do not change physical form in their process of cultural acquisition but mainly change location, the dynamics of the acquisitional-transformational process, if it is to be overtly expressed, may require association with some other medium that does undergo tangible or physical change. (It should be noted, however, that goods acquired from outside sources not infrequently may be intangibly transformed by blessings or ceremonies of purification. See Werner [1981:362]; Helms [1988:85]). Concurrently, qualities associated with skilled crafting—the imposition or exposition of order, the statement of morality contained in aesthetics— condition and control the potentially disruptive and dangerous atmosphere that exists whenever qualitatively distinct cosmological realms meet, as in circumstances of long-distance acquisition. Consequently, it may be legitimately said that dance, song, oratory or the wearing of ceremonial regalia produces long-distance goods as much as skilled travel through foreign realms produces long-distance goods. Not to be forgotten, either, is the power to attract that beauty is reputed to have, such that skilled (aesthetic) performances may be believed to contribute still further to the acquisitional process by causing the possessor of goods to part with them more readily.[16] It may also be the case that some form of beauty contained by the acquired goods themselves will be directly appreciated and valued for the qualities it expresses, as when the sleekness of piglets or the shimmering iridescence of feathers captures the appreciative attention of Kundagai traders. In such circumstances, the inherent attractiveness of the goods provides transformative music, too.

The close bonding between skilled crafting and the acquisition of foreign goods that occurs in market settings adds yet another dimension to the general interrelation between long-distance acquisition and artistic processes and personnel. Market activities become another of society's transformational events (along with initiation ceremonies, royal accessions, apotheosizing funerals and the like) where politically and ideologically significant activities necessary for continued reproduction of social life require the transformative and expressive powers of society's skilled craftsmen for their safe and proper realization.

In addition, skilled crafting and long-distance acquisition not only conjoin in the full expression of market processes when foreign goods enter society, but they can also be related, rather obviously, in the productive sense when acquisitional opportunities encourage the furtherance of crafting skills at home, as among the Baruya of New Guinea, where the skilled production ("crafting") of salt (requiring appropriate ritual and supernatural knowledge as well as technical expertise) provides a major "crafted" product facilitating the outside acquisition of necessary tools, weapons, and ornaments (Godelier 1986:80). Similarly, the skillful development of rhetorical abilities plays a major role in the acquisition of valuables from afar for Melanesian kula participants and the Ecuadorian Shuar, among many others (Leach 1983b:12; Hendricks 1988:223). Skilled crafting also yields desirable foreign goods in those intriguing situations where crafted items prepared for ceremonial use within society (for example, wood carvings) and traditionally destroyed after their ceremonial usefulness was over (for example, by being left to rot in the forest) are now saved to be sold to passing Europeans for Western goods or for cash with which to acquire desired goods at a later date (Gerbrands 1967:38; Küchler 1988:633 and 1987:240).[17]

The growth and intensification of various areas of skilled crafting in the Galla polities of southern Ethiopia as foreign trade developed during the nineteenth century provides a particularly good example of the complexities of a process that was frequently repeated to greater or lesser degree elsewhere in Africa wherever long-distance trade emerged as a result of European and Islamic contact. As Abir describes the situation, concurrent with the gradual centralization of Galla political organization, foreign merchants appeared more frequently in what had heretofore been a very politically fragmented and therefore very hazardous area for travelers. Consequently, collection of items favored by foreign merchants intensified. More gold was panned in gold-producing areas; ivory, which in the more remote areas had formerly been left to rot, was now collected; elephant hunting became more professionalized, which is to say, more of a "skilled craft" of sorts (see Chapter 9); various plants (coffee, coriander) which formerly grew wild were now cultivated and their fruits sold; and male civet cat farms were set up to acquire the precious musk more readily. All this activity increased the revenues from trade, such that Galla rulers became increasingly wealthy. They used this new wealth in a variety of ways (improved relations with allies and local dignitaries, support for small standing armies) but primarily to enlarge and embellish their courts and palaces, which endeavor, in turn, encouraged the development of various groups of artisans (Abir 1970 : 125–126).

Elsewhere in Africa, again after foreign trade items had been introduced, similar pressures to produce suitable products and skills that would permit the acquisition of foreign goods (particularly for elites who soon found them essential for court life) stimulated the development of professional groups of skilled elephant hunters (see Chapter 9) and of specialized traveler/traders who transported goods to places of acquisition, such as markets and European collection points. Many of these traveler/trading experts, such as the Yao and the Cokwe, were also famed for other specialized craft skills, including hunting, smithing, or weaving, in which they had excelled prior to becoming professional traveler/traders (Gray and Birmingham 1970 : 15, 19; St. John 1970 : 211–212).[18] Halfway around the world a similar development occurred (again in response to European contact) when the acquisitional possibilities opened by the early years of the fur trade intensified artistic and ceremonial life, including stimulating wood carving among the indigenous Northwest Coast peoples (Fisher 1977 : 21, 45).

Particularly interesting types of skilled crafting related to acquisition from afar are found in settings where specific acquisitional opportunities are explicitly recognized, developed, and exercised as a specific form of skilled craft. The state traders of nineteenth-century Asante are an excellent case in point, again with reference to European trade opportunities. Newly appointed official state or public traders (*batafo*), operating on behalf of the Asantehene (royal ruler), were assigned by the royal office a certain amount of gold which they were free to use as they wished and without any accounting for a period of two or three years. At the end of this time traders were expected to restore the principal to the king *and* to show a sufficient additional increment ("profit") "to support the greater dignity the King would confer," that is, to warrant their advancement and royal trust in their further usefulness to the court. If a trader failed to accomplish this "his talent is thought too mean for further elevation" (Bowdich, quoted in Wilks 1975:441, see also 440, 436–437).

Trading skills, in other words, constituted evidence not only of capability for wealth accumulation (the product of these skills) per se but also of "a mastery of relevant skills and knowledge" necessary to achieve and maintain a particular social and political status. In this case the required capability involved skill in managing the complexities of dealing not only with Asante but also with European and Muslim acquisitional systems (ibid.:450). It must also be understood that in nineteenth-century Asante wealth—gold dust in this case—was equated with the power of the state to pursue the policies deemed most conducive to the well-being of the citizenry (ibid.:444–445). Talent as a skilled "crafter of wealth," therefore, indicated a capability that would be applied not to the furtherance of personal profit or advantage but to the acquisition and transformation of outside materials into benefits for society at large, and was recognized and honored as such (see Chapter 8).

It is also possible to view cases of so-called "negative reciprocity" as acquisitional activities expressed as a recognized type of skilled craft. Consider the wording of an eighteenth-century comment on the attitude of Northwest Coast Indians toward European goods. As Fisher explains, "Because the traders operated largely outside Indian social sanctions, European property was not regarded in the same way as the property of other Indians. The traders were aliens and seemed extremely wealthy to the Indians, and their goods were looked upon as fair game. Yet Indians stole lightheartedly and laughed when they were detected, '*as if they considered it as a piece of Dexterity and did them credit ra[ther] than any dishonour*'" (Fisher 1977:14 emphasis mine; quoted from David Samwells' *Journal*). Such credible thievery, stealth, and dexterity brings to mind those culture heroes who are honored for prowess and cunning in raiding outsiders' cattle (as among the Pakot of west central Kenya; see Schneider 1973:163) as well as the role of Hermes, god of all persons and professions associated with distance or the outside (craftsmen, musicians, merchants, also athletes, heralds, and shepherds), as the cunning thief, the trickster, the "hero of *stealthy* appropriation" (Brown 1947:7).[19] Hermes, in other words, applies the same intellectual skill and supernatural aids (magic) to techniques of thievery as to other forms of outside-related activities, including more conventional forms of skilled crafting (ibid.: 11–12, 20–22).

Within the boundaries of society skilled crafting may generate long-distance acquisition, and acquisition may generate expressions of skilled crafting, but they both exist to the extent they do largely because both are fundamental to the existence and continued support of persons of influence. Political elites of all sorts, in their continual need to manifest their personal and professional qualities of honor and the ideals or epitomes of humanness they represent, in their association with the extraordinary beings and other phenomena of outside realms whose good will or beneficial attributes are believed essential to society's own well-being (and that of the lords themselves), and in their personification of the characteristics of the truly moral, the culturally ordered, and the civilized, build their homes and their cities with the finest materials and strive to adorn their communities, their dwellings, and their persons with the rich and exotic products produced by long-distance acquisition and by the most skillful artisans available.[20] It is through their support of both skilled crafting and long-distance acquisition that organizational, functional, and qualitative similarities between these two transformative modes become most apparent. It is in the service of elites, in the status of the elite, that skilled artisans and long-distance traveler/traders most easily find common cause in terms of who they are (socially speaking), what they do, how they do it, and for what reasons.

It is also in the context of meeting the demands of such influential persons that we can most readily see skilled crafting and long-distance acquisition as constituting a continuum of comparable activities in geographical space/time in which (1) the skills (and products) of local artisans may be augmented by (2) those of skilled masters from farther away whose spreading fame and reputations have brought them to the attention of equally reputatious elites, who then commission their personal services. The products crafted by both classes of skilled artisans may be augmented still further by (3) goods obtained by long-distance acquisition involving either (4) foreign traveler/traders, "experts in acquisition," who may also be invited to take up personal residence at the political center where, as valued advisors, teachers, religious specialists, and skilled artisans, they may constitute a type of foreign "good" themselves,[21] or (5) local traveler/traders who venture into the outside to derive such products from places too distant (or otherwise inappropriate) for the skilled artisans who created them to travel from personally.

8   *Qualities of Acquisition*

> Trading is the true test of man, and it is in the operations of trade
> that his piety and religious worth become known.
>
> — CALIPH UMAR,
> quoted in E. W. Bovill,
> *The Golden Trade of the Moors*, p. 236

The Flawed and the Ideal

For all of its glorification of the merits of the steady, ordered, domestic life at home, traditional society accords many of its greatest honors to those who venture outside, beyond its bounds, provided that they do so in a socially approved manner for socially approved ends. In like fashion, it also accords some of its greatest punishments to those who venture beyond for inappropriate and unapproved reasons, and exile constitutes one of the strongest statements of social displeasure. This is no accident, for the outside is a place reserved for individualizing, and either high merit and prestige or condemnation and opprobrium are accorded those who exceed the average and the ordinary, who venture beyond the social cluster at the middle of the normal curve.

Given the various dimensions of space and time, distance and direction that constitute the all-encompassing outside, the particular types of activities that can distinguish the outward-oriented individual are varied and diverse. Yet the fundamental qualities and characteristics attributed to those engaged in such endeavors are remarkably few and straightforward. Like the characteristics accorded the distant reaches of time and space itself, specialists in distance will be contrasted with the ordinary humanity of the social center in either positive or negative terms, meaning they will be recognized as either supra-human or subhuman, as exemplative either of ideal behavior that epitomizes the meaning of being human or of flawed behavior that degrades or dishonors the meaning of being human.

In Chapter 4 the attribution of these qualities to skilled artisans was considered by way of further appreciating the roles of these experts as transformative agents moving between and conjoining the social and the cosmological worlds and as persons well versed in the qualities and characteristics of certain aspects of the outside. It is now appropriate that we recognize the attribution of these same qualities to traveler/traders, the long-distance acquirers whose interests, activities, and capabilities as specialists in distance not only complement those of skilled artisans but also can be said to be subsumed under the general rubric of skilled crafting.

Appreciation of the fact that particular qualities are associated with traveler/traders is also extremely important when the political significance of their long-distance activities is taken into account, particularly when long-distance acquisition (like skilled crafting) becomes part of the portfolio of political interests and abilities required of aspiring or practicing men of influence. In addition, it is in this context of political association that such contrasts as there may be between the particular qualities accorded traveler/traders and those accorded skilled artisans become most significant.

Acquisition, as used in this essay, represents a higher order of appropriation; that is, given that appropriation of essential resources from the surrounding natural world is fundamental for human existence (as crafting in its broadly utilitarian sense is essential for the same survival), acquisition represents a particular quality associated with particular uses and expressions of appropriation (as skilled crafting represents a particular quality of basic crafting). The fundamental characteristic that distinguishes both skilled crafting and acquisition is extraordinariness and the fundamental quality attributed to them both and that basically sets them apart from more mundane activities is honor, referring to the esteem paid to (or due to) exemplary worth. Honor is associated with the good, the true, and the just, that is, with the proper expressions of whatever constitutes being ideally human. Honor also accords to the willingness to work to advance, maintain, or protect the social good. Persons who exhibit these traits are honorable persons, and the activities that reveal these traits in them are honorable activities. Yet honor, too, has its extremes; its end points to its own normal curve. Failure to achieve honor when honor is anticipated may produce shame and be considered a flaw in personal worth and a disruption in the uninterrupted flow of social proprieties. Conversely, successful attainment of honor through exceptional positive performance constitutes an ideal achievement and the attainment or expression of an epitome of desirable human behavior.

The honorable advancement, maintenance, and protection of the social good in traditional society involves understanding and advancing the
consubstantiality of life (see Chapter 7). This, in turn, requires understanding and proper expression of the life-sustaining features of the outer
reaches of the cosmos, whence human life and society are believed to have
originally derived and where the necessary support systems (both ideological and economic) are still headquartered. Religious specialists, skilled
artisans, and long-distance traveler/traders are all expert in obtaining intangible or tangible expressions of the cosmological life and energy necessary for the continuation of human society at home. In this respect formal religious activities, skilled crafting, and long-distance acquisition all
constitute honor-filled expressions of ideal human behavior. Moreover, for
long-distance traveler/traders, as with master artisans, the greater the
knowledge and the probing of the outside, meaning the farther the geographical distance traveled or the greater the obstacles conquered or the
more time spent in traveling or acquiring, the greater the attainment of
honor and prestige.

Just as many cultures have expected all persons to develop some degree
of skill in a craft as a prerequisite for cultural adulthood, so a certain
amount of physical and intellectual exploration of the geographical outside
may be expected of all culturally adult persons, or at least all culturally
adult men, as a prerequisite for the attainment of complete or ideal humanness. Thus a period of travel through or residence in foreign lands
may be considered a desirable or even necessary part of attaining full cultural identity and maturity. For example, in Tanzania, in the nineteenth
century, where Nyamwezi trade caravans traveled to and from the coast
several times a year, able-bodied men willingly signed aboard because
"porterage, on the long and toilsome journey, is now considered by the
Wanyamwezi a test of manliness"; "not one of them was allowed to marry
before he had carried a load of ivory to the coast, and brought back one
of calico or brass-wire" (Burton and Swann, respectively, quoted in Roberts 1970:66).

The "passion for journeying about" evidenced by Fang men as
nineteenth-century traders and twentieth-century dancers (Chapter 3) appears similar both in the prospects for material gain and the "successful
self-sufficiency" such travels provided (Fernandez 1982:419). So do the
travels of Mande young people who seek the "esteem and adulation" that
their society bestows upon those who, culture hero–like, travel to foreign
lands (as students or migrant workers) to seek both material rewards and
esoteric knowledge useful for improving life at home (Bird and Kendall

1980). According to Weiner, one of the purposes served by participation in the endless rounds of travel and acquisition known as the kula (Melanesia) is that individuals are periodically extricated from the entanglements of social obligations at home, allowing them to "regenerate the wealth and value of the self," in a sense to "craft" themselves as proper persons, by pursuit of fame through kula acquisition (Weiner 1983:165). In comparable fashion youthful Canelos Quichua were expected to enhance their social and intellectual development and their acquisition of personal power by traveling to distant areas, trading with strange people, and learning about the jungle environment. Similar trips were part of established initiation procedures for the young among the Murngin of Australia (Helms 1988:68–69, 165–166; and Chapter 3).

As an expression of exemplary or ideal humanness, a period of travel and knowledge of foreign countries may be particularly important for members of the political-ideological elite, whose younger members especially may be expected to travel as part of their training and preparation for eventual positions of high office or authority (Helms 1988:76, 98). Generally speaking, when expressed in the context of acquaintance with geographical distance, this manner of epitomizing the human condition involves the embellishment of ordinary experience and ordinary abilities by proved familiarity with a world that is different (compare Mills 1973:404). Such foreign experience may be particularly pertinent when positions of political authority accrue to those whose "power" is believed to derive from knowledge of distant places and peoples. Among the Shuar, for example, where positions of political leadership accrue to those who possess more vital energy or kakáram, foreign power sources are believed more potent than local ones. Consequently, it is "men who have traveled [who] are often elected to positions of authority" (Hendricks 1988:219, 232; see also Helms 1988:148–163).

Association with and knowledge of foreign domains as representative of exemplary humanness is also clearly evidenced when foreign traveler/ traders are heralded as introducing (culture hero-like) new traits of civilization to the peoples they encounter and among whom they may decide to stay. Roberts notes the "special status as foreign experts" that Nyamwezi could achieve when they settled (as the more enterprising tended to do) in distant countries. Some were noteworthy as traders and artisans; others gained prominence as chiefly advisors (Roberts 1970:68). When settling among established polities that are already centralized, such exceptional foreigners may become highly influential members of the chiefly or royal court. The Muslim traveler/traders (such as the Dyula and the

Hausa), who achieved positions as advisors, teachers, religious specialists, diviners, scribes, musicians, and praise-singers in royal courts of West Africa, are a well-known example of this phenomenon.

When exemplary civilizing "foreigners" replete with superior knowledge of distant places and things, and particularly if representative of some distant metropole, settle among politically more segmented peoples they may come to constitute formal political authority themselves. According to typical oral history accounts of such processes, after a period of traveling about "the newcomers establish their rule by superior knowledge, or intrigue, or trickery, or force. The new rulers bring in a new organization (and perhaps, again, new crops or technology), thereby ushering in a new social order where before, the story claims, a true or at least a civilized society scarcely existed" (Kopytoff 1987:50).[1]

In this assumption of political authority by foreign-derived travelers we may see a parallel of sorts with those skilled artisans who constitute foci of political authority through their abilities (as orators, managers of political-ideological events, or image-creators) to successfully impose order on potential social chaos. In the case of outside-derived political authority, however, the political skill that is evidenced appears as likely to involve exposition of form or power as to invoke imposition of order. That is to say, subordination to revealed authority is at least as characteristic of their political style as is maintenance of order (see Kopytoff 1987:36, 63). The capacity to effect political subordination or the acceptance of political attachment as part of socio-political maintenance, in turn, may derive at least in part from particular characteristics associated with experience of geographically distant realms in which expertise and power is evidenced not by exceptional (mystical) technical/supernatural ability to transform physical materials and behaviors but in the mystique accorded personal contact with the perceived mysteries of geographical-cosmological distance itself. This personal contact with powers resident in geographical distance appears to generate varying degrees of awe and fear among local populations, who may be more readily inclined to identify such foreigners (or their ancestors if the foreigners have been established for awhile) as embodying the power of cosmographically distant places.

In addition, the new organizations or techniques introduced from outside may be understood as formal expressions of that outside power, as expositions of the forms that geocosmological power may take. Similarly, the long-distance goods acquired from afar may also be said to be tangible manifestations or expositions of cosmological energy and power, and long-distance acquirers in general may be said to expose cosmological form and order by bringing such goods into the open purview of the homeland. To the extent that such authorities introduce organizational modes that reshape or transform society's original modes of operation or evidence craft skills (such as oratory) that actively impose order or perhaps represent formal religious systems embodying judicial traditions they will impose and maintain social order as well as expose and manifest political-ideological (cosmological) "forms" of power. But in the broader view the introduction of political authority itself becomes an aesthetic achievement of proper form and an expression of the epitome of true humanness in a world where "to be under no one at all, and dependent on no one, was to be utterly without status" and to be without a ruler was itself "uncivilized" (Kopytoff 1987 : 36, 63).

Unfortunately, the power that derives from geographical distance may be accorded negative as well as positive qualities by those at home. Long-distance traveler/traders may be regarded by society's mainstream membership with an awe and fear that places them at the bottom of the social spectrum rather than at the top and identifies them as flawed acquirers rather than as pinnacles of political-ideological achievement. Flawed traveler/traders are not so much associated with the lowest level of society as they are with that which falls behind or lies outside society and its political and moral proprieties. Thus, in some tales concerning the origins of political regimes introduced by foreign travelers from cosmologically distant places, the new arrivals are portrayed not as ideal civilizers but as deeply flawed (uncouth) barbarians who achieve political legitimacy by marriage to an autochthonous woman (Gillespie 1989 : 219–222). In the more immediate world, Plato, who had a distinctly negative view of traders and travelers, speaking with reference to coastal centers where travelers in the ancient Mediterranean world were likely to congregate (and which were ideally territorially separate from the *polis*), noted that the trade and traffic of a port "breeds shifty and distrustful habits of soul . . ." (quoted in Momigliano 1944 : 5). Similarly, Isocrates, speaking with reference to those who would disregard the virtuous life of settled land dwellers and embrace the unwholesome fortunes of the sea, comments that "sea-power causes injustice, indolence, lawlessness, avarice, covetousness" (Momigliano 1944 : 4, 6).

As many scholars have long made clear, the deficits attributed to the "flawed" traveler/trader have to do with honor and morality, with the exercise of goodness, all of which are judged to be lacking in this perspective of the character of outsiders, especially if they are foreign-born (Meneses 1987; Polanyi 1957a : 259; Aristotle 1962 : 30). The heart of the matter lies in the perception by society's mainstream members that flawed traveler/traders are not engaged in legitimate acts of mediation and transformation by which outside things are made available to those inside for the wider social good. Instead, flawed acquirers are said to emphasize private personal gain achieved at society's expense. Stated otherwise, flawed acquirers are frequently believed to be artisans of negative reciprocity who, however, insidiously invert and misuse these skills by focusing their cunning acquisitive capabilities not upon outsiders but upon the heartland, upon society itself (Harms 1981:198, 200; Rowlands 1987:62).

In some cases flawed acquirers have become so by allegedly allying themselves with supernatural forces of evil which could harm even the families of acquirers themselves (for example, by taking the lives of children) as well as other members of society as the price for their aid in acquiring wealth (Harms 1981:200, 203). Sometimes such negative relations were caused by practicing the thievery of retailing. Here the actions of flawed acquirers are regarded as doubly dishonorable, first, by being exercised entirely for their own personal benefit and, secondly, by achieving this benefit by taking negative advantage of other members of society (Aristotle 1962: Chapters 9 and 10; Polanyi 1957a:259; Austin and Vidal-Naquet 1977:13; Duby 1974:100; Wheatley 1971:285).[2]

Though the immorality of retailing is a widely cited example, the flaws in acquisition may vary depending on what particular qualities constitute honor. For example, the alleged improprieties may be decried because they allow unrestricted personal accumulation, ignoring social controls limiting the acquisition of wealth to an approved and finite social purpose (Aristotle 1962:22, 25; note 1, p. 26). Acquisition may go astray when itinerant merchants use military proficiency to go beyond necessary personal protection and to become brigands operating beyond societal restraints (Mines 1984:151–152; Kolff 1971). Similarly, achievement of wealth by long-distance acquisition may offend those whose honor is tied to acquisition of other types of things, particularly land (Ho 1959:333; Hasebroek 1933:8, 16–17), or whose honor does not allow them to be engaged with goods that are commoditized, lacking inalienable qualities.[3]

There are cases, too, where the honorability of long-distance acquisition is tarnished at least in part because the position of long-distance traveler/trader falls to persons who are denied regular avenues of honorable endeavor by the accident of birth. A case in point is found in the early days of the development of long-distance trade among the Galla of southern Ethiopia. Among the first of the Galla to turn to trade were younger sons of families who, because of certain particulars of Galla custom, could not share in the inheritance of their fathers. Such sons "found themselves in the awkward position of being left out of the traditional tribal organization" because they were not eligible for the customary age-grade initiation and turned to trade instead (Abir 1970:126–127).

On the other hand, flawed acquirers, standing as they do beyond the accepted bounds of social life, may be perceived by those who are more honorable as another source of outside benefits that may be legitimately tapped by persons whose job it is to obtain socially useful things from afar. Thus we find essentially the same phenomenon that was noted with respect to flawed craftsmen: given the commonality uniting the different dimensions of the beyond, those who stand outside in one sense may find common cause with those who reach outside in another. Just as families of socially unacceptable artisans may intermarry with socially reputable kings, so flawed acquirers (money-lenders, merchants-cum-ambassadors), as resource-rich social outsiders (and especially if foreigners), may become the confidants of resource-hungry elites and be trusted "almost as social equals" by kings and high lords (Ho 1959:333; Kolff 1971:215).[4] As a result, and again comparable to the situation of flawed craftsmen, although flawed acquirers themselves may be separated from the social continuum, the break between them and society proper may be bridged or mended by the value attached to the products they make available, just as the usefulness of the skills and the goods created by flawed artisans are accepted and appreciated even if the persons of the creators are not.

The Accumulation of Wealth

When properly conducted, acquisition of wealth from outside sources becomes a valued expression of high ideals, of the epitome of being human, and of morally appropriate behavior. Such acquisition becomes, in fact, the aesthetic expression of appropriation. Moral propriety or aesthetics where acquisition is involved generally means that there is no private or personal claim to acquired things, that sooner or later an appropriate share of the benefits of such acquisition will accrue to other segments of society by some expression of intra-societal distribution. Such dispersion, in turn, constitutes one of the transformative aspects of the skilled "craft" of acquisition.[5]

Although generous distribution is not the only form of socially responsible behavior that acquirers may follow, it probably has been the most common. Certainly much scholarly attention has been given both to the various forms that distribution may take and to the honor and prestige

that accrues to those who comply with generous distribution. Yet, although dispersal clearly requires prior acquisitional activities, the honor
that accrues to such generosity is not only distinct from but of a different
order from the honor associated with acquisition of things from afar. Acquisition, and especially long-distance acquisition, is a more dynamic type
of activity involving either personal travel into foreign parts or (especially
for high elites) vicarious association with those who do travel. As such it
speaks directly to the requirement that persons of influence be perceived
as persons of action, for it is through activity in general that power is
evidenced.[6] Generous distribution, in contrast, *when separated from prior
acts of acquisition,* appears to be inherently a more static or stationary endeavor, one that lacks comparable achievement-related activity *and* one
that is secondary, since in those settings where generous distribution is
required it must follow when acquisition has occurred lest the honor of
acquisition be forfeit.[7]

The prestige accruing to distribution in these situations is based on a
double negative: the good person is one who has not failed to be socially
responsible, who has avoided the penalty for personal stinginess. In contrast, the prestige accruing to acquisition is based on a single positive: the
good person is one who has appropriated exceptional things from afar.
Expressed in terms of a single system of rewards and penalties, the reward
is given for acquisition, while the penalty is affixed for failure to act with
the appropriate sense of social responsibility. The ideal, therefore, basically
lies in successful pursuit of the positive (acquisition) provided it is followed by successful avoidance of the negative (failure to distribute)
(Aijmer n.d.).[8]

Considered in its own right, successful acquisition (which can be explicitly encouraged by the admiration that is elicited by eventual generosity)[9]
involves accumulation of wealth—tangible or intangible "things" laden
with inherent and inalienable associations and worth, and for this reason constituting riches (Aijmer n.d.:7). The significance of the qualities,
the value, of such wealth is further enhanced because it extends beyond
the specific characteristics associated with particular goods to speak to the
qualities of the acquirer and/or of the polity served or represented.

Acquisition and accumulation of wealth, like capacity for travel, address
the personal capabilities of the acquirer, as was illustrated in Chapter 7 in
the discussion of Asante traders as "crafters of wealth." To villagers living
in the mountains of northwest Nepal, "Agonistic striving after wealth is a
way of proving personal worth in a context of explicit, measurable finan-
cial and social inequality" (Fisher 1986:186). In Benin, this same expres-

8-1.   Traders in Kumase, Asante. (From Mrs. R. Lee, "Stories of Strange Lands and Fragments from the Notes of a Traveller." [London, 1835]. In *Asante in the Nineteenth Century,* edited by Ivor Wilks. Cambridge University Press, 1975. Used by permission of Cambridge University Press.)

sion of personal worth by self-achievement, involving at least in part the acquisition of wealth, is recognized in the cult of the Hand. As Bradbury has explained, the hand (actually the hand and the whole arm), is regarded as a positive symbol of wealth and social achievement and of the things an individual has obtained with his or her own efforts, that belong to him or her as an individual rather than as a member of a kin group (Bradbury 1973:264, 265). The hand in the form of cult objects is thus served or worshipped (sacrificed to) particularly by those who have achieved. This includes people of wealth and high rank, women, if they are important traders, artisans, hunters, and probably warriors who are dependent on manual skills and physical strength and whose activities express individual enterprise and prowess.[10]

Evidence of the capability to acquire wealth may also indicate personal fitness for authority, "power moored to personality" as Salomon has phrased it (1986:95). It may herald the successful (ideal) attainment of knowledge and ritual efficacy as well as the personal state of spiritual purity necessary to elicit the supernatural aid required to obtain wealth.[11] It may speak generally of the ability to deal successfully with the outside and to obtain the benefits that follow therefrom:

[The concept of wealth held by the Northeastern Woodland Indians] connoted well-being—physical, spiritual, and social—positive cognitive and
animate states of being. Traditionally, when one accumulated wealth, particularly durable and portable wealth such as white shell beads, one was
accumulating the assurance of physical, spiritual, and social well-being.
Wealth, in this sense, was a kind of *medicine*. (Hamell 1986–1987:76)

   Mythical time and space converged in the furthermost regions from the
centre—at the world's rim, the rocky lands or rocky islands which lay beyond the great waters surrounding earth islands and at the threshold to
ritual lodges. Through visions, dreams, and heroic journeys, real human
man-beings had access to mythic time and space and to the powerful man-
beings dwelling there. Wealth, medicine, or charms were the tokens of successful encounters and ritualized reciprocal exchanges with this other
world. (Ibid.:77)[12]

Acquisition of wealth from outside can also express the concept of the
surmountability of culture (inside) over nature (outside). In a sense this
quality is expressed whenever humans successfully gain the assistance of
supernaturals through the eminently cultural acts of ritual in their various
appropriative activities in the natural world (Snyder 1975:158). The same
surmountability is similarly expressed by the possession of things from
that world that are filled with its inalienable qualities; the concept of
wealth itself connotes a transcendence or transformation from strictly
natural or physical things into value-laden things that expresses the ultimate human achievement of the "abnegation of the natural" and the "celebration of the supra-natural" or cultural (Snyder 1975:158–161).

   T. C. McCaskie has provided an interpretation of the meaning of wealth
and of the acquisition and accumulation of wealth in the nineteenth-
century kingdom of Asante that is richly illustrative of these points. The
wealth of Asante was pre-eminently expressed in gold, as dust or nuggets,
and the "entrepreneurial deployment" of gold underwrote the development of political centralization from "individual accumulators of surplus"
or "big men" (the *obirempon*, pl. *abirempon*) to territorially competitive
chiefships and, finally, to a unitary state presided over by the Asantehene,
the accumulator par excellence, the superordinate *obirempon* (McCaskie
1983:27).

   In McCaskie's opinion, gold was distinctive because it was substantively
mutable and as such served as a "transferential agent—something that
readily transgresses and conquers the vitally important Asante boundaries

between 'nature' and 'culture' " (ibid.). Similarly, the accumulator, the *obirempon,* by his achievement as proclaimed through "visible accumulation and public display," provided a "seminally powerful, a demiurgic model of attainment . . . [that] served throughout much of Asante history as the primary referent that defined the conceptualisation of the 'good' or 'admirable' citizen" (ibid.:27). McCaskie's explanation as to why accumulation was so valued to greater or lesser extent probably fits not only Asante but other cultures as well:

> The Asante were and are acutely aware that their culture, in the most literal sense, was hacked out of nature. And this understanding (which is historically and materially accurate) engendered the abiding fear that, without unremitting application and effort, the fragile defensible space called culture would simply be overwhelmed or reclaimed by an irruptive and anarchic nature. Thus the determination of culture, its preservation and enlargement, was construed as being about the domestication of the object—the wresting of control from nature.
>
> As a direct consequence of this view, the embrace of accumulation aspired to the universal—the endlessly indiscriminate as well as the objectively or identifiably valuable. In the former category, the ultimate reification was constituted by the incidental manufactures and artifacts of Europe, an enormous gallery of the haphazard, the trivial, the broken and the arcane. These were sedulously garnered irrespective of any primary considerations of utility or intentional function. Once acquired and hoarded, these (and other) objects might be safely ignored but never discarded; their assimilated presence was part of the most fundamental equation, the strengthening of culture (the realm of man) against nature (the realm of non-man). . . .
>
> But, of course, the imperative to accumulate found its most potent socio-political expression in the realm of the explicitly or objectively valuable. And the objects of accumulation in this sphere were endlessly elaborated over time; gold, subjects, land, women, guns, clothing, alcohol, and all the rest. Constantly underpinning this great edifice of accumulation was gold, the demiurgic substance, the yardstick of social attainment, the *nonpareil* of wealth, the measure of ultimate 'value' into which all other objects—at least notionally in material terms—might be converted. (McCaskie 1983:28–29) [13]

By the nineteenth century the accumulator as defender of Asante culture in the face of constantly encroaching nature was recognized and honored by the symbol of the Golden Elephant Tail, essential complement to the Golden Stool, representative of the collective identity of the Asante polity. It is noteworthy, as McCaskie emphasizes, that the Golden Stool was believed to have descended from the sky, while the wealth (the Golden Elephant Tail) that supported the Stool (the polity) derived not from the vertical axis of the outside but from its horizontal dimensions. The celestially-derived power of the Golden Stool provided the polity with cultural identity and with a point of ideological origins; the power of nature, as encapsulated in outside "things" derived by acts of accumulation and symbolized by the Golden Elephant Tail, provided the energy that activated the cultural/political order (McCaskie 1983:31).

To be sure, the Stool, that is, the state in the person of the Asantehene, held superordinant and ultimate authority over the Tail in that the state was the ultimate recipient or acquirer of the wealth accumulated by the *abirempon*. The state acquired the wealth of these ideal citizens (as well as of those less successful in acquisition) primarily by confiscating a man's wealth at his death. Nonetheless, prior to their demise the most successful persons of wealth, the foremost acquirers, were officially recognized and honored with the title of *obirempon* and conferment of an elephant tail whisk or switch, signifying the culmination of a lifetime spent in pursuit of the ideal and the reality of acquisition; the "accumulation of wealth in the highest degree" (ibid.:32; see also Wilks 1979; 1975:414–431).

Wealth and the Ancestors

In his discussion of the significance of the Asante state's ultimate appropriation of accumulated wealth, McCaskie explains that wealth accumulation not only expressed the dynamics of Culture vs. Nature but also related to the Asante understanding of the "logic of the historical process," the continuum of social reproduction from ancestors to living to yet unborn (McCaskie 1983:34; see also Weiner 1985, esp. 223–224). Within this context:

> All accumulation constituted an act of societal rather than individual increase—an obligatory aggrandisement or enlargement of the stock of human (Asante) capital, undertaken in conscious discharge of duties towards the achievement of the ancestors and of responsibilities towards the 'historic' future represented by the unborn. Thus, at its most fundamental, the accumulation of wealth was basically about the amplification of cultural space over historical time. . . .

... During his lifetime the individual accumulator of wealth received public or social acknowledgment of his achievement on behalf of society. . . . at his death, his accumulated wealth—the evidence of his capacity for and his skill at increase, the benchmark of his social responsibility— passed from his individual purview into culture. . . . (Ibid.:34; see note 17)

This transference was accomplished by the state's collection of death duties which McCaskie interprets as "a settling of accounts with history, the final item in the ledger that indicated the relative degree of the individual's success in contributing beyond his own gratification to the maintenance, enlargement and continuity of the realm of culture" (ibid.).[14]

The Asante method of settling accounts with history shows similarities with practices in which wealth is willed to religious institutions, as, for example, in medieval Europe when, after conversion to Christianity, the traditional pagan practice of burying wealth with the deceased was gradually replaced by bequests to the Church (Duby 1974:54–55). Another procedure for providing gifts to the state is recorded for Java:

There was a lake or rather an enclosed estuary in front of the royal palace, and each morning the chief steward came before his sovereign with a golden ingot of a certain weight. . . . Then, in the presence of the rajah, he threw the ingot into the lake. When the tide came up, it covered the ingots: when it receded, the ingots glittered in the sun. . . . But no one touched them as long as [the rajah] lived. When he died, his successor fished them all out, save one, and they were apportioned among the royal family, men, women, and children, generals and slaves of the royal household, and distributed to the poor and needy. The longer the reign the larger the number of ingots, and the greater amount of wealth to be distributed. (Sulayman, an Arab merchant, quoted in Quiggin 1949:267)

The Javanese kingdom in the person of the rajah, the Asante state in the person of the Asantehene, and the medieval European church in the person of the Pope all may be taken to represent the embodiment of the continuity of historic culture. In this capacity the personifications of the Asante state, the medieval church, and the Javanese kingdom provided the direct link connecting the living with the temporal/historical continuum of originating cultural ancestors and the yet unborn. The personifications of state and church constituted living ancestors, so to speak, and the wealth, the abundance, that ultimately flowed to them represented the re-energizing, or re-invigorating of the past and the future ancestral powers.[15]

Following this line of thought it appears logical that the same energizing of ancestral powers is believed to occur when wealth is buried with the deceased, most notably when quantities of accumulated wealth are buried with elites.[16] In addition, the accumulated buried wealth, the evidence of the deceased's capacity for, and skill at, increase, the benchmark of his or her social responsibility, tangibly validates his or her skills and capacities as an accumulator, as a responsible provider of social benefits. The quantity of burial goods thereby testifies to the deceased's qualifications to become a beneficent ancestor; indeed, the quantity of buried wealth becomes that ancestral potency, encapsulates that potency. It is not simply that such goods herald the status and social identity of the deceased or provide materials necessary for the trip to the beyond or for a comfortable after-life or remove valued goods from the accumulated stock among the living so as to aid future circulation of goods (though all these functions may result) but that such goods literally identify and create a functioning ancestor; as counterpoint, the name—the fame—of such an accomplished accumulator remains in the memory of those still living, providing means to contact, and thus to tap, his or her ancestral power (see also Errington and Gewertz 1986:102–103).[17]

Pursuing this point a bit further, and anticipating the discussion of the following chapter, the type of grave goods may become relevant to future ancestral power and potency. Archaeology and ethnography frequently attest that elite burial wealth takes the form of valuable natural goods or skillfully crafted goods. Such wealth expresses the capability of the deceased not only to accumulate wealth but, more specifically, to accumulate the type of wealth believed to encompass the potency either of nature or of skillful artisanry.[18] Acquisition of such goods and of the inalienable power encapsulated therein during the lifetime of the acquirer constituted a highly aesthetic or moral act indicative of the attainment of an ideal or epitome of humanness, evidencing as it did any of a number of highly desirable qualities, including a good working relation with the supernatural, and culminating in benefits both for society and for the acquirer as society's benefactor (see note 13).[19]

Burial or cremation of such goods and of their acquirer returns the physical form of all to the earth, the original source of both natural resources and of artisans' materials. This act transforms, recycles, or releases (sometimes by the breaking of goods before burial) the qualitative or inalienable aspects of both the acquirer as ideal, real, or purely cultural human being and of the goods as encapsulated potency to the reservoir of universal productive energies controlled and embodied by vitalized natural

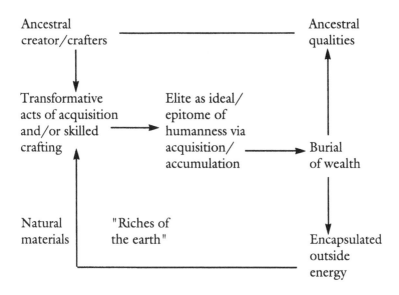

8-2.   Inside-outside cycle of accumulated and released "energies."

forces or by the corps of personalized ancestors (see Figure 8-2). Acts of burial, therefore, provide another situation of inside-outside transformation, one that is particularly crucial since it returns quantities of encapsulated energies back to the ancestral source and refreshes the ancestral stock itself.[20]

Such an interpretation may help to interpret not only routine elite burials but also more extraordinary cases where the deceased is interred with truly incredible amounts of goods. Robert Harms provides a description of such a circumstance in the central Zaire basin in the nineteenth century, when quantities of European goods could be acquired for ivory and slaves. He reiterates that as European trade made foreign goods available, chiefs and traders benefited most, acquiring weapons, currency items (shells, beads), cloth, and alcohol as luxury consumer goods. Cloth in particular was valued. "Wealthy people not only wore imported cloth but also saved large quantities of it to be buried with them as a way of gaining honor in the afterlife. . . . A rich man was buried with a great amount of his wealth because he wanted to show people in the afterlife what a great man he had been. Indeed, one purpose of gaining power on earth was to ensure its continuance into the afterlife" (Harms 1981 : 45, 149).[21] Again,

Sir Harry Johnston, who observed a Bobangi funeral in 1883, noted that the dead man had been placed in his grave with several layers of locally made cloth beneath him and was covered with piles of cotton cloth from the coast which represented a considerable amount of wealth. The largest bundle of cloth reported in the region was the one seen by Dr. Maes at a village near the Pool. It measured nearly three meters in diameter and three meters in height. All this cloth had been accumulated by the deceased during his lifetime. Because all people considered their burials important, even poor people tried to amass as much cloth as possible . . . a man who wore rags all his life might well have a store of cloth cached in his house to be used for his funeral. (Ibid.:192; see note 22)

The political-ideological and cosmological contexts of this curious behavior become clearer when we learn that Europeans, who had arrived in the Zaire basin from the coast in the 1870s with great quantities of wealth, were widely believed to live beneath the sea,

. . . where they wove cloth in large quantities. This theory may have arisen from the observation by Africans that when a ship was seen on the horizon, its masts were seen first, and then the hull, as if the ship were rising out of the water. White people were also associated with spirits of dead ancestors. This tied in with a widespread view of the slave trade which held that slaves went to America, died, and as spirits worked at producing sums of wealth unknown in the land of the living. Indeed, [it has been argued that] Mpoto, the name generally taken to mean 'the country where white people come from,' actually means 'the land of the dead.' A similar explanation was current in the 1880s among the Likuba, who said that when rich Africans died they went to Europe and became white. The cloth with which they were buried was their merchandise when they came back to trade (Harms 1981:210).[22]

Burying wealthy accumulators with treasure (meaning an aesthetically appreciated accumulation of energy-rich things) that the ancestors in some form will then return to again enrich the living is identical to yielding up accumulated wealth to the state, the church, or to distributional feasts that the living may again be served. It is also likely that the same goal is sought when hoards of precious things ("offerings") are buried in holes in the ground or cast into deep waters.[23] The same logic probably also underlies the practice of resting the foundations of temples, where deities and ancestors (who ultimately determine the extent of human well-being and the abundance of cultural life) contact the still living, on offerings of precious gems and other potent wealth (Clark 1986:87).

When wealth is composed of inalienable goods obtained from afar or skillfully crafted at home by the transformation of outside substances it can convey a range of interrelated political and cosmological messages based on the wealth of qualities such riches encode. Basically, the value of a store of wealth derives from the sum of the values of the constituent items of which it is composed, enhanced by the qualities that accrue to the concept of the accumulation of wealth itself. Acquisition of this sort essentially means a gathering in of inalienable qualities from power-filled places of origin somewhere in geographically distant space/time, so that the uninterrupted flow of cultured human existence, begun and continued by ancestral benefactors also located in cosmological space/time, may continue unabated. All those who honorably engage in this activity for the social good are evidencing an aspect of ideal human behavior, are acting "ancestrally." Those who achieve the highest levels of accumulation, either by their own efforts or those of agents working on their behalf, may anticipate an eventual apotheosis into the ultimate ideal human state of true ancestor-hood.[24] This is so because that treasure, the accumulation of which constitutes the very body and blood of kings, reaches beyond to constitute the potency of their gods, too.

9 *Naturally Endowed Goods and Skillfully Crafted Goods*

> From the Lega point of view, the top part of a pangolin tail is
> just as significant, just as charged with symbolism and meaning,
> as any of the beautiful statues.   — DANIEL BIEBUYCK
>   "The *Kindi* Aristocrats," p. 11

The Tangible and the Material

Up to this point primary emphasis has been placed on activities rather
than artifacts, on the significance, qualities, and interrelatedness of skilled
crafting and crafters and long-distance acquisition and acquirers. It now
becomes necessary to broaden the discussion somewhat to differentiate
more carefully among the types of things that are acquired from afar. I
shall distinguish between two broad categories of outside products—
those considered to have been skillfully crafted and those considered to be
naturally endowed—provided an initial caveat is held in mind. In compar-
ing and contrasting these categories it is important to realize that, while
such a dichotomy may be heuristically useful and often prove to be ethnographically valid, the particular types of objects or artifacts that are attributed to one or the other category in particular cultures may not always
be in accordance with the outside observer's opinion or assumptions concerning what constitutes natural as opposed to crafted things. This is particularly true with respect to the category of natural things, which in some
cases may include manufactured items.

A case in point concerns woven reed mats in frontier provinces of the
Inca empire, which seem to have been regarded as a part of the "wild" or
natural resources automatically belonging to the Crown (Murra 1980:
96–97). Although these mats were manufactured by technical skills, their
production apparently lacked the aura of supernatural assistance that provides the distinctive sacral quality that is always part of the process of true
skillful crafting. Conversely, seemingly natural things may be regarded as

skillfully crafted by those who produce them, as in the case of the spec-
tacularly long yams grown in parts of New Guinea. As Roscoe describes
it, "Long yam cultivation is an esoteric art" requiring not only proper
stock and sophisticated knowledge of how to prepare seedlings and yam
holes but also supernatural skills and assistance as evidenced in proper use
of secret magical potions and powders (1989:221).[1]

Sometimes, too, a sharing of common qualities, such as color or design,
may inter-relate a seemingly obvious natural vs. crafted distinction. As
Morphy points out with respect to Yolngu art (Northeast Arnhem Land,
Australia),

> The distinction between natural and cultural designs must not be too rig-
> idly conceived, as things which are called *miny'tji* [roughly 'painting,' hav-
> ing color and regularly recurring design] are all believed to be the result of
> consequential action; *miny'tji* are meaningful designs. The design on the
> back of a turtle is seen as its design in much the same way as the design
> painted on a human body is seen as belonging to and representing a
> clan. . . . Myths explaining the form of natural designs are analogous to
> those relating to cultural designs; indeed natural and cultural designs are
> frequently seen as two manifestations of the same thing. (Morphy
> 1989:24; bracketed material mine)

Although, as these examples indicate, care must be taken in assigning
things to one or the other category, some degree of differentiation between crafted (cultural) and natural things appears nonetheless to be ethnographically valid. When applied to anthropological interpretations, however, a skilled crafting–naturally endowed pairing would seem to suggest
most obviously a variation on the well-worn prestige-subsistence or non-
utilitarian-utilitarian dichotomies which have been widely expressed in
the literature over the years. Generally speaking, however, while skilled
crafting as used in this essay is related to the more familiar prestige or non-
utilitarian category, naturally endowed as conceived here is totally unrelated to the utilitarian or subsistence domain.

Both skillfully crafted things and naturally endowed things are contrasted with "ordinary" material things in the same sense as prestige, ceremonial, luxury, non-utilitarian, or nonconsumable manufactured things
are contrasted with subsistence, utilitarian, necessary, or consumable
things (see Figure 9-1). Both skillfully crafted and naturally endowed
things partake of general characteristics that have been adduced for the
prestige, ceremonial, luxury, or non-utilitarian sphere. As Appadurai has
stated it, these are goods "whose principal use is *rhetorical* and *social*,

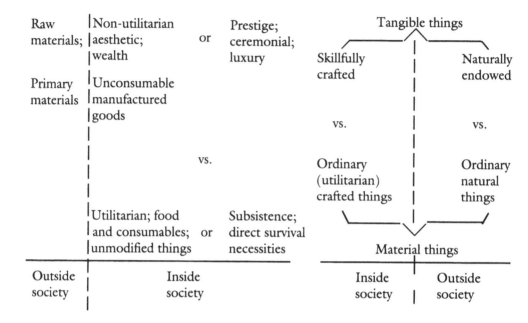

9-1.   Anthropological classifications of categories of "types" of things.

goods that are simply *incarnated signs*. The necessity to which *they* respond is fundamentally political" (1986:38). In addition, Appadurai notes, the luxury register is characterized by restriction to elites, complexity of acquisition (the "scarcity" issue), semiotic virtuosity,[2] specialized knowledge as prerequisite for "appropriate" consumption, and a high degree of linkage in this consumption to body, person, and personality (ibid.).

Goldman states the characteristics of such goods somewhat differently and from a perspective that is closer to the approach enlisted in this essay. Speaking specifically of the centralized polities of Polynesia, his emphasis is on durable goods that were elite-associated, scarce, and "for the most part products of *honorable* production and destined for *honorable* use" (1970:476). To speak of honor-related goods and activities, he notes, is a rephrasing of the notion of the "prestige economy" in which "the center of attention [is] ... on *form*, the correct way of doing things ..." In addition, honor-related or prestige activity was "concerned either with ritual associated with the gods or with chiefly power, which was basically sacred power" (1970:479).

In the context of non-centralized societies, Anderson, speaking of New

Guinea peoples and particularly of acquisitional trade, notes a contrast between subsistence items and "necessities" on the one hand and goods "valued for aesthetic rather than subsistence reasons" (for example, fine plumes and shells) on the other (1979:35). Harding, also with reference to New Guinea (the Sio) and taking issue with the commonly used distinction between utilitarian and non-utilitarian goods, states the contrast as between food and consumables (betel, tobacco, lime) and "durable, manufactured goods" constituting "wealth" (along with valuables and money) (1967:57, 72).

Harding further identifies three qualities which individually or in combination are exhibited by wealth items, at least among the Sio: considerable labor is required to produce them; they are durable; and they are circulated to meet important social obligations. He notes that ornaments of shell and teeth are "perhaps to be regarded as wealth par excellence, since they qualify on all three counts of labor, durability, and convertibility."[3] In contrast, "perishable manufactured goods, things quickly worn out, and slightly modified or unmodified implements" are conceptually opposed to wealth as things that are "nothing" (1967:73).

Since I consider both skillfully crafted things and naturally endowed things to be structurally related to the prestige/ceremonial/wealth/non-utilitarian sphere, they may be expected to contain or exhibit many of the qualities and characteristics identified by Goldman, Appadurai, Anderson, and Harding. Quite a few have been identified in preceding chapters, where skilled crafting in particular has been specifically associated with qualitative concepts of ideal behavior, honor, and eliteness, with persons of political influence, with aesthetics, and thus with the concept of morality. In addition, particular emphasis has been given to characteristics and significance of acts of skilled crafting and of long-distance acquisition, including particular types of labor required to produce or obtain such things. The theme of convertibility has been broached, too, in the context of responsible acquisition and qualitative transformation.

Most, but not quite all, of these qualities also identify the naturally endowed category of things which will be discussed further here. Naturally endowed things constitute a conceptual category of goods obtained from the natural or physical (as opposed to social or cultural) realm which (in contrast to the Sio perspective on unmodified "ordinary" things) are accorded significant qualitative value in their natural state without additional human modification. Naturally endowed things are distinct from ordinary things of nature by virtue of being accorded extraordinary qualities that place them in a higher conceptual realm in a manner directly comparable to the distinction that the same contrastive qualities create between skillfully crafted goods and ordinary utilitarian crafted goods.

It is for this reason that skillfully crafted and naturally endowed things may be properly identified as *tangible* things, composed of and exemplative of particular values or qualities, rather than as merely material things, characterized by physical properties alone (Taylor and Aragon 1991:29). Although in a universe traditionally believed to be unified by a general consubstantiality of life virtually all landscapes and all earthly things are regarded as forms of or as containing quantities of such life-energy or power (Ingold 1987:73), some things contain exceptional amounts or express particularly potent concatenations of such power, or are regarded as more closely associated with the ultimate cosmological or ancestral creative sources of such power. It is because of the exceptional quantities or extraordinary qualities that these unique goods are believed to possess— as evidenced, for example, in distinctive markings, designs, color, odor, sound, or brilliance (Morphy 1989)—that they are regarded as being particularly endowed and, therefore, as highly desirable as codifications and encapsulations of cosmic power.

It should be emphasized that in no way are such naturally endowed products regarded simply as raw or primary materials whose value lies in their potential for being processed into some form of manufactured good. Naturally endowed goods are conceptually complete in and of themselves and are not simply regarded as the first stage of a lengthier production process, although they may be—and frequently are—modified in form by some manner of skilled crafting. Yet such modification even of naturally endowed material is by no means insignificant. On the contrary, it is the act of crafting, the "labor factor" cited by Harding or, stated more completely, all that such crafting implies in traditional society, that seems to most clearly differentiate naturally endowed things from skillfully crafted things, that allows us to speak of them as separate categories of things, and that, frequently, though by no means inevitably, seems to accord skillfully crafted things with enhanced political-ideological or cosmological value in those circumstances where such a comparison becomes possible or necessary.[4]

Generally speaking, the most highly valued natural things, the things that are believed to be especially cosmologically endowed, are those associated with political-ideological honor, with the ancestor-related ideal or epitome of being human, and with political and cosmological space/time associations. Such naturally endowed things (like many tangible forms of skilled crafting) are valued as personal ornamentation or as insignia of office or rank, forming vital parts of the regalia and costuming that crafts or transforms specific private individuals into society's high elites and in-fluential leaders (Kuper 1973). Such objects also become vital components of transformational social events or identify and relate constituent social sectors with portions and processes of the wider cosmos. For example, speaking of the Kwakiutl, Goldman notes that,

> Complementary properties were matched with rank . . . so that canoes and slaves, and seals [skins] and sea otters [skins] circulated only among the highest chiefs. Yellow cedar bark robes and sewed mink blankets were given to commoners; all other forest mammal skins went to chiefs of middle rank. If the mink skins, which were in fact quite uncommon, are ignored, the religious principle that relates emblematic and complementary properties becomes reasonably clear. Highest rank is associated with the sea, the primary source of wealth, middle rank with the forest beasts, and lowest rank with a forest tree, whose bark is its 'skin.' (1975:136)[5]

Kwakiutl thought, as Goldman relates it, not only accords highest rank and greatest wealth-value to things (specifically mammals) from the sea but also clearly distinguishes between the world of animal life and "the bloodless but living character" of certain trees, that is, between a more energetic, dynamic, highly valued, and thus elite-like portion of the out-side and an alive but passive, lower valued, and thus commoner-like por-tion of the outside. Comparable associations may be found in many other societies where select animals and their pelts (lion, jaguar) are associated with the elite while "lesser" forms of animal life symbolize either lower status commoners or lesser, non-civilized outside peoples (nomads, bar-barians) in the eyes of settled folk (Gossen 1975; Pasztory 1983:71, 278). "Before coastal cloths were known, chiefs, elders, and other prominent men were distinguished by their exclusive right to wear serval, lion, and leopard skins, while others wore barkcloth and more common animal hides" (Alpers 1975:21 regarding the Yao).

Gemstones provide another widely recognized example of highly valued natural goods—"riches of the earth"—particularly noted for the qualities with which they have been endowed (Oppenheim 1977:203; Sahagun 1963: Chapter 8; Evans 1976:61–62, Chapter 6). Here, again, qualitative ranking is not uncommon. Feldman, speaking of Mesoamerica, distin-guishes between tribute gems that were the most highly valued, divine gems marked by intrinsic holy properties and used for fortune-telling, and minor gems "used for adornment which were neither so rare nor so important in native ideology that they were considered of great value per se; that is, their value came from the work that went into shaping them, not the material that composed them" (1985:91–92).

Feldman's comment again interjects the subject of skilled crafting into consideration of naturally endowed things. Indeed, in spite of reasonably clear ethnographic as well as analytically useful distinctions between skill-fully crafted things and naturally endowed things in general, it is difficult and perhaps unnecessary to isolate completely the subject of naturally endowed materials from that of skilled crafting. Not only do certain expressions of skilled crafting utilize naturally endowed materials, but there is a widely held belief (see Morphy 1989:24–28) that skillfully crafted things and naturally endowed goods are all part of a single energy-charged landscape, even though energy concentrations are not evenly distributed therein.

> One of the features of the [sacred geography of Southeast Asian states] is that there is no sharp break between the natural and humanly-built landscape. Outcroppings of rock, stone *lingga,* sacred hills and mountains, and the architecturally constructed 'mountains' used as palaces and navel-cities all can have a common meaning in this geography: they are the locations or nodes in which the forces that animate the universe can collect. (Errington 1983:201)[6]
>
> *Sumange'* [the life-energy which makes the world happen] is in everything or pervades everything, not only humans, but rocks, trees, houses and artifacts. Like bodies, they are visible supports or collection-nodes. But these items support *sumange'* in different degrees or concentrations . . . (Ibid.:228; see also Errington 1989:66)

In such a world, of course, the focusing or collecting of natural energy may be further enhanced by skilled crafting which pulls together the energies and potencies of the various natural goods of which the crafted item is composed: "It is the spirit of the tree, the spirit of the fibre, and the spirit of the elephant that go to the making of the composite drums, which are honored equally with the names of the dead kings" (Rattray 1927:186).

Skillfully crafted things and naturally endowed things are also comparable in those circumstances when obtaining a presumably naturally endowed substance requires the same combination of supernatural aid and technical knowledge that informs artistic production. Salt-processing is a good case in point when it is remembered that, in addition to its strongly utilitarian features, in traditional societies salt was also a highly naturally endowed product. Salt frequently was considered to be a distinctly supernaturally-related material that could be obtained from spirit-owned sources only by a combination of both technical and supernatural skills (Godelier 1986:80, 130–134; Andrews 1983:3, 11–13, 86 and passim). Similar combinations of technical skills and supernatural aid have long been considered essential for successful hunting, too, another very ancient form of skilled craft oriented to the acquisition of naturally endowed things from outside realms.

Hunting

Hunting as a mode of skilled behavior which provides many naturally endowed goods, not only shares many attributes of both long-distance acquisition and skilled crafting but also may be directly and explicitly associated with either long-distance acquisition or skilled crafting in particular ethnographic circumstances. In addition, characteristics accorded skilled hunting have long informed the formal qualities of leadership and political influence in both simpler and more complexly organized polities. This is so because, above and beyond its role in subsistence, hunting, like both skilled crafting and long-distance acquisition, is exemplative of that realm of uniquely human thought and expression that reaches beyond the limitations and restrictions of the domestic, the subsistence-oriented, the local, and the kin-based to relate human inquiry and experience to a wider realm that lies beyond. Indeed, hunting may constitute one of the oldest modes (other than shamanism) of association with the characteristics and qualities of the outside realm and thus with temporal/spatial distance.[7]

Consideration of select aspects of hunting is also useful for this essay since in the ethnographic present hunting, not unlike skilled crafting but in partial contrast to long-distance acquisition, though involving the outside frequently occurs closer to home, in nearer forms of distance that adjoin the settled heartland or that constitute a liminal zone between home and the farther reaches of the beyond. Hence, from the perspective of the heartland, the naturally endowed materials obtained by skilled hunters may at times conjoin with the products of equally skilled artisans to provide counterpoint for the goods (crafted or naturally endowed) obtained by long-distance acquisition from geographically more distant reaches.

Fundamentally, hunting, like skilled crafting and long-distance acquisition, expresses concepts of transformation. It constitutes a type of anomalous behavior that links the civilized realm within with the wild or uncultured world without with the ultimate goal of achieving benefits for the former and a sense of control over the latter (Ingold 1987:117).[8] Not surprisingly, this activity is believed to have originated with ancestral creators and culture heroes who now may serve as exemplars for contemporary hunter-heroes following in their footsteps.[9] Appropriate to its involvement with a portion of a thoroughly energized and vitalized universe, successful hunting (particularly of the most ideologically powerful and potent animals) requires mastery of both technical skills and modes of supernatural contact, communication, and manipulation.[10] Consequently, highly skilled hunting also may exemplify the achievement or expression of ideal human behavior, may be considered to represent an epitome of humanness, and in that context may be associated with beauty and truth, that is, with moral or civilized behavior.[11] Conversely, as might be expected, in some settings hunting (probably because it entails killing) may also constitute flawed behavior conducted by low status or impure persons sometimes thought to be not fully human (meaning they are considered socially or physically deformed). Nonetheless, flawed hunters may enjoy a special relationship with persons in high positions of power.[12]

All of these characteristics closely ally hunting with skilled crafting. Indeed, skilled crafting and successful hunting not infrequently appear to be regarded as variations on a common theme. Expertise in both may be expressed by the same individual, such as the Dan (Liberia) blacksmith (the leading man of influence in his community) who is also the "leading carver of far and wide" as well as "a very good hunter" (Himmelheber 1963:97–99; Cline 1937:140, 121, 123). In comparable fashion, men of influence among the Shuar (southeast Ecuador) are both skilled orators and skilled hunters (Hendricks 1988:220). Relating hunting to the origins of polities (see Chapter 10) as well as with skilled artistry, "Baghirmi [Sudan] tradition claims that the first king arrived from Yemen with one hundred wooden trumpets and one of copper, which only the hunter Lubadko had the right to blow on behalf of the ruler" (Herbert 1984:235).

McNaughton explains why this conjunction of skilled activities is found among the Mande, where hunters may also be smiths. His discussion may well be appropriate for many other societies, too. Speaking of "the energies that animate our world, the energies referred to by the Mande as *Nyama*, which give life to all living things and provide the momentum for every act undertaken in the world," he says,

> Hunters, through their science and the *daliluw*, learn to control enormous quantities of this energy, and that is one of the reasons they are so distinguishable from other citizens. Sorcerers, heroes, hunters, and certain pro-

fessional artists—like the sculptors and the oral historians—control this energy to an extent that greatly surpasses most people, and so they are afforded much respect, and often they are held in awe, even fear. (1982:56)[13]

This shared commonality of exceptional abilities that relates hunters and skilled artisans[14] reflects ancient ideas about the commonality of qualities constituting the diverse physical materials of the tangible world. For example, Eliade discusses Malayan miners' beliefs that tin is alive, possessing many of the properties of living matter such that it can move from place to place, reproduce itself, and develop special affinities for certain people. He explicitly notes "the animal behaviour of the ore: it is alive, it moves at will, hides, shows sympathy or antipathy to human beings—a conduct not dissimilar from that shown by game towards its hunter" (1962:54). In somewhat comparable manner, Eskimo stone carvers who have replaced traditional hunting with sculpting find explicit parallels between successful hunting and good carving. The same linguistic term is used to express both the search for the right kind of game and the search for suitable stone. Another common term relates the manner of working with (hunting) animals with the manner of working with (carving) stone. Finally, it is recognized that comparable end products of self-prestige and food and other supplies for family are achieved, whether by animal by-products or by money from sale of sculptures (Graburn 1976:49, 55). To the ancient Greeks, this same sense that a commonality in aptitude, attitude, and behavioral disposition united various forms of crafting and hunting was expressed by attribution of the quality of *metis,* "practical and cunning intelligence," to both skilled artisans (blacksmiths, orators, weavers, carpenters) and hunters (also fishermen) alike (Detienne and Vernant 1978: 307–308).[15]

Involving, as it does, the acquisition and conveying of desirable goods, forms of "wealth," from outside (Aristotle 1962:21), hunting also exhibits similarities with acquisitional trade and travel (Polanyi 1957:258) and is recognized accordingly: "Wealth came originally through fishing, hunting, and trading . . ." (Oberg 1973:56 regarding the Tlingit; see also Alpers 1975:18). "The ideal person was one who was not lazy, who was up early, hunted all the time and was enterprising in trade" (Goldman 1940:370, 344 concerning the Alkatcho Carrier). Similarly, among the Nunamuit Eskimo, where "a man became recognized as a rich man by amassing wealth through his abilities as a hunter, trapper, and trader. . . . a person had to spend years learning how to catch animals and to trade effectively. . . . The ideal of all little boys was to grow up and become an important umialik, a successful trapper, hunter, and trader, and to be called a good man for his generosity by the people around him" (Gubser 1965: 181, 183).

Among the Panare of Venezuelan Guiana, community leaders evidence prestigeful acquisitional ability by leading their groups in trading trips to the Creoles, in tapir-hunting drives, and in fish-poisoning expeditions (as well as in religious ceremony and in dealing with resident foreigners such as visiting anthropologists) (Dumont 1977: 211). Hunters and traders have also shared the good fortune of safe travel under royal protection if they worked and journeyed as agents of the king: "No heathen can be perfectly secure in his person and property beyond the precincts of his sovereign's jurisdiction, excepting, however, the character of ambassador, whose person should be held inviolate, that of king's merchant or trader which is equally sacred, hunters of elephants in the king's name, and on his account; and lastly, men of rank, or others whose influence or interest at court is powerful enough to gain for them a travelling protection by the use of the king's name . . ." (Dupuis, quoted in Wilks 1975: 17).

Particularly noteworthy for this essay are instances in which skilled hunting served as precondition for later involvement in long-distance trade and travel. In the case of the Yao, particular community ritual behaviors that maintained states of ritual purity and social order while men were away from home were followed first for elephant hunting and then applied to "the closely related institution of caravan trade which . . . may reasonably be regarded as an extension of elephant hunting in terms of its social implications for the Yao village" (Alpers 1975: 19; see also Lamphear 1970: 86, 89). Similar extension of a traditional hunting milieu into trade occurred on the Northwest Coast of North America where, in response to the European fur trade, European woolen blankets gradually replaced traditional animal skins in ritual activities, seeming to imply that these European "pelts", and thus Europeans themselves, carried the same high-level ideological significance (as sources of outside beneficial wealth) as traditionally had accrued to animal skins and the animals they represented (see discussion above; also Helms n.d.).[16]

Finally, in this brief acknowledgment of the close associations between skilled hunting, travel, and the acquisition of valued things from afar, we may note the activity of certain Mande hunters, particularly the truly great hunters, who seek to develop their skills and knowledge of the bush, and thus their reputations, by traveling many kilometers to study with already famous hunters with knowledge not available at home. "Such trips were generally of six months' duration but could be as long as eighteen. The hunters went out in groups of two or three, and sometimes they traveled alone. The goal was to acquire a name for oneself by proving one's ability and knowledge, while simultaneously expanding both ability and knowledge" (McNaughton 1982:91, note 5). In addition, traveling hunters returned with valued goods, trophies of their wanderings and tangible evidence of the success of their ventures, including pelts, tusks, and horns of elephant, hippo, buffalo, antelope and bundles of tails from all animals killed, a bundle as large as the hunter was skilled (ibid.).

The Skillfully Crafted vs. the Naturally Endowed

Just as skilled hunting shares qualities of both long-distance acquisition and skilled crafting, so naturally endowed things and skillfully crafted things may be interpreted as conceptually comparable encapsulations of cosmological powers and of human transformational activities. However, in situations where either skillfully crafted things or naturally endowed things are available to fill a particular function, skillfully crafted goods may be accorded higher value and preferred over naturally endowed ones. An example may be found in situations where fine fabrics, whether locally crafted or acquired by long-distance acquisition, have superseded the use of highly valued animal pelts and leathers in royal or elite costuming (Balandier 1968:166–167).[17]

Reasons for a preference for the crafted over the naturally endowed are varied and not always clear. In some cases it may represent the civilizing imposition of a foreign political or ideological power over a local population, as in the introduction of Muslim practices in West Africa (Levtzion 1968:92).[18] The rationale may also lie in qualitative contrasts made between passive and dynamic forms of expression in the sense that the passive exposition of cosmic form and power expressed without further modification by naturally endowed things such as animal horns or skins, shells, or iridescent feathers contrasts with the opportunity for active imposition (shaping, creating) of cosmologically ordained form by skilled human artisans working with mutable substances such as clay, ore, paint, or fiber. In other words, the contrast may lie in the greater amount of work that can be invested in crafted things especially if that skillful labor increases aesthetic quality[19] and imbues goods with socially valued inalienable qualities of their human (social) production (Bell 1949:23; Polanyi 1966:189).[20]

The best of both worlds, the naturally endowed and the skillfully crafted, may be acquired, however, when finely crafted materials, such as fabrics, are obtained as skillfully (even magically)[21] produced things from afar and are thereby further endowed with the additional empowerment that distance provides. Thus Mughal rulers of eighteenth-century India, who surrounded themselves with a wide range of legitimizing symbols of rule derived from "as many earlier or contemporary rulers as possible," ". . . sought to enhance the prowess of their own armies by dressing them in scarlet English broadcloth" (Bayly 1986 : 304).[22] In their search for temporal/spatial symbols and associations of legitimation these same Mughal rulers (not unlike their Asante counterparts) also developed an insatiable desire for foreign (European) novelties. "European writers tended to see the demand for novelties as a childish desire for trinkets. Actually, the profusion of novelties in a court was considered another mark of great kingship. It bespoke vast and varied realms, connections with far-off kings; as God the ruler of the universe had created all manner of beasts and objects, so his earthly shadow must rule over a profusion of creations" (Bayly 1986 : 305).[23]

There may be a significant contrast, however, in how the godly and ancestral powers encapsulated in the profusion of creations are perceived when they are associated with the potency of naturally endowed things and skillfully crafted things, respectively. Speaking of the Luwu of Sulawesi (Celebes), who feel that all artifacts and aspects of landscape as well as people are pervaded with a life-energy, *sumange'*, Errington notes that certain energy-filled things, such as pieces of old china, old iron pots, and knives that are found in the ground, are valued and cared for as talismanic "leavings" containing ancestral potency but that these ancestors are regarded as impersonal and anonymous, "detached from any particular person or former person." In contrast, energy-filled "leavings" of past rulers, such as ornaments and regalia, are identified with a specific named ancestor who descended from the Upper World to become the first ruler of Luwu (Errington 1983 : 230 and 1989 : 33). Extrapolating from this intriguing data, it can be suggested that one of the important differences between things regarded as naturally endowed and things regarded as skillfully crafted—and one of the characteristics that may contribute to the higher value attributed to the latter in some circumstances—is the type of ancestral association each allows.

The encapsulated potency associated with naturally endowed things reflects an anonymous, generalized, all-encompassing or less specifically "humanized" primordial creative force. The human capacity for skilled crafting, in contrast, usually relates to specific personalized ancestral creators or deities whose dynamic transformative abilities are energetically recreated by the skills and labor of human artisans. Consequently, products of skilled crafting are directly linked to the same personalized ancestral beings and to their labors, their *acts* of transformative creativity. Things that are naturally endowed with potency, while power-filled and celebratory of the energies of original Grandfathers and Great Spirits, do not in and of themselves reflect the same type of energetic human connection with specific ancestral powers conceived as epitomes of ideal creative humanness. Nonetheless, when energetically gathered and accumulated by acts of acquisition both naturally endowed things and skillfully crafted things provide means for earthly humans, whether lonely initiates, traveling traders or hunters, or powerful rulers, to herald their own personal identification with the lords of the universe.

10 *Acquisition and Political Authority*

For the king had at sea a navy of Tharshish with the navy of
Hiram: once in three years came the navy of Tharshish, bringing
gold, and silver, ivory, and apes, and peacocks. So king Solomon
exceeded all the kings of the earth for riches and for wisdom.

— I KINGS 10:22—23

Elites and the Outside

A human being, in contrast to other organisms, Ingold reminds us, ". . .
is an intentional agent, a person, to whom nature appears as a world apart,
the medium in which he inscribes his work" (1987:104). The nature of
that work, and the significance accorded it, reflect the equally universal
human belief (at least in traditional societies) that energetic and powerful
forces are contained within and emanate from this world apart, this outside realm (Balandier 1970:106). Situated in the midst of this dynamic
cosmic universe, organized human society constitutes a "world within a
world" (Shorter 1972:100), a microcosm of controlled, productive, civilized moral order whose members believe themselves to be both separate
from, yet intimately interconnected with, the forces of the beyond.

There are always some individuals who are more closely related to the
delicate, often dangerous, necessity of effecting viable links between the
heartland and the world that lies without. In myths and tales these are
society's heroes, noble in character, distinguished in valor, honored for
exceptional service to their people, and heralded as exemplary of the human ideal. In the generally less distinguished immediate and everyday
world these are society's influential individuals—shamans, bigmen, chiefs,
kings—held responsible for the general prosperity by virtue of their abilities to successfully interact with and acquire the dynamic properties of
the universe. "The essence of majesty (and the essence of power?) was the
monarch's participation in two separate hierarchies: the earthly and the
cosmic. In one guise, the king of Nepal was a divine actor in an earthly

realm; but in another, he was a mortal figure in a cosmic hierarchy" (Cannadine 1987 : 11).

The success of persons of influence, as contemporary approximations of ideal humans who are associated with the outside world, is judged by their abilities to be informed about, understand, manipulate, and ultimately acquire socially desirable things therefrom. Such successful association is expressed both by direct actions involving the beyond and by activities that serve as metaphor for this essential quality of leadership. Although the actions and metaphors that define authority and leadership within this context are diverse, all such activities are characterized by concepts and processes of creative transformation which, when tangibly expressed, require that natural and/or crafted things from cosmologically outside realms be intellectually and sometimes materially reworked in some manner so as to fit within the cultural matrix at home.[1]

Thus we find influential persons associated with acts of skilled crafting proper, sometimes when skilled artisans are recognized as society's political leaders, sometimes when persons of authority seek to attract and associate (subsidize) craft specialists with their compounds and courts, sometimes in the sense that rulers are encouraged or expected to develop expertise of their own in one or more skilled crafts (see Chapter 5). Such interests are gravely misunderstood if construed as mere royal hobbies or leisured indulgences, for they stand instead as metaphors for rulership as ideal expression of creative outside-inside transformation, that is to say, for the original ancestral creation of cultured human existence itself.

Similarly, we find persons—and statuses—of authority closely associated with hunting as expression both of the dynamic interrelationship between the world of human existence and the realms and powers of the outside and, more specifically, of the political and ideological legitimacy assigned to or assumed by those skilled in such acquisitional relations. Speaking of tribal Baruya of New Guinea, where inside-outside relationships are used to legitimize gender-related dominance, Godelier summarizes:

> It is in the forest where man receives from the great trees the sap that eventually becomes his sperm; it is there where he hunts, kills, tries his strength, his endurance, and his mastery of the means of destruction; it is there where he sends his spirit to mingle with the wind, which will bear it away to the Sun; it is there where dwell the souls of dead ancestors, who stand guard over the territory of their children. In a word, it is by adding to the powers of 'civilization' [the village and women's agricultural world]

those of life in the 'wild' that men establish their superiority over women and legitimize their domination. (1986:73; bracketed material mine)

A comparable need for identification with the powers of the primordial or ancestor-filled wild underlies much of the interest of chiefs and kings of more centralized societies with powerful naturally endowed wild animals and with the hunt, too.

Nor is it surprising to find that skilled hunters (like skilled artisans) may be recognized as influential leaders either in reality[2] or in myth, where they appear as civilizing ancestors-cum-culture heroes frequently arrived from afar;[3] that established rulers may seek to associate skilled hunters of renown with their courts and entourages;[4] or that rulers themselves place great emphasis on hunting as political-ideological "sport" or as royal display.[5] In like fashion royal lords or their positions may be metaphorically identified with qualities associated with select beasts of the wild (elephants, lions, leopards, jaguars, bears, llamas, cassowaries, dolphins); indeed, may even be believed to share transformative powers with such animals such that the king becomes a leopard and the leopard is a king just as the jaguar or the bear is a shaman and the shaman is a jaguar or bear (Ingold 1987:248–249, 251; Henderson 1972:276–277). Like Baruya men, high ranking nobles, chiefs, and royal leaders as dynamic hunters attempt to exemplify the virtues and qualities of "real" people attributed to all types of specialists involved with some form of outside-related activities; virtues and qualities that also relate them to epic hero-hunters of the creative ancestral past (Goldman 1975:52–53; Hanaway 1969:22, 25, 27; Finnegan 1970:133; also references in Chapter 9, note 9).

Hunting also constitutes one of the earliest mythical-cum-historical statements that things derived from a cosmologically defined outside belong to or are the responsibility of persons in positions of political-ideological authority. Among the Barotse not only do game and fish in public waters and wild fruits belong to the tribe, through the king, but in addition "some parts of certain game are royal property—the ground tusk of an elephant, lion skins, leopard skins, parts of a hippo, and eland switches and sinews and some meat—and these have to be rendered to the king while the hunter keeps the rest" (Gluckman 1965a:103). Such items constitute "things of kingship" (ibid.:153) not only among the Barotse but in many other polities as well. "When Bini hunters killed an elephant, one of its tusks had to be taken to the palace where there were carvers to fashion it into whatever the Oba wished" (Attenborough 1976:72; see also Sutherland-Harris 1970:252; Shorter 1972:136; Dumett 1979:50–51). Similarly, among the Kimbu of West Tanzania, "Swarms of bees, animals, and deposits of iron ore belonged . . . by right to the chief" (Shorter 1972:136), just as in the Inca state and other Andean polities, "All 'wild' resources were considered the crown's" (Murra 1980:97; see also Salomon 1986:83, 95; Moziño 1970:47 note 4 regarding the Nootka).

By the same token, things that exist in the cosmographical beyond may be actively acquired by the crown, which is openly associated not only with more immediate wilds but also with distant strange, exotic, often holy places whence, because of their profound cosmological association, knowledge, wealth, and treasure may be derived (Helms 1988). Generally speaking, the realms that provide such cosmologically charged things represent portions of the universe held to be distant from the heartland because, in addition to geographical location,[6] in some manner or to some degree they are considered qualitatively contrastive. For a population settled on agricultural plains, the high uncultivated mountains that seem to touch the sky not only stand in ecological contrast but also may be charged with sacred potencies and with fearsome beasts and uncivilized beings, while those settled along open and busy river highways may find the depths of the forest to be equally replete with supernatural mysteries. Similarly, land folk virtually everywhere find lakes and seas, and the things derived therefrom, to be by definition "unusual, unique, new, perfect or monstrous" and thereby "imbued with magic-religious powers" (Eliade 1958:13).

From such potent and distinctive outside settings all manner of unusual and unique things may be obtained through the auspices of prestigeful tribal leaders and royal lords who not only are associated with the holiness of mountains and the deities of the waters but may personally venture into such locales either by physical travel[7] or by ritual transformation,[8] or who may arrange for desired things from afar to come to them, as the Sumatran kings of Śrīvijaya received natural goods from tribal peoples of the forested interior and crafted wealth from long-distance trade via the sea (Hall 1985:79–90).

Elites as Acquirers

The mechanisms by which the acquisition of long-distance goods and political authority are conjoined are ethnographically diverse, but in general we find that, as with both skilled crafting and hunting, professional acquirers or traveler/traders may themselves be granted leadership roles and authority;[9] that persons of influence may seek to attract traveler/traders to

10-1.   Gifts from the Aegean for presentation to the pharaoh. (After Norman de Garis Davies, *The Tomb of Menkheperrasonb,* Plates 4, 5, The Metropolitan Museum of Art, 1973. In Emily Vermeule, *Greece in the Bronze Age.* University of Chicago Press, 1964. Used by permission of The Metropolitan Museum of Art.)

their courts or retinues;[10] and that established rulers may become personally active in the conduct of various modes of acquisitional activity. In such capacity chiefs and kings may take personal initiative to organize caravans,[11] encourage other political functionaries to act as crown agents for long-distance acquisition,[12] or facilitate or protect the activities of foreign traders.[13]

In the same spirit, monarchs may also act to protect the morality of the acquisitional process. As Duby notes, regarding the Carolingian era of medieval Europe,

It would be incumbent upon the ruler (whose ambition was to revive the Empire, and who, anointed by bishops, was becoming more fully aware of being God's instrument) to act as guarantor of order and justice, and keep special watch over [trade]. Morally suspect because it brought into play the profit motive condemned by the Christian ethic, trade called for strict control. Consequently, the king was in duty bound to pay particular attention to it. He supervised and legislated, and writings emanating from the palace bear numerous traces of his preoccupations. (1974:97)[14]

Such preoccupations safeguarded the marketplace and ports of trade, and were expressed by attention to court etiquette and formalities when traveler/traders presented themselves before the throne.[15] In return, royal leaders acquired further tributes, taxes, and obligatory presents.[16]

Underlying all this activity are basic concepts relating acquisition to the continual need to control, harness, and transform cosmic energies essential for the continued well-being of society and, by extension, heralding the qualities and abilities of persons who successfully indicate their ability to conduct such vital operations. "A big man is defined as one who 'has.' Specifically he has all of those things which are both the requisites and the manifestations of totemic power. . . . Conversely, a rubbish man has and controls nothing; he is described as a dog, picking up the scraps left by others" (Errington and Gewertz 1986:101). Even more specifically, persons of influence, as acquirers and persons of accumulated wealth, are personally honored and granted political legitimacy for their exceptional understanding and cunning manipulation of outside powers such that, more than most individuals, they are able to rise above the mundane and the ordinary aspects of mere survival. The acquisition and ritual transformation of symbols for wealth "stood for man's greatest achievement—his abnegation of that which is natural to him. Potlatching was . . . the final ritual in a series by which the Skagit transcended the limiting aspects of human biology, in accordance with their definition of what is 'supernatural'" (Snyder 1975:161 speaking of Puget Sound peoples; see also Scoditti 1983:271; Wilks 1979; Fisher 1986:135, 176; Lindstrom 1984:304; Errington and Gewertz 1985:449–452).

In other words, the king as accumulator becomes the fountainhead of society's prosperity, and the act of acquisition in itself becomes a mark of exceptionality, exclusivity, and ability to control, and allows the cultivation of a kingly image: "There have been three of these princely visitors [Islamic *sharifs* as traveler/traders] at Coomassy during the reign of Sai Quamina [Osei Bonsu], and none ever came so far to the south and west before; a circumstance that induces the present sovereign of Ashantee to arrogate to himself a greater degree of glory than his ancestors ever enjoyed" (Dupuis, quoted in Wilks 1975:311, first parenthetical remark mine).[17] Similarly, tangible accumulated wealth becomes a succinct encapsulation of these same qualities and of this image as well as inalienable tangible manifestation of cosmic power itself.

Given the political and ideological enormity of the acquisitional task and the related necessity of operating at the cutting edge of moral person-hood in the face of the constant enticement of immoral self-enrichment, it is no wonder that morally conducted acquisition and accumulation fol-lowed by socially mindful display and distribution may be trumpeted near and far by skilled praise-singers and bards (Smith 1962:313). The artful and aesthetic verses of these skilled artisans of words further transform suc-cessful acquisition and accumulation of tangible things into reputation, honor, and fame that flow outward again into space and time, with poten-tial to achieve the ultimate reward of immortality reserved for those whose attainment of the human ideal entitles them to join the company of ances-tors (Munn 1977:50 and 1986:15, Chapter 5; Bauman 1986:138–146; Poole 1982:103). In this manner acquisition also comes to signify the moral qual-ity of life, and the accumulation of wealth may signify the honorability of a life-span and fitness for attaining ancestorship. The size of the death duties collected from the estates of wealthy Asante *abirempon* bespeaks accumulation as quality (Wilks 1979:11), as do the burials of quantities of wealth at the deaths of successful accumulators, and distributions of quan-tities of wealth items at mortuary feasts (Kan 1986).

For those at the pinnacle of political authority, the sum of successful acts of acquisition may signify the quality or the condition of an era of kingship or of social-political (also meaning sacred) history (Hastrup 1985:67–68) in a manner directly comparable to the statement achieved by skillful construction of cosmologically-oriented temples, palaces, and capi-tal cities. Thus the quantity of gold bars "sacrificed" by the Javanese king to the waters of the estuary and retrieved therefrom for distribution at his death (see Chapter 8) seems to testify to the quality (length and pros-perity) of his reign: "A king was remembered for the number of gold bricks left behind. The days of his reign, remembered by the number of gold bricks available for redistribution to his people, symbolized the king's ability to keep the system prosperous. According to Abu Zaid, it was for leaving behind great wealth that a king was rewarded with a place in his-tory" (Hall 1985:286).[18] It was in the same spirit that in medieval Europe "The ruler's treasure house was the seat of his power. He needed to amass the most delectable treasures hidden within the earth; silver, and above all gold and precious stones. Kings had to live surrounded by marvels which were the tangible expression of their glory" (Duby 1974:52).

Ultimately, both acquisition and the recognition attained thereby connect acquirers with the activities and qualities of ancestors. Persons of influence have ability to acquire to the extent that they have achieved control over, or the cooperation of, the powers of the outside and of the dead as ever-living ancestors (Ingold 1987:273).[19] They have authority to do so by virtue of ancestral precedent: as chiefly culture heroes originally acquired benefits from creator gods, so contemporary chiefs must acquire benefits from distant lands, foreign peoples, and other outside powers (Sahlins 1981:29–30). Foreign or outside personages, in fact, may be considered living representatives of the continuing potency of ancestors.

Excerpts from Oswalt's description of an Alaskan Eskimo feast indicate that honor to the dead visiting from afar was paralleled by receipt of wealth items from human visitors from afar. First came the invitations to living and dead alike: "A year before a Great Feast [to the Dead] was held, special invitation staffs were placed near the coffins of the persons being honored, and songs of invitation were sung at the graves. As the date in January for holding the five-day ceremony approached, special messengers carried invitations to villages as distant as 200 miles, and hundreds of guests might attend." On the designated date, "The audience assembled in the kashim . . . and the souls of the commemorated dead were thought to gather in the fire pit." Drumming and songs then welcomed the guests and set the scene in which "Those from afar were expected to present the hosts with gifts of considerable value, such as caribou skins" (Oswalt 1979:265). Later in the proceedings a return gift of food and water were offered to both the deceased and the living guests. An even more explicit example is provided by Seguin (1986:488–491) with respect to the matrilineal Tsimshian who regard fathers' lineage members, foreigners, animals, and supernaturals all as interrelated outsiders who reside in a cosmologically different world from the Tsimshian proper and who make available to the Tsimshian various supernatural powers and means for success in various activities, including curing and carving (see also Kan 1986:198; also Chapter 11).

Acquisition and Ancestral Conditions

Involvement by means of acquisitional trade with spatially/temporally distant realms and locales is, by definition, involvement with universal origins and with cultural creations and creators. Consequently, just as skilled artisans are continually repeating the creative transformational acts of cosmic creator/crafters, so long-distance acquirers are effecting a continuation of original ancestral acts of cosmic integration, control, and transformation.

Involvement with distant realms by the acquisition of goods from geographically distant places highlights activities that are seen to combine, organize, and symbolically stabilize diverse dimensions of the near and the far; highlights, in other words, the imposition of order as a fundamental cosmological-political principle (Seeger 1987:60). The tribal leaders, chiefly elites, and kings who conduct this activity are in effect repeating the unifying, organizing, stabilizing, and constructive acts of the original mythical creators and builders of the ordered universe. Goldman expresses this point as it may have been conceived by the Kwakiutl:

> Powers link donor and receiver, and ultimately interlace all classes of beings and all cosmological zones. If the Kwakiutl have indeed in mind a grand conception of linking together all the disparate parts of their universe, the responsibility for carrying out the plan falls on their chiefs. In the religious sense, the chiefs are the assemblers, the concentrators, and the managers of supernatural powers. Their first ancestors began the task and each generation repeats it. . . . The human chiefs go out into alien realms and deal with alien beings to accumulate *nawalak* [personally held power originally acquired from supernatural beings], and to concentrate it in the ceremonial house. When they have become centers of *nawalak* [good things, such as salmon] come to them. . . . The power to attract derives from *nawalak* and demonstrates its possession. Some supernatural beings in the oceanic worlds originally gave *nawalak* to humans. . . . In exchanges of *nawalak* and *in the collections of the treasures that promote the increase of life and property,* the human being is the actively energetic agent. He is the primary intruder into other worlds—though not the only one—the primary collector and ultimately the central unifier or perhaps the only reunifier of the universe of life. (Goldman 1975:198–199; bracketed material and last emphasis mine)

With respect to the acquisition of "treasures that promote the increase of life and property," the Suyá of the Mato Grosso (Brazil) regard their history

> as the gradual incorporation of items taken from monstrous outsiders that are used for the benefit of the collectivity in its enduring circular village. Narratives recount that they obtained fire from the jaguar, corn and garden crops from the mouse, names from enemies underground, body ornaments from cannibals, and so forth. Contact with other groups in the more recent past added material culture and songs from [many tribal groups] and Whites. Even such events as raiding ranches and hijacking a

FUNAI plane may be interpreted as reflecting a general perception of the way collective good is served by dramatic (sometimes sly) confrontation with powerful outsiders. (Seeger n.d.: 3–4; 1987: 44, 52–59)

In comparable fashion, though from a different perspective, Rowlands describes how among West-Central African peoples temporally distant ancestors together with living elders, who were the embodiments of ancestral purity, constituted a "projection on the living of the ideal world of dead ancestors" that stood in contrast to "the natural order as the source of power which no society can be without yet exists as an alien substance of external origins" (1987: 55). Such natural power had to be domesticated or transformed for social benefit by rituals invoking ancestral protections and by other strategems (alliances, gift exchange, diffusion of royal regalia) that brought this external arena within the bounds of moral order. The political effectiveness of a chief depended greatly on his abilities to work toward this end. His efforts included extending gifts of crafted things, believed to be literal embodiments of ancestral substance, to notables of adjacent populations. In return, ritually essential naturally endowed products (camwood, sasswood) were acquired from distant forests. These and other goods obtained from distant sources (including Europeans) "were selected and valued because they were a visible demonstration of the power of ancestral order to incorporate an alien and potentially hostile world and subvert it to serve its own purpose" (Rowlands 1987: 60–61).

Considered in very general terms, the approach to outside realms by the Suyá and by Kwakiutl chiefs seems to contrast with the approach of the West-Central African chiefs to the extent or in the sense that the Suyá and the Kwakiutl appear to emphasize the attraction of beneficial powers and tangible treasures from the outside (including geographically foreign realms) in order to energize and civilize the social and ceremonial center, while the African chiefs attempt to expand their moral center toward the outside so as to encompass and thereby convert and harness portions of the cosmographical beyond. In both approaches (which will be considered in more detail in the following chapters) political leaders, as embodiments of original ancestors, effect continued contact with supernaturally potent foreign locales where original expressions of creative forces, powers, and energies indicative of the temporal past continue to be actively evidenced.

By effecting such transformative cosmological connections, political leaders provide obvious evidence of a quasi-ancestral identity and an elevated completeness of their own. To greater or lesser degree they are seen as purer or more "real" than other persons in body and behavior, as

tangible beings physically manifesting the qualities of the ideal and the
sacralized in human form as opposed to the more mundane existence, relatively devoid of such qualities, that may be the fate of ordinary folk (Henderson 1972:270, 322−323; Goldman 1975:52; Gesick 1983:2). Indeed, some
persons of authority, even while yet living, seemingly surpass the basely
human condition altogether by becoming political-ideological icons. As
such they are transformed not only by attributes of sacrality, distinctive
behavior, and exemplary personal qualities but also by richly textured and
elaborately designed costumes, gems, and other regalia often derived and/
or crafted from materials obtained from geographically distant, mystically
charged domains by long-distance acquisition or equivalent acts, such as
hunting. Such costumes and regalia elevate and transform the very person
of the chief[20] into an aesthetically (and thus morally) potent, supra-human
"crafted object" indicative and expressive of the lofty qualities that constitute the "sheer ideal" (Geertz 1980:130−131; Arhin 1970:369−370).[21]

So ennobled, such "crafted" lords are totally embued with and fully exemplify the ancestrally-related concepts of ideal purpose and achievement
that are associated with acquisition and skilled crafting and that are expected to culminate ultimately in the well-being of the polity. As crafted
icons that relate to more elevated realms of humanly conceived existence,
such lords also unite the diverse spatial/temporal dimensions of the universe as represented in both the acquisition of culturally energizing, supernaturally potent materials and powers from horizontal distance and the
uniquely human capability for creative, aesthetically informed skilled artisanry, activities that have potential to raise every member of society toward
the epitome of humanness.

PART III

CENTERS AND ORIGINS

11   *Superordinate Centers*

> The imperial sons all followed; all officials, civil and military, the
> headmen of the barbarian (states), all stood according to their
> positions. Rare birds and beasts were all deployed before the
> altar. Since the start of the T'ang, decorated items and
> processional equipment has never been so resplendent.
>
> — OLD T'ANG HISTORY
>
> describing an offering to the river Lo by the Empress Wu,
> in David McMullen, "Bureaucrats and Cosmology," p. 227

Outside Centers and Ancestral Powers

"Every society links its own order to an order beyond itself, and, in the
case of traditional societies, to the cosmos" (Balandier 1970:101). In for-
mulating these links every society also recognizes two centers or focal
points associated with the inclusive sense of distinctive cultural identity
and transformative creativity that marks its members as uniquely human.
One center, the most immediate and most tangible, is situated in the here-
and-now of an existing society. It is formalized in the persons and declarations of political and ideological leaders, in moral codifications, and in
the impressive compounds and courts, rituals and regalia where social,
political, and ideological proprieties are formally presented. The other
center is situated somewhere in the cosmological outside. It may be located either on the vertical axis of spatial/temporal distance that places
outside centers "up there" (or "down there") or on a horizontal (geographical) axis of spatial/temporal distance that places outside centers
somewhere "out there" (Figure 11–1). Regardless of location, spatially/
temporally outside centers are regarded as foci of initial cultural origins
and creation, and thus as places of cosmological power. They are perceived as settings for initial transformations, as ultimate sources of cultural benefits, as homes of deities, culture heroes, original skilled artisans,
and ancestors, and as continuing fonts of energizing spirituality and of
political-ideological legitimacy for the physically alive and active members
of society (see Turner 1972:210–213, 226, 229–230).

The beings, inherent qualities, and purported activities attributed to

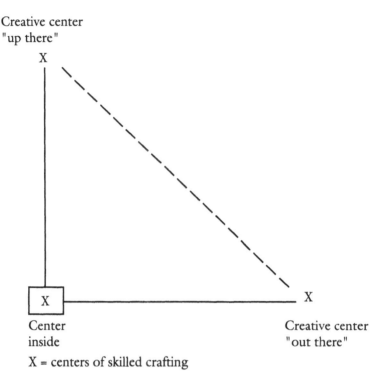

11–1. Locations of creative centers.

outside centers are basically the same regardless of location since the vertical and horizontal axes of the outside are but variant dimensions of the same external realm. The formal expressions of these supernaturally charged beings, qualities, and activities, however, will vary according to the center's location, that is, whether it is situated in a vertical or a horizontal dimension of the outside.

If the outside center of origins is located on the vertical axis, direct physical or material contact is not possible for living persons. Tangible manifestations of the centers' qualities will appear instead at the political-ideological center of living society, where political and religious specialists engage the intangible outside center by rituals of divination, appropriation, appreciation, and manipulation. Concurrently, diverse skilled artisans, re-creating the acts and abilities of original creator/crafters, provide aesthetic manifestations and encapsulations of the creative qualities and powers of the outside center.

If the outside center of origins is located on a horizontal cosmographical axis, however, direct physical or material contact is possible. Tangible manifestation of the center's qualities not only may be expressed by leaders and artisans in the home society but also are found at the center-out-there itself where skilled artisans (as original creators) continue to produce power-filled artifacts that may be directly acquired by the home society by the skilled craft of acquisitional trade. Alternatively, skilled creator/crafters from the outside center may be enticed to grace the social heartland in person just as living representatives of the otherworldly powers who dwell and govern at the distant center may periodically visit. In like fashion, persons of influence (or their representatives) from the center at home may travel in diplomatic pilgrimage to the sacred distant place over the horizon.

Regardless of their dimensional settings, all political-ideological or cosmological centers, as places of cultural origins, are associated with concepts of ancestral powers. Ancestral powers, however, are not restricted to specific creative centers, and it is necessary to differentiate among those that are so related and those that are not.

Judging from ethnographic data, ancestral powers or powers associated with origins are identified either as anonymous in character or as personalized in character, the two constituting either distinct types of powers or variations on a continuum of powers. Anonymous powers of origin are associated with the cosmological outside realm in general, while personalized ancestral powers are associated with specific centers as places of cultural or human origins and with specific ancestors. To take a representative example, native residents of the island of Aoriki in the Eastern Solomon Islands (see also Chapter 4) believe that

> There are two separate orders of deities: one called the *ataro ni mwani,* 'deities from humans,' the other *ataro si fenua,* 'deities of the island.' The deification of spirits that occurs in the great -murina [funeral] celebration involves the former, deities derived from human spirits. The deities of the land do not have personalities. They were present in and around the community before humans arrived; they made the environment usable, productive, and fertile. Thus, the deities of the land make it possible to amass material wealth. . . . The deities derived from human spirits guide human destinies, give power, and protect people from alien spirits and enemies. . . . The two classes of deities have no direct interaction. The only link between them is the humans who worship and depend upon both, but in different ways. (Davenport 1986:103–104; bracketed insertion mine)

A similar distinction that seems to reflect end points of a continuum of ancestral power is recognized by the Bugis-Makassarese of the polity of

176 CENTERS AND ORIGINS

Luwu (South Sulawesi or Celebes) in Southeast Asia. As was noted in Chapter 9, villagers, guided by voices in dreams, often excavate from the earth old artifacts (pieces of broken china, old iron pots, knives) that are treasured as ancestral fragments or leavings. However, "The ancestor who produced the leavings is anonymous, so the villagers' relation to the ancestor is impersonal, detached from any particular person or former person. But villagers connect themselves to the ancestors by cherishing these potent leavings as talismans, tapping ancestral potency through caring for the objects" (Errington 1983:230). In contrast to these things from the earth are power-filled objects ("regalia") associated with the polity, the realm, of Luwu that are regarded as leavings of past rulers and that were initially brought down to earth from the Upper World by the ancestral culture hero and first ruler of the polity, Batara Guru. These objects associated with initial cultural founders and the succeeding line of ancestral rulers identified the center, the core, the navel of the polity (Errington 1983:230–231; 1989:121–129).[1]

Whether anonymous or personalized, chthonically or celestially associated, ancestral powers are believed to be part of a continually operative outside realm that constantly makes power available to energize cultural existence. To be made operative, however, cosmological powers must be identified, frequently in tangible form, and actively sought and acquired. In this study two categories of tangible cosmological powers have been identified: one focusing on naturally endowed manifestations of original or ancestral powers; the other on skillfully crafted manifestations of original ancestral power. We have also delineated some of the qualitative characteristics of skilled crafting as a distinctive human activity and have further argued that in some respects acquisitional trade, by which tangible goods may be acquired from outside, constitutes a distinctive type of such crafting. It now remains to relate specific type of tangible goods acquired from afar with type of ancestral power and with the cosmological location of creative centers where, as places of cultural origins, skilled artisans transform and create.

Here again, two basic patterns may be discerned. The first emphasizes acquisition of naturally endowed tangible manifestations of anonymous ancestral power from geographical outside realms. Polities exhibiting this acquisitional pattern are those whose outside cosmological center is located on the vertical axis, requiring that tangible expressions of personalized ancestral power by means of skilled crafting be created at the political-ideological center of the cultural heartland itself. This center thereby re-creates the ancestral world to which it is linked by a vertical *axis mundi* (Figure 11–2, pattern one).

The second acquisitional pattern emphasizes acquisition of skillfully crafted tangible manifestations of personalized ancestral power from a geographically (cosmographically) distant locale. Polities exhibiting this acquisitional emphasis are those whose outside cosmological center is situated at a distant point along a horizontal axis. Given the visible and material geographical location of this outside center, where skillfully crafted goods may be physically produced by living artisans, it is possible for the acquiring society to obtain skillfully crafted tangible manifestations of personalized ancestral power directly from this center, to which it is linked by a horizontal *axis mundi* (11–2, pattern two). (It should be noted that this tie does not obviate the value of skilled crafting at home, which may replicate or further transform crafted goods obtained from afar. Nor does it prohibit acquisition of potent naturally endowed things from anonymous powers of the outside).

These two models linking acquisitional emphases to broader cosmological paradigms have obvious parallels with other contrastive political-cosmological or political-ideological models of traditional society. Balandier, for example, working largely with African materials, senses a distinction between societies that seek to dominate the cultural-natural-cosmological world wherein they are centered and those that approach those worlds not to exercise dominion so much as to see "their own extension and reflection" (1970:101–102, 107; Chapter 5). Similarly, McKinley distinguishes between the Hindu-influenced cosmos of Southeast Asian states which "had its sacred center *in the middle* of a kingdom, and . . . required the priests of a royal cult to activate the radiating influence of this mystic point" and the indigenous "tribal" world where "the mystically charged points in the tribal universe tended to lie *outside* the village deep in the forest, or in the upper-world or the under-world. Shamans were required to bring the sacred power of such outer zones back into the village" (1979:318).

The approach that I have taken to such contrasts attempts to go a step further by relating both models to a common traditional cosmological framework (see Chapter 13). Because of the *qualitative interchangeability* of its spatial/temporal axes or dimensions, this general cosmological structure allows several distinctive adaptations to the outside realm as variations on a basic theme concerning the need to acquire and transform tangible manifestations of cosmic powers from without for the benefit of those within

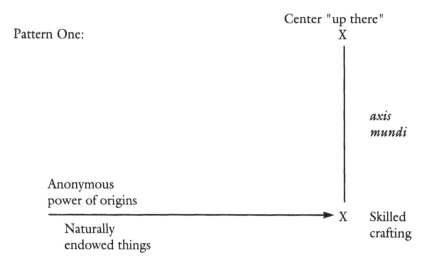

Personalized ancestral power of center "up there" related to home center by vertical *axis mundi*

Acquisition of naturally endowed things from geographical outside as manifestation of

Anonymous outside powers in cosmographical realm

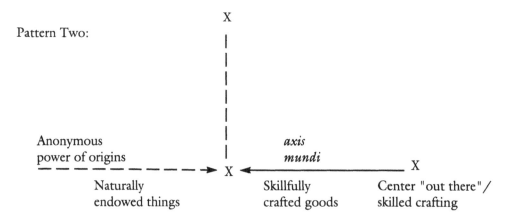

Personalized ancestral power of center "out there" related to home center by horizontal *axis mundi*

Acquisition of skillfully crafted things from geographical outside as manifestation of

Personalized outside powers in cosmographical realm

11–2.   Cosmographical associations and patterns of acquisition.

the cultural heartland.[2] It should also be reiterated that the identification of particular long-distance goods as naturally endowed or skillfully crafted things is an emic determination in every case. Ideally, therefore, this distinction cannot be definitively made simply and solely on the basis of an outside observer's independent opinion as to what constitutes the presence or absence of skillful human modification unless that opinion rests on an appropriately informed perspective. "The capacity of a traded object to yield information does not depend on its functional characteristics but is derived from subjective meaning attached to it by the local and distant societies respectively" (Chaudhuri 1985:18).

Superordinate Centers

Scholarly discussions of relationships between centers and outlying regions commonly employ terminological pairings such as independent and dependent, core and periphery, or heartland and frontier, all of which have their virtues in particular contexts but none of which seems quite appropriate or satisfactory for the perspectives considered here. The problem lies basically in the rather negative implications or marginal connotations of terms such as dependent, periphery, or frontier when used to identify regions or places that, in fact, contain their own definitive characteristics vis-à-vis a center. To be sure, from the perspective of the center outlying regions may well be (indeed, as non-centers by definition virtually must be) considered devoid of certain characteristics judged essential for delineation of the center. In that sense contrastive terminology, which must be negative or derogatory to the same extent that the center is positively defined, may be expected as part of the process by which the center defines itself. But even for centers this deprecation does not mask—is not intended to mask—the fact that outlying regions or domains contain specific identifying characteristics of their own. In fact, when more impassionately described, the relationship may be seen to reflect more of a sense of where superordinance is to be recognized and deferred to.

Superordination is defined (by Webster's New International Dictionary) as "the relation of a universal proposition to a particular with the same terms." Contained here is the implication that the difference between the universal and the particular is one of degree, not of kind. Recognition of this characteristic is fundamental for our concern with cosmological or political-ideological centers and for understanding relationships between centers and non-centers. For example, in traditional cosmologies in which the creative outside center is located on a vertical axis, the fundamental superordinate relationship recognizes that outside center as the universal point of origins and the setting for original expressions (by creative ancestors and culture heroes) of cultural means to obtain or create the fundamental moral order required of a structured, harmonious universe. The "particular with the same terms" delineates the characteristics of the earthly center as a reduced version of the superordinate original. Here, by means of diverse forms of skilled crafting heralding the legitimacy of the political and ideological authority of the focal line of personalized ancestors, the ideal of the cosmic moral order is re-created and re-expressed in tangible terms (Geertz 1980:13, 17–18; Errington 1983:198–199).

Furthermore, operating within the same context and concept of superordinance and of superordinate relationships, the earthly center believes itself to be charged with the moral obligation to repeat or continue the task of manifesting moral legitimacy and ideological centrality in the face of the non-moral or the less moral on this earth and of extending the spread of cosmic order in geographical territories that lie beyond where uncivilized peoples and impersonal or anonymous (authochthonous) powers predominate. Such efforts, in turn, may be expected to rebound to enhance the fame and the glorification—and thus the moral strength—of the center such that the earthly center (as represented by its political-ideological elite) now believes itself to be superordinate to whatever lies cosmographically beyond.[3]

The center generally pursues its charge by presentation of various types of skillfully crafted and aesthetically/morally instructive regalia to the leadership of those foreign peoples who (in the eyes of the center) still languish in ignorant amorality. The success or benefit of this mission is tangibly evidenced, in turn, by the center's acquisition of exotic naturally endowed foreign things from the cosmographical outside realm; things that not only bespeak the center's continued outreach but also serve to increase its ideological and political potency by virtue of the autochthonous powers believed to be inherent in that which is exotic, curious, or different.[4] The purpose or charter of the center's expansionistic mission and the legitimacy of its claim to that charge derive from the earthly center's identification with a superordinate, vertically located, ancestral outside center, while the energizing of that charge derives from the center's own superordinate acquisition—the seemingly inveterate collecting—of power-filled naturally endowed things from the horizontal, cosmographical outside dimension.

From the perspective of the earthly center, the situation with respect to cosmographically distant regions is closely comparable to the seeming paradox surrounding flawed artisans or flawed long-distance acquirers, whereby the category of personnel is deemed unfit for admission to respectable (moral) society although the items crafted or acquired may be welcomed and highly valued. In the eyes of superordinate centers, geographical outside realms constitute flawed domains in that the beings resident there, like flawed artisans and long-distance acquirers, are judged to be devoid of proper understanding and acceptance of the moral truths, the civilizing ideology and standards of ideal humanness, associated with the personalized ancestral power that links the center with its own center-of-origins up there. Consequently, cosmographically outside beings, being amoral and unrefined because they lack this link with the personalized ancestors of the center, are morally flawed and thereby properly deemed "barbarians" (Schafer 1967:12–13, 57–58, 99–100; Cartier 1982:7–11).

Nonetheless, such failings are not thought to obviate the presence and value of anonymous or impersonal autochthonous powers that may be encapsulated in the grotesqueness of rare animals, the strange appearances and behaviors of foreigners, and the curative or protective benefits of a wide range of other naturally endowed resources—precious stones and minerals, rare and aromatic woods, spices, drugs, and herbs, tails, horns, furs, and feathers of exotic birds and animals, not to mention the living forms themselves—as well as useful knowledge concerning the potencies of such goods commanded by the barbarians (Soustelle 1961:68; Schafer 1963; 1967). Constant acquisition and sometimes physical transformation (crafting) of a range of such diverse things bespeaks, for the center, both the inherent superiority of the truths of ancestral morality that can expand against and ultimately defeat and encompass the flawed chaos beyond its borders and the ability of the center to acquire beneficial products and powers for the ongoing well-being of society from the mysterious and spiritually dangerous but potent lands outside.

Ethnographic descriptions of this cosmological and acquisitional perspective are diverse and sometimes wonderfully graphic in their particulars, as in the widespread pre-Columbian Mesoamerican conception of the orderly, bright (diurnal), celestial world and its terrestrial cultural centers as corresponding to and connected by the straight lines and orderly configurations of woven textile, while the dark, chaotic, uncontrolled portions of the universe (the night sky, the wilds of nature, the cavern-filled underworld especially as Land of the Dead) correspond to a confused, disorderly mass or ball of tangled, twisted strands of thread (Klein 1982, esp. 1–12; see also Schaefer 1989–1990; 1991). That portions of this tangled outside realm could still provide potent and highly valued naturally endowed things is evidenced by the acquisition of a wide range of products (colorful feathers, precious and semi-precious stones, cacao, gold and other metals, animal skins, marine shells, cotton) from territory beyond the marches of major empires by various professional traveler/traders including the famed pochteca, whose rigorous journeys took them to distant lands perceived as chaotic and unconsecrated (even though well populated) wastelands beyond the sphere of the moral heartland and directionally associated with Lands of the Dead (Chapman 1957:126; Helms 1988:88–93).[5]

Equally well-known examples of vertically centered exemplary polities seeking to establish acquisitional connections with geographically and spatially/temporally distant wilderness are found in Southeast Asia, where contrastive qualitative concepts run through the hierarchy of social structure within society as well as identify the character of connections beyond the realm (Geertz 1980:107–108; Gesick 1983:2; Errington 1983:199–200; Tambiah 1977). Here a concept of the center, epitomized in the person of the ruler as still, serene, exquisitely refined and elevated manifestation of the ideal toward which cosmological power is channeled and by means of which it is accumulated, transformed and contained, contrasts with concepts of the outside as low, coarse, debased, and possessed of activity, with dynamic sources and forms "out of which power wells up" (Geertz 1980:109; Errington 1983:200; Anderson 1972). As Gesick has expressed it, speaking of common themes shared by Southeast Asian polities,

> Linked with the conviction that living beings were ordered along a continuum from the bestial to the sacred [there is] a circular conception of space in which potently charged centers were thought to radiate power outward and downward toward less-charged peripheries. . . . at the extreme periphery civilized, cultivated lands and villages gave way to jungles and mountain ranges—'wild' territory beyond the reach of the center's power. These territories were by no means impotent; on the contrary, they were filled with power; but it was anarchic, chaotic, primeval. Only a person who was extremely 'central' in himself could, by meditation and self-discipline subdue these forces. Indeed, settled, civilized, 'tamed' space—the kingdom, the state—was believed to be the product of the meditation and spiritual power of such 'central' figures—powerful ancestors, the king. . . . (Gesick 1983:2)

The process of resource acquisition from various lower or outside entities is interpreted by Errington as evidencing deference of the outside realm to the superordinate center (in this example, the polity called

Luwu). Both the goods and the dynamic act of travel to the center expressed this relation.

> Sometimes these tokens were of material value; one Toraja polity from the mountainous area near Luwu was required to bring as its offering buffalo horns filled with gold dust, panned from mountain streams. Sometimes they were not; a Bajo group living in the Gulf of Bone near Luwu's center was required to bring a coil of rope. Gifts can be thought of as 'tribute,' but it would be misleading and misreading to imagine that their primary purpose was to augment the bigger Navel-Center's coffers, although in some cases they may have done so. These gifts were not primarily loot. They were materialized tokens of deference, just as people materialized deference in their bodies by the act of travelling towards the Center and, once there, used deferential speech and posture. (Errington 1983:221)

In addition to deference, acquisition of such gifts and "tributes" is also in accord with the prevalent belief in Southeast Asian states that the ruler should "concentrate about himself any objects or persons held to have or contain unusual power." Hence palaces were filled with an array of sacred and extraordinary objects and human beings collected and guarded in order that the ruler might absorb and accumulate the power which they encapsulated (Anderson 1972:12, 35).[6]

With respect to the act of travel, from the point of view of the accumulating center, the movement (travel) of outside persons to the center in itself may constitute both an expression of the center's capacity to obtain politically and ideologically beneficial—and necessary—"things" from afar and recognition of the center as exemplative focus of the human ideal (Colson 1962:616; Strathern 1983:78; Lessa 1950:35, 37, 42). In this acquisitional setting the concept of the ideal is often manifested by the requirement that representatives of the still uncivilized and amoral outside realm be present in ceremonial attendance during public rituals of state when the superiority of the center is formally evidenced. The tangible reality and legitimacy of the high moral and political-ideological achievement of the center is officially validated at least in part by its exposure to representatives of that portion of the cosmos still ungraced by its virtues but who are expected to be irresistably drawn to and attracted by the beauty, the alluring and aesthetic (moral) splendor, of the center. By inevitable consequence, not only would the moral superiority and thus the centrality of the polity be affirmed but tangible benefits, such as merchant ships, also would be successfully summoned or drawn by the "blowing winds of virtue" (Toby 1984:223).[7]

Toby describes the efforts of seventeenth-century Japanese lords to develop highly publicized ceremonies of state complete with visiting delegations of foreigners (Korean and Ryukyuan) who were also forced to engage in very public pilgrimages to shogunal shrines and to participate in the highly skilled art of court etiquette and protocol (Toby 1984:205, 208, Chapter 5, 72–76). The intent of such high visibility visits was to evidence the civilizing effect of the center upon barbarians, who as a result had "not ceased to come for trade" nor failed to present the proper congratulatory letters on the proper state occasions. Such visits also were intended to signal the legitimacy of the ruling line, and to evidence the growing power of the center as demonstrated by the fact that the "transformative powers of [the] country's virtue had reached abroad to foreign lands" (Toby 1984:205). They were directed, too, toward attaining the still broader goal of "'neither books, nor technology, nor profit' in shogunal diplomacy, 'but the establishment of international order'", that is, of an ideal "world order" (Toby 1984:218–219, 173).

Scholarly discussions of the various mechanisms and stratagems utilized by the traditional empires of the Far East—most notably China—to develop such ideal world orders have frequently emphasized economic and political efforts of imperial centers to attain imperialistic outreach as evidenced, for example, by the bestowal of rich and valuable skillfully crafted gifts on foreign local leaders, such as those of the northern, western, and southern frontiers of China, who in turn provided tribute and submission to the throne. Yet it is also frequently remarked that these bestowals of imperial compassion were often worth more than the local products acquired in return. In the perspective adopted in this essay, however, the generous bestowal of rich, crafted gifts by the center (as well as the extensive hospitality showed to visiting delegations) is not directly balanced against anticipated material returns but is viewed as a very high-level form of praise-singing by means of which the morally appropriate generosity of the imperial center, personified by the Son of Heaven himself, was publically heralded[8] while, simultaneously, inalienable tangible elements (regalia) of the Chinese moral-cultural order were dispersed to the outside[9] and valuable naturally endowed resources were acquired therefrom.[10]

Returning to the superordinate center itself, the rationale for requiring that foreign barbarians be in attendance at public ceremonies of state (see chapter epigraph) or that they send congratulatory letters at times of royal successions as recognition and validation of the legitimacy of the central order's superordinance may seem valid as given for states such as Japan and China. Yet the concept that recognition by barbarian outsiders is somehow necessary if legitimacy is to be properly acknowledged still seems to attribute an exceptional degree of political-ideological significance to these morally flawed and socially low-status foreigners.

The answer may lie in either or both of at least two possibilities. Barbarians, deriving by definition from an uncivilized, amoral outside realm that falls beyond the ancestrally ordained cultural order of the center, may convey or encapsulate a concept of the original primordial or anonymous outside power that preceded the creative transformations of personalized ancestors. Thus their attendance or their congratulatory letters may reflect the attraction (beauty) that the world of aesthetics and of "ideal" humanness is assumed (by those at the center) to have for those less blessed, or it may represent acknowledgement of the controlling, transformative power and ultimate victory of ancestrally guided cultural order over the flawed chaos of the pre-cultural world. Alternatively, however, the ritually significant presence of barbarians may signify that the imperial/ancestral power and legitimate authority of the center has significant roots or origins in qualities associated with cosmographical as well as celestial realms, that is, barbarians may constitute or represent a conception of primordial power not entirely divorced from that represented and encapsulated by the imperial lineage.

This interpretation follows from the widely held tenet of traditional cosmologies in general that the horizontal cosmological axis shares qualitative attributes of the vertical cosmological axis, meaning that in some manner or degree foreigners, even low-status ones, may represent or be related to personalized ancestors of the center just as flawed artisans and long-distance acquirers may be suitable companions for kings. For superordinate polities, such as traditional China and Japan, the predominantly impersonal or anonymous nature of powers associated with the geographical outside underlies the general interpretation of foreign peoples as barbarians and identifies their tangible products as naturally endowed rather than as skillfully crafted. Nonetheless, the primordial outside realm also represents the very concept of original or ancestral beginnings, of origins, and association with a concept of Origins by definition legitimizes whatever political authority is identified with it.

Therefore, the presence of at least select outsiders at state occasions may represent or commemorate both the concept of origins and the concept of ancestors made tangible. Which is to say, the presence of such visitors particularly at times of imperial succession may be taken to represent attendance by the ancestors in the guise of the primordial. As such their presence validates the legitimacy of the ruling lineage of the state by attesting to its association with origins.

In addition, given the primacy of the vertical axis, the original location of the personalized ancestral creative center for superordinate political ideology (see Figure 11–2, pattern one), it is not surprising to find that foreign barbarians, living somewhere in the horizontal or geographical outside realm, may be seen as ultimately deriving from the vertical or celestial dimension of the beyond. Such an interpretation is suggested by comments elicited by a visit of a barbaric Ryukyuan embassy to Tokugawan Japan to the effect that "Ryukyu was originally descended from the Heavenly Clan [i.e, Japanese] . . . and is now a vassal of the August Country [Japan], as is Korea. . . ." (anonymous pamphleteer quoted, with parentheticals, in Toby 1984:209). Consider, too, the comparable Southeast Asian view that the ancestrally ordained and continually accumulated power and light of the center, exemplified by the highest elite, flows downward and outward, losing potency and fading into darkness as it moves toward the cultural peripheries and toward the outside and as its bearers, peripheral kin lines increasingly distant from the core of the ruling authority, drop lower and lower in status and thus increasingly become identified as commoners or outer people (Errington 1983:199, 202–203; Geertz 1980:16–17).

Considered in broad mythical/historical terms, it is entirely conceivable that such outer people eventually may drift entirely beyond the cultural-moral pale and become identified as foreign barbarians lacking civilized ideals altogether. Yet a sense of original association between the center and at least some of those beyond may linger to underlie a generalized recognition of geographical outsiders as related, albeit in an unrefined sense, not just to autochthonous powers but to vertical ancestral powers as well.[11]

Broadening the ethnographic data base, identification by an inside or central core group or polity of a category of outsiders as related to vertical ancestors, as physical manifestations of the quality of ancestors, and thus as valuable legitimating witnesses, appears explicitly in other polities. Let us consider the Northwest Coast Tlingit, for whom an "inside/outside" opposition was a crucial element of their world model in general (see also Sutlive 1978:66–68).[12] The Tlingit held periodic mortuary potlatches (the Tlingit equivalent of transitional ceremonies of state) to commemorate a prominent deceased elite member of the lineage and to confer recognition of status (title) continuity on successors. As Kan explains (1986), on such occasions the host group—the central or inside group—as members of the matrilineage affected by this death and transitional situation, invited their paternal/affinal relatives to attend as non-consanguineal outsiders and guests who would serve as mediators between the host matrilineage and that matrilineage's deceased kin. This association between outsiders and deceased ancestors was expressed by the belief that, while the tangible forms of potlatch gifts were given to these guests, the spiritual essence of the gifts became the property of the dead. Such a correspondence suggests the attribution not only of a direct relationship but also of a qualitative identity between deceased matrilineal insiders and living non-consanguine outsiders.[13]

Furthermore, in these proceedings the visiting guests were thought to act as representatives or impersonators of their own deceased ancestors, which again suggests that it was as visiting living ancestors from outside that they were able to effectively relate their hosts with the hosts' own ancestral line. In addition, the guests' presence was required as prerequisite for revalidation of the hosts' claims to the sacred crests that validated the continuity of the hosts' ancestral family line and identity.[14]

While some of the best known and most fully developed examples of superordinate centers are found in centralized societies, particularly pre-industrial states and empires, the ethnographic literature also indicates that significant attributes of the dominant center with a collectors approach to outside acquisition is also found in non-centralized societies, too. Indeed, it is present to at least some degree in any setting in which a polity extends its skillfully crafted symbols and encapsulations ("regalia") of political-ideological identity to at least select outside groups and/or acquires naturally endowed resources from some portion of the geographical outside realm. The absence of a formalized political centrality in such settings may complicate our investigation, however, for de-centralized political organization generally necessitates a less focused or more individualized approach to dealings with outside realms. Consequently, it may also require that we identify patterns in such outside activities by extrapolating from the presence of a few individual or select characteristics of outside involvement rather than by direct evidence of the obvious presence of all postulated criteria.

In some respects the Huron of northeastern North America may provide a case in point, though the situation is complicated (as it is for most ethnographically known societies) by European contact and by trade in goods that seem genuinely to reflect ecological contrasts and subsistence needs (cornmeal, dried fish, skins for clothing). Yet, as Trigger emphasizes, other important items, such as beaver skins and the wealth derived from the fur trade, were not simply of commercial or economic signifi- cance but provided "means of realizing the traditional values of [Huron] society" (1976:429, 63). I would suggest, in addition, that both furs and European trade goods were regarded as naturally endowed items derived from outside realms and that the Huron regarded their society as super- ordinate with respect to the foreign societies providing these goods.[15]

This assessment rests largely on evidence that the Huron regarded them- selves as culturally/morally superior to both the northern Algonkians, who provided furs, and the French, who provided wealth items for furs. Most telling in this respect (given the normalcy and ubiquity of ethno- centric views in general) is the fact that the Huron did not bother to learn the languages of the northern tribes with whom they were involved, ex- pecting the latter to learn theirs instead.[16] Similarly, "Foreigners who experienced difficulty in learning to speak Huron were regarded as lack- ing in intelligence" (Trigger 1976:65). This condemnation included the French, who were also deemed physically unattractive because of their unnatural (presumably meaning non-human or subhuman) and disfigur- ing beards, which were considered the cause of their intellectual deficien- cies (1976:432).

With respect to Huron perceptions of the French, it is also interesting to note that the Huron "believed that only the oldest and most experi- enced French headmen were capable of crafting iron knives and kettles and that the king made the largest kettles. For this reason, they asked only seemingly important Frenchmen to do the more complicated jobs of mending and altering European goods" and did not understand why the French were not more compliant in meeting their requests (Trigger 1976:429). Trigger further notes that the Huron probably attributed much of the technological skill of the French to magical acts. These excep- tional skills, however, apparently did not redeem the general low opinion in which the Huron held the flawed French. Rather, the Huron seem to have regarded the French as flawed artisans and attributed such powers to the supernatural endowments of nature rather than to cultural skills. "Since supernatural powers were believed to be inherent in nature, the possession by the French of a particular kind of magic was no indication of their intrinsic cultural superiority. There is little evidence that the Hu- ron regarded the French as superior to themselves, while there is much evidence that they regarded them as inferior" (ibid.:430, 433).[17] Indeed, Huron recognition of the magic of French technological skills may have been directly comparable to their attitudes towards Algonkians as flawed purveyors of useful magical skills. Although the agricultural Huron regarded the hunting and fishing northern Algonkians with considerable condescension,[18] the latter were also believed to possess powerful spirit charms for which the Huron were willing to pay a great price, for they valued the assistance of these spirits in the more uncontrollable areas of Huron life (hunting, fishing, fighting, gambling, love) (Trigger 1976: 65, 79).

Similar types of relatively uncentralized superordinate societies are also described for New Guinea, where it further appears that inside/outside contacts, especially in the area of ritual culture, may have contributed to increased social ranking and political centralization for some polities (see Harrison 1987). By way of example we may briefly consider salient characteristics of the Murik, located along the northern coast of Papua New Guinea near the mouth of the Sepik River.[19] The Murik have been involved with a number of outside groups, including riverine and bush peoples with whom they deal in seemingly straightforward subsistence items (sago palm starch, fish; but see Gewertz 1980 regarding the symbolism of power also associated with these products). In addition, the Murik traditionally acquired nuts, garden produce, fishing nets, unfinished shells and teeth, and pigs from offshore islands. Of these, pigs and perhaps also shells and teeth, were especially desired for ritual purposes. "For the ambitious traditional Murik male, nuts and garden produce are of secondary importance. For him, pigs, the essential currency in the local ritual cycle, are the *raison d'être* of overseas trade, and he goes to the islands armed with pig-buying magic" (Lipset 1985:83). In return, the Murik made available to their island suppliers a number of crafted goods including worked baskets and "a surprising variety of manufactured ornaments" including headbands, vests, tiaras, bodystrings, necklaces, armbands, earrings and rings of finished shell, dogs' teeth and/or boars' tusks (presumably incorporating the unworked teeth and shells acquired from overseas). They also exported music and dances of sacred male cults to the islanders and to other coastal people (Lipset 1985:83).

The Murik appear to represent a superordinate center because they provided skillfully crafted products, including expressions of their own identity as proper humans (i.e., the male cults), to island societies interested in acquiring these items as critical components of their own indices of cultural identity (Lipset 1985:72, 83–84; see also Chapter 12). Lipset explains the intent of this activity from the perspective of the Murik as the center. The right to perform the major sacred spirit dances associated with Murik men's cults falls to the eldest sibling of the descent group which owns each dance, and may be extended to outside islanders by the same descent group representative, who also displays and presents crafted boars' tusk insignia, symbolic of the identity of the descent group, along with the dance. Presentations of this material are intended to invest the acquiring islanders with the symbols of membership in the descent group, which is to say, the Murik have attempted to expand select aspects of their social (village) world into the overseas realm by crafting "fictive kin" (Lipset 1985:73, 84). According to Lipset, the benefit for the Murik lay in extending a moral context, based on the skillfully crafted expressions ("the rhetoric and symbols") of kinship statuses, within which further acquisition could take place (ibid.). In this manner the Murik proceeded with the dual task of formally expanding the moral universe of the center (which, *a propos* of the discussion above, also formally related outsiders to Murik ancestors) [20] and acquiring valuable outside resources from this now enlarged morally proper context.[21]

When kinship-like associations are extended to outsiders in this manner, such associations provide a means not only for honorable but also for manipulatable access to the source of desired outside goods. Such manipulation via the symbols of fictive kinship (including associated ancestral connections) seems comparable in this context both to the purportedly irresistible aesthetically-drawn attractions achieved by decorating and adorning humans and canoes, as in the kula, and to the controlling rituals used in so many other settings to entice invisible outside spirits or Masters of Animals to assist acquirers to successfully hunt or fish or obtain other outside resources. When considered in this light, extensions of fictive kinship statuses, like attention to aesthetics and controlling rituals, again suggests that, from the perspective of superordinate centers, "people" as a component of the outside realm may be perceived by the "true humans" at the center as particular tangible forms or physical manifestations (encapsulations) of the more generalized powers of the horizontal dimensions of the cosmos rather than as true moral human beings in their own right.[22]

Finally, a few words concerning superordinate centers and their outside realms elsewhere in Oceania. The realm that centers on Yap and its outer islands in the Western Carolines is a case in point. Yap provides prepared or crafted goods (turmeric, combs, bamboo, fine small grass purses, shell scrapers), including facilities for canoe-making, as well as essential plant foods, to outer islands and enjoys a wide reputation among these islands as a place of spirits located beyond the horizon where sky world and sea world merge (Goodenough 1986:558; see Chapter 12). The mythical founder of one of the paramount centers of Yap is also regarded as first chief of the outer islands and Yapese magicians, whose powers were held in high regard, could be called upon to perform rituals beneficial to the outer islands.[23] In return, Yap had access to a range of goods from the islands (coconut and coconut palm products, mats, various shells) including three (pandanus mats, coconut oil and a special type of fiber loincloth) valued as offerings to Yapese ancestors.

Communications between constituent groups in this world-order was accomplished by using the language of the superordinate group as well as by means of pseudo-kinship ties, in this case modeled as parent-child roles. In recognition of these kin ties visitors from the outer islands offered prayer offerings to Yapese ancestral ghosts. Yap also used the threat of magically induced perils, such as bad weather, to enforce both the identification of Yap as the center, a seemingly god-like place of cosmic powers, and the acquisition of desired goods (Alkire 1965: 122; Lessa 1950:45; Lingenfelter 1975:147, 149, 151).

An interesting variation on the general theme is found when the relationship between Yap and an important neighbor, Ulithi, is taken into account, for Ulithi appears as a sort of staging area for Yap both in long-distance acquisition and in skilled crafting (Lessa 1950). Indeed, it can be suggested that Ulithi essentially served as a crafting and long-distance transformational agent for Yap. Though Ulithi regarded Yap as superordinate, outer islands regarded Ulithi as superordinate (Lessa 1950:27, 32, 45).[24] Travelers with goods designated for Yap actually stopped at Ulithi, whence Ulithians commanded the final stage of the voyage. It was at Ulithi that the woven mats and decorated fiber loincloths were prepared as religious offerings to Yapese ancestors, and it was from Ulithi that information from Yap was communicated to outer island chiefs and that valued goods from Yap were extended farther into the outer island population. Ulithi may thus be regarded as a lower status segment of the center (Lessa 1950:38, 39, 41, 44; Labby 1970:86–88, 106), providing the transformation stage between the truly distant outside realm and the center proper. In so doing Ulithi served much the same purpose that long-distance traders and specialist artisans do in chiefdoms and states, for Ulithians conducted the actual transporting or transforming of outside materials destined for elite lords. In consequence (and again like artisans and traders), Ulithi, itself believed to have been created and populated by Yapese spirit-ancestors, also served as a source of strength and repute for the center (Labby 1976:106).

12 *Acquisitional Polities*

> During my field work among northern Athabascan I listened to
> awed accounts of the remarkable powers of the neighboring Bella
> Coola. The Carrier Indians married into Bella Coola families, just
> as Kwakiutl marry into other tribes to acquire for themselves at
> least a connection with the treasures of another world.
>
> —IRVING GOLDMAN
> *The Mouth of Heaven,* p. 16

Characteristics of Centers-Out-There

For traditional societies world-wide the ultimate source of cultural legitimation derives from whatever constitutes ideological origins, and the true
center of cultural identity and especially political legitimation is located at
the place of origins, wherever that may be. For living societies in the here-
and-now origins by definition connotes distance, and distance is defined
by temporal/spatial referents that contrast with the immediate. In the
model of cosmological order associated with superordinate societies, as
discussed in Chapter 11, the location of the temporally/spatially distant
center of cultural origins and legitimation lies on a vertical cosmological
axis that generally relates contemporary society and its originating ancestors with a celestial world. There are many other societies, however, that
locate the temporally/spatially distant center of legitimating origins on a
horizontal cosmological axis that generally relates contemporary society
with a place, a center, beyond the horizon. This is not to say that such
societies do not recognize more vertically related connections but that essential qualities of the vertical are obtained by association with a place out
there rather than with a place up there.

That this can be so reflects the widespread cosmological tenet that the
outside is not uni-directional but constitutes an all-encompassing multi-
directional realm completely surrounding the social heartland, and that
the temporal/spatial dimensions or "directions" of the outside essentially
are qualitatively interchangeable. Consequently, it is entirely reasonable to
identify cosmographically distant places as equal in quality to celestially

(or even chthonically) distant places and to recognize foreign people and foreign objects from such geographically distant locales as ancestor-like conveyors of legitimizing authority and regalia. As Kopytoff has summarized it, speaking of African polities, "Legitimacy is sought by associating one's origins with mythical events, prestigious historical figures, and grand polities known in the region but often rooted outside of it" (1987 : 72; see also Geertz 1977 : 168).

Throughout this essay I have noted several examples of comparability between geographically distant points, directions, beings, powers, or things and vertically distant points, directions, beings, powers or things. Comparability between deceased ancestors and visiting foreigners is one case in point. Another involves the association of wealth items, such as dentalia shells (California tribes) or cowries (Ojibwas), obtained from distant lands with supernatural spirits of the above or below (see Chapter 6; also Taylor 1981 : 657, 671). In comparable fashion, in many areas of West Africa things of the Earth are dealt with through traditional indigenous religious practices while things of God fall under the aegis of Islam introduced by Muslim outsiders who ultimately relate, spiritually speaking, to the distant center of Mecca. These newcomers also introduced not dentalia shells or cowries but horses, a form of wealth to which local inhabitants attributed a range of political-ideological and ritual meanings related to the various powers, sacred and secular, of the immigrant foreigners who also provided political and ideological leadership (Goody 1971 : 63–71; Thompson 1974 : 74).

In yet another setting we find foreigners deriving from the geographically distant sea correlated with powers from the earth. Balandier describes the situation that developed in the kingdom of the Kongo, where the original creator, Nzambi, governed the order of the world and the course of lives. He notes that among the spirits unleashed by Nzambi were deceased clan elders (*bakulu*) who were believed to live in subterranean villages near woods and streams whence they became involved in the undertakings of their still living descendants (1968 : 246–247). Balandier then says,

> The *bakulu* and the Europeans who landed in the Kongo in the late fifteenth century seemed to be related by an extraordinary kinship. They were incorporated into a single landscape, a single symbolic universe. The newcomers came from the water (their caravels were compared to whales) and had the white color of relatives who had gone to the village of the dead. They arrived bearing riches and armed with instruments which

demonstrated their power. They came to speak of God and lands unknown. The analogy seemed obvious: these White, these *mundele,* were
emissaries who heralded the return of the ancestors. They were going to
build the 'society of below' on earth, to divulge the secret of the true life,
of power and abundance. (Ibid.:253–254; see also Harms 1981, discussed in
Chapter 8)

Finally, there is a brief myth relating to the kula, that most famous institution for the exploration and appropriation of the wealth of horizontally situated worlds beyond, which, in an interesting structural rever-
sal, derives outside vertical powers from defaulting outside horizontal
experiences:

> An interesting myth localised in Yalaka tells how the inhabitants of that
> village, prevented by custom from seeing the world on Kula expeditions,
> attempted to erect a high pillar reaching to heaven, so as to find a field for
> their adventurers in the skies. Unfortunately, it fell down, and only one
> man remained above, who is now responsible for thunder and lightning.
> (Malinowski, quoted in Leach 1983a : 143)

If we turn more specifically to cosmographically distinct places of
origins we find that identification of such locales must be rather specific in
assignment, that such focality is not accorded to just any distant setting.
On the contrary, since the very concepts of center and of origins contain
criteria distinguishing uniqueness and emphasizing primacy, it is to be
expected that the locations of cosmographically distant centers-of-origin
also will be distinguished by unique cosmological qualities. It is reasonable
to expect that a geographically distant setting that is designated as a cultural place of origins for a given group may be recognized as such because
it is believed to constitute a particularly charged point or direction of cosmological contact between various dimensions of the outside. Because of
this conjunction it is a place where ritual can bring the gods into contact
with humans. Which is to say, any distant locale where such ritual occurs
can become a power point, a center-out-there, where power is material-
ized, just as the marketplace (see Chapter 7), central city, central temple,
palace complex, or craftsman's workplace[1] of the heartland denote major
points of ritually activated conjunction between cosmological realms of
heaven, earth and underworld (Eliade 1959:12–17; Schele and Freidel
1990:67).

A center-out-there, for example, may be associated with the horizonal
spot at the west or the east where earth and sky are believed to meet and

where the sun, the original celestial traveler and archetypical bringer of benefits, rises above the horizon or plunges beneath it; it may be correlated with the mouth of the river where the dead may move on to celestial or underworld abodes or ancestors transfer from the celestial realm or from the underworld to the terrestrial world (Helms 1988:27–28, 44–45). Such a place may be associated with positive, power-filled points where distant high mountains, tall waterfalls, or gigantic trees seem to pierce the sky or where sea and sky meet at islands on the horizon, places where ritually charged kula transactions may be conducted (Schaefer 1989–1990; Tambiah 1983:192–198) or where spirits dwell:

> From an island-centered perspective, the sky world and the sea world seemed to merge at the horizon. Beyond the horizon, or beyond the ultimate horizon was only a vast, unified expanse. Ponapeans knew of Yap . . . but they had never been there. For them it was a spirit place beyond the horizon, where 'Soaring Yap' in the sky and 'Diving Yap' under the sea were equally parts of Yap. For Truk's people also, Yap was in legend regularly a spirit place. The deep sea, moreover, ruled by the god *Sowunóón* 'Lord of the Deep,' was a continuation of the spirit world. Places well beyond the horizon were figuratively, if not literally, places in the sky. (Goodenough 1986:558, see also 559)

In short, centers-out-there, located at crucial cosmological junctures, may be considered directly comparable in ideological significance to the distant places at the "edges" of the earth, sometimes visited by shamans in trance or in person,[2] where various giants or earth-bearers, pillars of stone, or cosmic "seams" are believed to effect contact between the terrestrial world and worlds above or below. As Klein puts it with reference to Mesoamerica, such places become "the interface between night and day, death and birth, and hence, end and beginning" (Klein 1982:15, see also 12, 14).

In addition, cosmographically distant places of origin, like any center of cultural origins be it situated out there, up there, or at the cultural heartland, should also be places of transformative crafting (Figure 11–2). That is to say, it is no accident that the Popol Vuh reports that the Quiché lords, who either literally or mythically traveled to a great kingdom across the sea to the east to obtain political legitimation, returned therefrom with the regalia of office—canopies, thrones, musical instruments, feet and feathers of birds and animals, ornaments, and the written truths of the Popol Vuh itself (Tedlock 1985:54–55, 203–204).[3] Strathern reports a comparable belief from New Guinea, where "an old Northern Melpa informant . . . told me that the *Kewa wamb* (= sky people, sometimes pictured as cannibals . . .) dropped valuables at the place where the 'legs of the sky' (*mukl timb*) reached the earth, i.e. at the end of the earth; and people there worked shells into shape and sent them along trade routes" (Strathern 1971:235).[4]

Of course, when identified as a place of skilled crafting, the cosmographically distant outside locale, as center-out-there, also is recognized as a geo-political entity where a living leadership directs a range of activities associated with earthly affairs as well as with spiritual matters. From the point of view of the home society, skillfully crafted and aesthetically valued things associated with that outside place not only signify (by definition, we may assume) the ideal or the epitome of the distinctive quality of humanness associated with a place of political-ideological origins but also convey inalienable links with the transformative powers of the ancestor-like creator/crafters who made them and with the moral order represented by such a center. By extension, these skillfully crafted and qualitatively charged goods also link the acquiring society with the creative center's political-ideological elite who, in turn, stand as representatives or as conduits (through ritual) of the even greater legitimizing power associated with the personalized ancestral potency associated with that cosmographical locale and its lords. "In the Chinese world order, only the Son of Heaven received the Mandate directly from Heaven. . . . The Yi throne [of Korea] [was] . . . [u]nable to receive its Mandate directly from Heaven, [and so] it turned to the Son of Heaven as a mediator" (quoted in Toby 1984:171, first bracketed material mine).

The possibility that the acquisitional heartland may actually acquire tangible crafted items from the center outside is, of course, a major point of contrast distinguishing horizontally located outside centers from vertically located ones; a contrast that imbues acquisitional activities with tremendous import. Yet, even as polities linked with vertically situated centers-of-origin must craft their own tangible expressions of power in imitation or re-creation of ancestral creator/crafters so, on occasions when direct acquisition is not possible, societies that are exploring horizontal linkages to power-filled places may attempt to imitatively craft the potent tangible expressions of the outside's power in order to acquire something of that transformative power itself. As Abramson relates from the Upper Sepik region of New Guinea,

> . . . European objects are often imitated by primitives for various reasons. This phenomenon, which also serves to introduce foreign motifs and styles into the indigenous visual vocabulary, seems to occur most frequently in

the so-called 'cargo' manifestations. Such foreign items as rifles, letters, air-planes, and canned goods, and such foreign behavior patterns as military marching, close-order drill, office work, communicating via short-wave ra-dio, and so on, are imitated, equivalents being manufactured (in the case of the objects, out of traditional materials, barkcloth, vines, wood with ochre paint, etc.). This imitation is thought by the New Guinea people to be a possible path to the riches and power possessed by Europeans by means of the magical principle of similarity. Such reasoning is also behind much of the common Sepik use of such foreign objects as flags, Christian crosses, and other European official symbols as motifs for decoration of bamboo lime-containers and ceramics and in tattoos. These apparently are regarded by the natives as 'power' symbols or personifications, rather than as symbols with the particular referents they possess in European contexts. Thus, the depiction of Kaiser Wilhelm on a Middle Sepik lime-container was probably motivated not by a reverence for the German Im-perial crown, but rather by the same respect for spiritual power that is ex-pressed by a rendering of the first ancestress of the tribe. (1976:264–265)[5]

When, as is perhaps more often the case, tangible skillfully crafted goods are acquired directly from outside, the associations they convey may be expressed by a number of related concepts ultimately correlated, as we have seen, with the political-ideological significance of spatial/temporal distance combined with the power signified by skilled artistry. These attri-butions, as they relate to geographically distant peoples, places, and things, may be contained within an even broader temporal/spatial pattern of meaning attributed to "significant" crafted objects in general. The in-terpretation given by Suriname Maroons to the diverse range of artistic things, both locally crafted and obtained from outside, that codify and express the qualities of their lives and culture is concisely illustrative: "Ma-roons . . . view an object in terms of its general historical and cultural context, associating technical and aesthetic features with the particular tribe, region, or village where it was made and the historical period it represents" (Price and Price 1980:193).

Yet even within this general frame of reference, distance or production by outsiders can bestow a sense of quality judged to be lacking in local products: "'Before the advent of the horse, a good many buffalo robes were bought from the Pend d'Oreilles and Flathead . . .' by the Coeur d'Alene, whereas afterwards they were no longer dependent upon others for this article *except* for the especially good ones they got from the Plains tribes." Plains tribes, in turn, considered a range of items, including bows and arrows, made by Plateau peoples to be superior to their own (Jablow quoting Teit 1966:12, 13 my emphasis). Similarly, "The finest examples of [metal ornaments, elaborately decorated weapons and utensils] were attributed to craftsmen of the more populous and technologically complex peoples of the interior, such as the 'Mandingo.' The Gola always looked upon their own products of this kind as cruder and less attractive than those that came to them from certain other peoples north of the Mano River, or from the eastern highlands" whence some Gola blacksmiths had received their own training (d'Azevedo 1975:49; see also Bayly 1986:308–309).

Even if the original producer is unknown, an object that gives evidence of having been crafted within a context of skilled artisanry (that is to say, by someone guided by aesthetic qualities) may be appreciated as such (d'Azevedo 1975:69). Given the general belief that technical expertise alone is insufficient for successful artistry, such skillfully crafted foreign objects (like those regarded as naturally endowed) may also be interpreted and valued as containing exceptional supernatural power or as having been produced by magical means (Bayly 1986:306; Eliade 1962:27; Appadurai 1986:52; Guy n.d.:3). In addition, as has been frequently mentioned before, skillfully crafted foreign-derived things are accorded the quality of inalienability. These goods not only encapsulate the powers and qualities of the strange and the beautiful in their tangible form but also are believed to provide a direct link with the extraordinary power of their distant places of creative origins. This, of course, is why such items are so often sought or accepted as pieces of political-ideological regalia. Such key symbols combine the mystery of exotic distant origins and the aesthetics of skilled crafting that together embody ancestrally defined moral order and potency and herald the creation of the polity.[6] By acquiring regalia from a geographically distant outside locale or, alternatively, acquiring an artisan from that distant place or knowledge of crafting techniques (Herbert 1984:250–251), an acquisitional polity publically identifies and acknowledges not only the superordinate status but also the other-worldly nature of that distant place; recognizes it as a cosmologically distinctive and therefore politically legitimizing center-out-there.

In addition to whatever historical particulars may relate the heartland to its superordinate place of beginnings, it is as a consequence of cosmological identification with distant space and time that such an outside locale can be conceptualized as a place of political-ideological origins associated with specific or personalized ancestral powers. And it is a further consequence of the cosmological identification of such outside centers that the leadership of acquisitional polities can pursue ties with such centers without necessarily entailing politically fatal local opposition to such subservience. On the contrary, this seemingly delicate position for an otherwise autonomous polity is readily resolvable when it is understood that such political and ideological deference along a geographical axis may be perceived as closely comparable to that which accrues to the proud authorities of polities where the point of cosmological contact and political-ideological deference is with vertically distant gods and ancestors. In both cases the polity's legitimate leadership is communicating with another world, another realm of existence, and such cosmological brokerage is always highly honorable, at least when properly conducted with the well-being of society in mind (Kopytoff 1987:36).[7]

Concurrently, cosmological identification as creative places of cultural origins reifies such outside centers as sources of potently charged tangible expressions of energizing cosmological power and of cultural (moral) propriety. These treasured objects are created by transformative artistic crafting conducted by supernaturally assisted specialists, and are skillfully acquired, again with supernatural aid and protection, by the leadership of acquisitional polities; a leadership that seeks tangible means to bring to life their own identification with, and privileged participation in, the supra-natural world of creative gods, ancestors, and legendary heroes who are the ultimate legitimizers of human authority (Fraser and Cole 1972: 313–314).

Such arching political goals also serve to emphasize another significant point of contrast broadly distinguishing acquisitional polities relating primarily to horizontal *axes mundi* from superordinate societies relating primarily to vertical *axes mundi*. Horizontally connected polities that seek to acquire skillfully crafted goods, particularly regalia, from geographically distant centers-out-there are basically emphasizing the strengthening and legitimizing of their own political centers. They are seeking to empower and enhance their own centeredness in opposition to whatever centrifugal local forces may seek to reduce or diffuse the power of that sense of centered concentration. Vertically connected superordinate centers, in contrast, appear to have their own political centeredness more firmly structured internally. They seek instead to expand their scope of influence or their range of control whether such be defined politically, in terms of offensive control over outside peoples, or cosmologically, in terms of defensive control over outside powers in whatever form they may take. That is to say, superordinate centers seek to express not their centeredness so much as their centralness, while acquisitional polities seek to emphasize the reverse (Spencer 1987:374).

The Acquisition of "Civilization"

Acquisitional societies relating to horizontally situated centers-out-there are fairly easy to spot in the ethnographic record, since the diagnostic criteria include not only imitation, generally by persons of influence, of styles of dress and ornamentation, household furnishings, architecture, or design motifs of foreigners but also, and especially, crafted ceremonial items, household furnishings, forms of dress, or other regalia acquired directly from outside societies.

One case in point concerns the Nafana state of Banda (Black Volta River area of Western Ghana), one of a number of polities involved with the Asante state (particularly during the eighteenth century) in an association tangibly expressed by acceptance of Asante art forms and Asante political regalia (Bravmann 1972). According to local traditions, the Nafana, already established as a polity, came into contact with Asante when they were defeated in a war with the latter and their chief, Sielongo, formally asked to pay homage to the Asantehene. In return for accepting this situation,[8] Sielongo was given various symbolic gifts (salt, palm wine) and a white Asante chief's stool. After Sielongo died, however, it became customary for the Nafana to blacken the personal stool of the chief in the manner characteristic of Asante but not of the Banda who, though they themselves had traditionally recognized the importance of ancestral stools as tangible representations of their own lineages (stools were named after the founders of families), had not blackened them. The stool originally acquired from Asante, however, now was formally blackened and consecrated as an ancestral stool of the state. This practice was then extended to the ancestral stools of all Sielongo's deceased predecessors as well as those of his royal successors. It appears to clearly acknowledge a shifting of the ancestral *axis mundi* of Banda chiefs from the vertically distant domain of traditional ruling lineage ancestors to the horizontally distant center of Asante (which had acquired its own original ancestral golden stool from the sky).

Keenly aware of their own political independence, succeeding Banda chiefs were somewhat sporadic in meeting obligations requested by Asante (such as attendance at important Asante state festivals). Yet they periodically assisted Asante in various ways and thereby added to their Asante-derived regalia a number of gold-hilted state swords (used as messenger swords and for swearing allegiance of lower chiefs), a palanquin, and a set of arm bangles as well as a talismanic white stool for the Queen Mother[9] which was periodically replaced by replicas also made in Asante. Other chiefly ornaments (gold bracelets and rings) and textiles for costumes were acquired from Asante, too, as was a brass-studded chair-of-state like that used by Asante paramounts, obtained "in order to augment the regalia of Banda and thereby to increase the prestige of the state" (Bravmann 1972:169). A number of state-related Asante-type festivals, in which Asante-like objects could be used, were also adopted. The Asante language became widespread as a second language and was always used in rituals employing imported Asante regalia. Forms of political and military organization were patterned after Asante, too. That all of this was far from superficial copying is evidenced by the fact that "When Banda-Ashanti relations deteriorated in the nineteenth century and items of regalia were no longer presented by Kumasi, Nafana chiefs *traveled south to Ashanti to commission artisans to produce these objects,* which had become a necessary part of Nafana culture" (Bravmann 1972:164–165, emphasis mine.)

Finally, Bravmann relates that special significance is accorded to those objects of Asante-derived regalia which are the first known examples of each particular type of imported object. Although over the years most items of Banda regalia have been acquired from Asante, "since the tradition of *making* regalia never really took root among the Nafana" (ibid. 170), the pieces originally received directly as gifts from specific Asante-hene on specific occasions are accorded special recognition. In the paradigm followed here, these original pieces of regalia can be said to encapsulate most meaningfully the sense of political-ideological origins and to relate most directly to the specific personalized Asante ancestral creators of legitimate Banda chiefship; thus they are imbued with the strongest quality of inalienability relating Banda with their cosmographical center-out-there.[10]

Basic characteristics of the Banda tie with Asante can be found in numerous other settings. The association of the elite of various frontier societies with the traditional Chinese empire, personalized by the Son of Heaven, is perhaps the best known case in point. Here, too, Chinese-derived crafted goods, including silks and satins, fine clothing and accessories including robes of state and other court attire, musical instruments, domestic furnishings, fine wines, titles, ceremonies, court etiquettes and procedures, even mandarins as resident advisors and learned Chinese books, were avidly sought and acquired by rulers of adjacent polities. Each of these lords, with the aid of such regalia, "began playing the role which he thought he should play, since the gift from the Chinese emperor in the form of court dresses had lifted him above his tribal folk and since the title seemed to give him additional power and privileges" (Eberhard 1965:138). Not the least of these privileges was access to the celestial mandate of political legitimacy available by way of the Son of Heaven (Schafer 1963:26–27; Farquhar 1957:62–64; Yoshinobu 1983). In like fashion the inalienable quality of sacred relics of early Christian martyrs acquired by political-religious elites of medieval Europe via the Pope from the vast treasury of the Roman catacombs provided prestige and enhanced legitimacy, by way of the horizontal tie with the sacred center of Rome, for numerous abbots, bishops and kings, although, on occasion, ambivalence concerning further earthly geo-political implications led to surreptitious acquisition of relics by theft rather than by open gift (Geary 1986:182–186).

The acquisition of highly valued goods, including carved slit gongs, curved boars' tusks, and breastplates of dogs' teeth, from mainland contacts by Manam islanders of Papua New Guinea is highly suggestive of a comparable situation, though in this case the setting appears more diffuse, and successful acquisition was interpreted as a kind of victory over outside providers (Lutkehaus 1985:130). Yet the ups and downs of the political fortunes of Manam aristocratic lineages rested largely on continued success in obtaining large numbers of such valuables (ownership of which was the supernaturally affirmed prerogative of the aristocracy) from their mainland contacts. Although the center supplying such items took the form of trading partners located in a number of villages scattered along the mainland north coast, that is, the postulated "center-out-there" was more a "region-out-there," the type of items acquired by the Manam suggests that mainland peoples and polities were accorded at least some of the unique and distinctive significance that accrues to sources of crafted political-ideological paraphernalia.[11] In this case the acquired goods included "most of the important objects associated with their secret cult: *garamut* drums, masks, bamboo flutes, and the finery (e.g., feathers, baskets and shell ornaments) with which newly initiated males were decorated. While the Manam could provide their basic subsistence needs themselves, they were dependent upon the mainland peoples for the necessities of their ritual life" (Lutkehaus 1985:137).

In a comparable case involving the Manambu of the middle Sepik River region, who also acquired qualitatively charged crafted goods and activities from the outside, a specific center is indicated as source, not only for the Manambu but for a considerable number of other groups, too: the complexly organized Iatmul, "princes of the Sepik," and "major exporters of symbolic goods in the region" to smaller and less complexly organized polities (Harrison 1987:495–496; Roscoe 1989:227). As is frequently the case in such situations, adult Manambu became bilingual in the language of the outside center (the Iatmul, as superordinate center, remained monolingual; see Chapter 11). The Manambu acquired magical spells and whole ritual complexes from the Iatmul, including male initiation rites for which expert Iatmul supervisors were imported. Such ritual entitlements were the property of particular subclans, and those subclans with ties to the Iatmul "tended to gain more important positions in ritual" than those not so favored (Harrison 1987:496, 498).

Finally, by way of expanding the range of ethnographic coverage, it is appropriate to acknowledge the very considerable political-ideological significance of the coastal Bella Coola for the Alkatcho Carrier of central British Columbia, particularly during the nineteenth century. As Goldman has indicated,

> many features of the potlatch-rank complex, if not the entire potlatch ideology, were derived from Bella Coola. . . . A study of noble names held by the Carrier leaves no doubt that these come from the Bella Coola. The Carrier themselves are fully aware of this fact, and claim that not only did they get all their honorific names from Bella Coola, but that they sought Bella Coola craftsmen to carve their crests for them. Further, while the Alkatcho Carrier rarely invited the Upper Carrier to their potlatches, they always included the Bella Coola among their guests. (1940:338)

The Bella Coola, though despising the Carrier, nonetheless welcomed them as visitors to their own villages, too, partly because the Carrier provided valuable furs but also because, like other superordinate centers mentioned in Chapter 11, it was deemed necessary to have flawed outsiders present at their winter ceremonies (Goldman 1940:339). Concurrently, by means of personal ties, particularly marriage, with daughters of noble Bella Coola families (who thereby acquired access to furs), the most energetic and successful Carrier were able to "acquire for themselves at least a connection with the treasures of another world" (Goldman 1975:16) and thereby enhance their political-ideological standing at home:

> Bella Coola-Carrier intermarriages were not very common [for] not only did the Bella Coola endogamic tendencies restrict such alliances, but the economic strain upon any Carrier family entering into a series of affinal potlatch exchanges and the necessity of participating in the rivalrous pot-

latches more or less upon Bella Coola terms was more than most Carrier families could sustain. Therefore, only a few Carrier individuals, the successful hunters, the shrewd and energetic traders, the lucky gamblers, were able to acquire enough wealth to participate upon a basis of relative equality in Bella Coola potlatches. These individuals, having acquired 'big names' from the coast, apparently formed the first Carrier aristocracy. (Goldman 1940:344; see also note 13)

The several examples of acquisitional polity-superordinate center associations briefly described in this and the previous chapter readily relate to the theme of interregional systems delineated in a variety of ways in the professional literature, particularly those approaches that focus on a dominant center and its attempts to expand a measure of political hegemony to culturally dependent or peripheral societies so as to encompass them within a single political-economic-cosmological network, realm, or world order. Within this perspective such peripheral or (as I prefer to see them) acquisitional societies may be interpreted as simply representing the flip side of the outreach orchestrated by expansionistic core polities in which they constitute satellite components of larger regional or imperialistic networks that focus on the center.

The primary danger inherent in such a perspective has always been the strong tendency either to emphasize the perceived unity of the whole and the adaptive operational smoothness of the alleged system (whether expressed in economic or ideological terms) or to emphasize the primacy of potentially disruptive stresses and tensions allegedly emanating from exploitative activities of a perpetually domineering center towards its continually subordinated but restless periphery. Both approaches share at least one inherent weakness in that they take a predominently unitary approach to complex situations that, in fact, contain not just a dominant center but a number of equally vital, centered, and self-identified political foci, each of which follows its own political-economic and political-ideological agendas geared to strengthening either its centeredness or its centralness.

To be sure, potential incompatibilities between acquisitional polities strengthening centeredness and superordinate centers expressing centralness can create very dynamic situations depending on how forcefully the respective polities pursue these goals or how closely or directly interactive they become in such pursuits. Yet, when considered in overall systemic terms, the situation is neither entirely one of functional unity nor entirely one of constant domination and exploitation. On the contrary, more detailed investigations of the actual dynamics involved in such associations reveal that, especially when considered over the long run (and when dealing with traditional non-industrial or pre-capitalist societies), both the unity and the exploitative dominance considered characteristic of the ongoing system are easily overstated. Many so-called frontier or peripheral (acquisitional) polities, though they maintain political-ideological associations with a superordinate center, successfully avoid both lasting exploitation (indeed, exploitation from the center may not even be attempted) and any really significant degree of overall cultural assimilation by the center. Some may periodically accept a degree of political dominance by the center only to periodically challenge at least some aspects of the center's geo-political presence. Some may adhere to outward form for the advantages to be gained while avoiding full acceptance of the system. Others may purposefully use improper titles when communicating with the center's ruling elite, or fail to acknowledge on diplomatic missives the calendrical date proclaimed from the center, or neglect to send congratulatory diplomatic missions to the center on occasions of state, or attempt to acquire the invaluable inalienable qualities of foreign regalia by theft so as to avoid undue political implications. At times the superordinate center, for reasons of its own, may present its own gifts with more emphasis and enthusiasm than the acquisitional polity, for reasons of its own, may wish to muster in return. Alternatively, acquisitional polities may fervently seek to acquire regalia denied them by a superordinate center which wishes to more tightly control the extent and direction of its influence and its expansion.[12]

In short, when considering the overall nature of long-distance associations between superordinate centers and acquisitional polities, it is essential to recognize the distinctiveness, in the immediate world of the here-and-now, of all polities concerned in spite of or in addition to the political-ideological attributions that separately relate each polity with one or more of the others in terms of cosmological space/time dimensions and contexts. In the particular perspective I am employing in this essay, interaction between such polities essentially expresses not involvement of all within a single all-encompassing system but an overlapping of several essentially separate and distinct cosmological realms in which each acquisitional polity or superordinate center basically regards its outside protagonists as either helpful or threatening cosmological elements. Each polity thus seeks to acquire or encompass (by acquisitive trade, diplomatic missions, fictive kin ties, sometimes theft or warfare) such aspects of that potent outside realm as best fit its own political-ideological programs and paradigms (Hevia 1990; Roscoe 1985, esp. 522–526).[13]

The major challenge for those who wish to explore the dynamics of such relationships in "inter-galactic" terms is to understand how such separate and distinct cosmologically based interactive frameworks can functionally interdigitate. One avenue to explore recognizes the flexibility contained within the basic tenet of traditional cosmology in general that holds that the multiple directions constituting the outside realm may be qualitatively interchangeable. That is to say, the basic precondition that separate political legitimacy be attainable for each polity (at least in its own eyes) may be met by the qualitative complementarity of vertical and horizontal *axes mundi* that herald as equally honorable, in the respective eyes of the respective leaderships, the acquisition of skillfully crafted regalia from ancestrally defined centers-out-there by acquisitional polities and the acquisition of naturally endowed things from the cosmographical outside realm by superordinate centers seeking to implement and energize the ancestral legitimation deriving from places of origin up there.

Yet, while the potential for complementary interactions between the various centers and acquisitional polities may rest on this convenient cosmological flexibility, the dynamics, tensions, and stresses in the respective world orders that result reflect the fact that the more immediate goals for both superordinate centers and acquisitional polities are directed to one-way appropriational activities focusing on acquisition of ideas, behaviors, and tangible crafted or naturally endowed things that manifest political-ideological legitimacy or cosmological powers necessary for the continued functioning and social reproduction of society. This is not to deny that two-way exchange relationships expressing mutual ties of alliance may at times develop. But, when they do, as periodically happened, for example, in the Chinese oecumene, it may be taken to signify that former acquisitional polities have become more completely encompassed within the internal organizational framework of the expanding superordinate center where, as within the boundaries of any polity, relational rules and modes of exchange apply (Chapter 6). Many acquisitional societies, of course, tend to drift in and out of such associations with their cosmologically superordinate centers, to the consternation of in situ political leaders no less than of anthropologists and historians.

The fundamental complementarity and interchangeability of vertical and horizontal *axes mundi* is also evidenced by the fact that acquisitional polities linked by horizontal *axes mundi* to superordinate centers-out-there (with vertical links of their own) may themselves act as superordinate centers vis-à-vis the surrounding outside world, creating a down-the-line pattern in which a series of acquisitional polities appears, each serving as a source of ritual and regalia for others, with the whole ultimately related to a primary superordinate center. A case in point is found in the chain of linkages among polities of the Sepik River (somewhat simplified here) beginning with the Iatmul from whom the Chambri and the Manambu (and perhaps also the Sawos) acquire magical spells, shell valuables, carvings, pottery, and other aspects of ritual culture. Bush peoples farther in the interior, in turn, eagerly acquire similar elements of ritual culture from the (to them superordinate) Chambri and Manambu (Harrison 1987:495–497; Roscoe 1989:227; Errington and Gewertz 1986:99–100, 106–107).

A different type of vertical-horizontal complementarity may be expressed with respect to the creative transformation contained in the concept of skilled crafting. As we have seen, in the superordinate centers characterized by vertical *axes mundi* such transformations involve in situ production by skilled artisans utilizing locally available or long-distance acquired material resources (trees, ores, precious stones, dyes, etc.) which will be shaped and given tangible form at the center. For some acquisitional polities, the same result, the same availability of qualitatively significant crafted things, is achieved by transforming natural things that are either locally available or acquired from more distant outside realms into skillfully crafted things obtained directly from the center-out-there by means of brokerage activities by which natural resources of the anonymously charged outside realm are exchanged for crafted products from the superordinate center. The skilled artisans in this case are those influential persons of the acquisitional polity who manage this movement of goods, who transform the natural products of one dimension of the cosmological beyond into crafted goods from another dimension of the cosmological outside. They do so with manipulative or transformative skills which, like all skilled transformations, combine technical expertise and supernatural assistance. In this case, however, the beings and powers that must be manipulated belong to horizontal rather than vertical cosmological directions.

Successful Ainu leaders may provide a case in point. According to Ohnuki-Tierney, these "ideal men" are good hunters and fishermen who can obtain a surplus of fur, fish oil, or other natural resources which they then exchange for foreign crafted goods, including Japanese lacquerware, swords, turquoise beads, and clothing desired primarily for use as offerings to Ainu deities (1974:74–75, 76). The Miskitu of eastern Nicaragua, whose superordinate center-out-there was England, overseas to the east, provide another, more complex, example. The significance of the English as originators and validators of Miskitu cultural and political legitimacy is evidenced in myths attributing the creation and legitimation (origins) of the highest Miskitu political position, the so-called kingship, to the English Crown. The British also provided crafted regalia of kingship (a crown, a written commission) as tangible record of English-derived legitimation. The same legitimizing symbolism accrued to certain British manners and material goods—tableware and table manners, wearing apparel, household furnishings, and areas of learning—also adopted by Miskitu kings and other leading political figures.

By adopting political regalia and the manners, customs, crafted goods (including guns) and even, to some extent, language of their overseas cosmographical originators, the Miskitu, in turn, acquired symbols of cultural and political superiority (as well as military dominance) vis-à-vis indigenous tribes living to the west, in the mountainous interior of Central America where diverse native groups regarded by the Miskitu as morally and culturally flawed (rude, subhuman) beings, sought a measure of protective isolation. These interior peoples provided the Miskitu with unworked or only partly worked resources (rough-hewn canoes, game, skins, calabashes, net hammocks).[14] In addition, as a result of Miskitu raids, they themselves came to constitute a type of natural resource as war-captive/slaves. By means of acquisitional trade the Miskitu then transformed such captives and a wide range of other natural goods (tortoise shell, india rubber, skins, canoes, gum copal, dyewoods) into English-derived crafted items (including cloth, machetes, guns, powder, and domestic accoutrements). As successful raider-traders and transformational agents the prestige and reputations of Miskitu leaders flourished, too (Helms 1969; 1983).

Finally, it is not surprising to find that successful management or transformation of resources available via horizontal linkages may provide both political and ideological means and motivation for an acquisitional polity to (re)emphasize vertical cosmological links of its own; to shift identification from a horizontal center-out-there to a vertically situated one, that is to say, to become a separate superordinate center in its own right (Tambiah 1977 : 84). An excellent case in point is found in Schneider's discussion (1978) of the shift in political-ideological linkages between the eastern Mediterranean, long the resplendent superordinate center of the European theatre, and northern Europe, composed of various acquisitional polities linked to that center (see also Rogers 1983 regarding medieval Korea). This readjustment was accompanied by development in northern Europe of a key crafted symbol, black cloth, to signal separation from its long-time Mediterranean center-out-there (Byzantium, Rome) which was represented by its own skillfully crafted key symbol, resplendent polychrome textiles (Byzantine and Renaissance Italian silks). Additional breaks or re-orientations in formal ideology (the rise of monasticism and then of Protestantism) and acquisition of its own outside realm of naturally endowed resources in the New World both heralded and assisted further development of northern Europe as a region of independent political and ideological centers now linked less to Rome and more directly to authenticating celestial origin points of their own; new superordinate centers that would seek to acquire beneficial resources from their own new world of developing acquisitional (colonial) polities.

13 *Conclusions*

> Social types are not isolated creations, wholly independent of
> each other, and each one an original entity, but rather the result
> of an endless play of combination and re-combination, forever
> seeking to solve the same problems by manipulating the same
> fundamental elements.   —CLAUDE LÉVI-STRAUSS
>   "The Bear and the Barber," p. 10

In Lévi-Strauss' view, the arenas within which societies combine and recombine explanatory elements are located either on the level of nature, with its "taxonomic system of natural species" as expressed in totemism, or on the level of culture with its "social system of trades and occupations" as expressed in castes (1963:9). In complementary fashion, we may hypothesize that traditional societies combine and recombine basic elements of a commonly conceived cosmological structure in which critical aspects of the social universe of the heartland are related to the ideological universe outside.[1]

Stating the matter from the perspective of Western paradigms, one manner of interpreting the diversity of elements constituting the traditional world, an interpretation shaped and informed by explanatory devices based on our own prevalent belief in the consubstantiality of matter, appreciates the role played by ecological diversity in enriching the range of material resources available for human use. Yet another perspective, shaped and informed by explanatory devices based on indigenous belief in the consubstantiality of life forces, appreciates the role played by cosmological powers in enriching the diversity of tangible resources available for human use (Reichel-Dolmatoff 1976). It is also understood by proponents of both the ecological and the ideational perspectives that, in terms of social dynamics, it falls to the leadership of any given polity to officially direct or take responsibility for the acquisition and transformation of outside resources, whether such resources be defined as economically material or ideationally tangible.

Comprehending the conceptual frameworks and underlining basic assumptions within which these political tasks are conducted is crucial, because somehow, in ways that still remain all too opaque to us, this acquisition, manipulation, and transformation of resources, broadly defined,
historically has helped to fuel the developmental growth and complexities
of human social and political organizations. At this point proponents of
ecology and of ideology (symbology), respectively, generally find little in
common, for they usually approach the basic problem from separate and
seemingly irreconcilable perspectives. Yet further light might be cast upon
these still elusive cultural processes if we could appreciate more fully the
transformative, and thus politically significant, interchangeability of certain resources in traditional political systems. This interchangeability has
long been understood by members of traditional societies but we, from a
different cultural background, will fail to fully appreciate its significance
unless we comprehend similarities and complementarities in certain dimensions of culture that we have generally kept analytically separate. The
interpretations in this essay are an attempt to move along such lines by
postulating a common indigenous conceptual framework concerning cosmological structure and politically significant acts of transformation within
which economic concepts of long-distance trade and resource acquisition
and symbolic concepts and activities of artistry and ideology can be
combined.

Such juxtapositioning can suggest interesting similarities of varying degrees of interpretive import that at the very least may help to overcome
some of the conceptual barriers that so frequently have separated our analytical categories; at the most such juxtaposings may cast additional light
on fundamental cultural processes. Hunting, for example, is readily recognized as a kind of long-distance contact requiring entry into geographical (cosmographical) outside territory in order to acquire desired goods.
To obtain these resources hunters (and/or facilitating shamans) frequently
contact and negotiate with a mystical master of the animals who controls
access to the game, even going so far as to ritually invite the master of the
animals to the hunter's camp or home to be hospitably wined and dined
by ceremonial ritual in hopes of maintaining a fruitful rapport (Ingold
1987:245–273). It is in exactly the same spirit of intent that chiefs or their
acquisitional trading agents contact and negotiate with foreign rulers or
other persons of influence who are also resident somewhere outside and
who also control access to desired foreign resources, at times extending
chiefly hospitality and courtly etiquette (ritual) to visiting rulers, diplo-

mats, and trading agents who arrive from afar with stores of exotic and valued goods.

Similarly, as this essay has argued at length, acts of acquisition of skillfully crafted goods from a superordinate center-out-there by the leadership of an acquisitional polity may be understood to carry the same political-ideological significance as acts of skilled crafting at home. Skilled crafting gives tangible, culturally meaningful form to outside-derived powers and qualities, bringing such powers and qualities literally into view for the heartland. In like fashion, acquisition of skillfully crafted goods as well as naturally endowed things from an outside realm also literally brings power-filled items, qualitative forms, into view for the heartland. By so doing, of course, skilled acquirers are accomplishing the same goal as skilled artisans. They are, in fact, conducting a form of skilled crafting themselves, thereby conveying to the home populace their personal control of the requisite technical and supernatural skills and abilities required of those who deal with the beyond. Ultimately, the leadership of both superordinate and acquisitional polities, as skilled crafters/acquirers, are evidencing direct association with ancestors as concept and as personages and with ancestral powers, which is to say, with the fundamental political validation and legitimation that derives, by definition, from association with the concept of origins.

As Rabineau, Fernandez, and others have pointed out (Chapter 5), proper conduct of other aspects of traditional political leadership also constitutes an art, one requiring maintenance of proper social and community relationships through exemplary behavior. Exemplary behavior, by definition, is that which serves as an archetype or ideal model deserving of imitation. The most exemplary—most honorable—in this context is that which again recreates and embodies ideal qualities of the recognized ancestors, those predeceased exemplars who have survived the oblivion accorded to the qualitatively less fit and thereby come to constitute and represent "pure quality." Their living representatives and descendents face the constant challenge of reflecting such qualities anew, particularly by superior conduct in select activities deemed to require and, therefore, to be expressive of the necessary ideal attributes. The possibilities are varied, but in general these activities include (though they are not restricted to) all those forms of outside involvement which can be conducted for the benefit of society. Hence, in addition to various formal religious (including shamanic) activities, skilled hunting, acquisition of naturally endowed resources, acquisition of skillfully crafted things, and the many expressions of skilled crafting itself, broadly defined, are all areas where the ideal, the epitome of human intent and behavior, may be expressed.[2]

Given that these diverse types of activities can convey comparable expressions of ideal human intent and behavior as well as comparable evidence of political legitimation by association with origins, it follows that they should also be politically interchangeable depending, for any given polity, upon historical and environmental (ecological) particulars as well as on the limits and/or opportunities inherent in local social organization. Being interchangeable in quality and political significance, these acts, in the aggregate, also allow for considerable manipulation by political hopefuls or already influential persons who, being both mortal and therefore (still) imperfect, are constantly challenged by personal ambition and/or social pressure to continually provide fresh evidence of successful attainment of society's high expectations.

When successful, such transformational experts also have at their disposal means by which they themselves may further rise above or be distanced from the ordinary, the commonplace, and the mundane. The very great importance of being able to give tangible evidence of such capabilities as a condition for further authority or political influence is evidenced by the fact that acquisition of tangible forms of politically significant ritual and regalia may actually precede the further development of real authority and/or formal positions of authority (Harrison 1987; Helms 1979:20). That is to say, successful acquisition or production of politically significant things from afar, in whatever form such outside-related things may be expressed for a given society, may constitute the growth-point of an evolving polity (Harrison 1987).

At least part of the power of such outside-related activities may reside in the also very important fact that these endeavors emphasize personal initiatives, motivations, skills, capabilities, and achievements in a manner that at least initially, or in the acquisition stage of their outside involvement, frees individuals from the constraints and demands of the local, the domestic, and the kin-based group, that is, of the world that dominates life within society (Benet 1957:212; Helms 1988:63−64, 76−78). Assuming that such outside activities are regarded as socially useful and desirable, society even positively rewards such individual achievers with prestige and elephant tails, with personal fame and renown, with positions of political authority and responsibility, even with an immortalized name. Sooner or later, of course, society co-opts the tangible fruits of these endeavors by placing limits of one sort or another upon individual earthly accumulations, perhaps by requiring immediate distribution of goods, or payment of death duties to church, state, or kinsmen, or burial of goods as recycled ancestral potency. Similarly, society also eventually co-opts the impact of such individualism. In this life, this may be accomplished by conferring formal political offices or influential roles that are crucially strengthened by personal quality but that also act to "depersonalize" the individual (Fortes 1962:86–87) by transforming him or her into an ideal form. Alternatively, such an individual may be formally excluded from social life as flawed. In an afterlife, society may similarly co-opt individualism by conferring the depersonalized or ideal status of ancestor (Davenport 1986).

Yet, even though achieving individualism may be channeled, socialized, or co-opted, personalized acts of skilled crafting and of acquisition are constantly repeated. Indeed, they must be constantly repeated. Repetition constitutes reassurance that the energizing link between society and its cosmological realm and ancestral creative centers is still effective, still functioning. Repetition evidences that acquirers or artisans are still capable of mediating between realms, can still activate the power received from without and encapsulate or transform that power for the social good. Repetitive acts of acquisition or skilled crafting are means of continuing the communication between living human beings and the ancestral world by carving, painting, or weaving, by song or dance, or by acquisition of exotic goods (Schaefer 1991).

Constant repetition of such activities also constantly reaffirms the unquestionable truth, the sacrality, of the cosmological system, its organization, and its mode of operation, and thus reaffirms the legitimacy of those political and ideological roles claiming their authority in terms of these cosmological tenets. Constant repetition of such transformative activities also seeks to reassure not only that a political-cum-cosmological order exists but also that it operates in tandem with the constant demographic, economic, and political fluctuations and perturbations that, from the perspective of political economy, constitute social reality and social norms. Constant repetition of transformative acts that either expose or impose order allows a sufficient degree (or sense) of shifting order in the face of constant flux so that under normal circumstances society achieves the necessary adjustments, large or small, to its ecological, demographic, even ideological world by frequent, flexible, manageable processes of change rather than by more abrupt jolts that could threaten social dissolution. In the process the cosmology and the actuality of political structure and operation are matched to achieve a reasonably functioning fit between action and legitimation (Tambiah 1977:81, 92).

Critical to successful political-ideological management of flux by reassertions that order is inherent at least in the ancestrally ordained and directed portion of the universe is the belief that direct and active contact can and must be maintained with critical components of that universe. Hence naturally endowed or skillfully crafted things acquired from outside and behavior or things crafted by society's own artisans are believed to be not mere representations but actual encapsulations or embodiments of cosmological power (Johnson 1989). These encapsulations and embodiments can then be put to use either to enhance social order within or to energize the expansion of social-political order outward into those more benighted portions of the outside realm that represent the ever-present threat of social-cum-cosmological disorder. Similarly, as Roscoe has noted (1989: 227–228), the centers-out-there that serve as superordinate cultures of power and which may appear to some observers to be distinguished for their "superior scale, sociocultural complexity, and/or military prowess" also, and perhaps primarily, may be recognized for their focality as centers of activities (including various forms of skilled crafting) that create or demonstrate original sources of political-ideological power. As such, cosmographical centers "out there" are but re-creations of cosmological centers-of-origins "up there."

In exactly the same sense, those who attain high achievement in matters of acquisition, accumulation, and transformation are but recreating the roles of primordial ancestors even as they garner both the credentials and the amassed cosmological energy that, regardless of how it is distributed in tangible form, will allow their own apotheosis into future ancestors. It is therefore entirely appropriate that both lineage houses and primate cities should be constructed and ornamented by skilled artisans from near or far under the auspices of lineage elders and high kings and that both the paths leading from the village plaza and the roads stretching outward from the city gates should point toward spatially/temporally distant places where tangible naturally endowed or skillfully crafted manifestations of the qualities of distance are available to those seeking to acquire them for their own home centers.

Reflecting these cosmological verities is the compelling fact that, in seeking and acquiring as well as crafting such objects, the choices made by acquisitional traders or artisans or by the rulers whom they may represent are not arbitrary, but, as Hodder has emphasized (speaking within the rubric of exchange systems), "are appropriate within a cultural, ideological, and historical context. Objects come to have meaning as members of categories opposed to other categories, and as nodes in networks of associations and evocations. Any adequate analysis of exchange systems must consider the way in which the symbolism of the artifact legitimates, supports, and provides the basis of power of interest groups" (1982:207). Combining the domains of "exchange" and "acquisitional trade" as differentiated in this essay, Hodder has also emphasized that

> The associations and contexts of exchanged artifacts can be examined between regional units and at different distances from sources. Each artifact type may have different values and meanings within each local context, and the exchange of objects between cultural units and the maintenance of boundaries between ethnic groups may be based upon, and may manipulate, such differences. There is a link to the within-unit contexts in that whether artifacts cross or do not cross between ethnic groups is related to their meanings within each unit. It is thus necessary to examine variations in symbolic associations over space. (1982:208)

Furthermore, "concern with the forms of the transactions themselves is inadequate, since the social effects of exchange depend on the different symbolic meanings of the artifact types in each context. Exchange must be understood in relation to these differences of meaning." In short, "The functioning of exchange depends on the choice of an object within an ideological framework" (ibid.).

It has been the intent of this essay to suggest a general ideological framework judged to be broadly valid for traditional society as a whole and to suggest some of the fundamental categories of meaning and symbolism that accrue to vital artifacts of acquisition within that framework. In so doing I concur with Hodder that

> There is more to exchange than *economic* advantage—even if social advantage is included in that term. Exchange involves the transfer of items that have symbolic and categorical associations. Within any strategy of legitimation, the symbolism of objects is manipulated in the construction of relations of dominance. The exchange of appropriate items *forms* social obligations, status, and power, but it also *legitimates* as it forms. A fully contextual approach to exchange must incorporate the symbolism of the objects exchanged." (Ibid.:209)

Though Hodder speaks with reference to the general perspective of "exchange," his point is equally valid, indeed even more so, when considered in reference to a general perspective of "acquisition" as discussed in these pages. The biggest difficulty to be faced and overcome in grappling with this issue is that the relevant data not only derive from societies with a general interpretation of the composition and functioning of the world that is significantly different from our own but that they also reflect critical aspects of this "world view" as it impacts upon the manner in which the earth's resources are identified and utilized. This is not a new problem; just one that has been very difficult to resolve, especially for processual issues. In 1857 the German philosopher, Schelling, in his "Philosophy of Mythology," observed "Here we must not ask how the phenomenon must be turned, twisted, distorted or minimized still to be explicable from principles we have determined not to depart from, but: in what direction must our ideas be enlarged in order to be commensurate with the phenomenon" (quoted in Schmitz 1963 : 155).

This is the true creator, the waver
Waving purpling wands, the thinker
Thinking gold thoughts in a golden mind,
Loftily jingled, radiant,
The joy of meaning in design
Wrenched out of chaos . . .

—WALLACE STEVENS
"The Sail of Ulysses" (*Opus Posthumous,*
ed. Samuel French Morse [New York:
Alfred A. Knopf, 1957], p. 100)

Notes

CHAPTER 1

1. My interest in this juxtaposition of particular activities was initially piqued by the various attributes of the Greek god, Hermes, who was associated with the Thief, the Shepherd, the Craftsman, the Herald, the Musician, the Athlete, and the Merchant, as well as with mental ability and magical powers associated with actions as culture hero. Hermes was also recognized more generally as the "giver of good things" (Brown 1947; Helms 1988: 111–113, 114; 1987).

CHAPTER 2

1. Goldman explains this contrast in a more general setting: "The literal is asocial because it differentiates by person rather than by category; it is transient because it does not enter into binding concepts; it remains within its given sphere and has the social disability of utmost parochialness. Finally, it is a raw event and therefore incomplete. The metaphoric, literally a transfer from one sphere to another, endows the event with the added significance of merger and of compression; it . . . is a transposition, a move into a precisely defined state that establishes the social viewpoint. . . . which can be rejected only at the risk of defying the concept of community" (1970:516).

2. Over-communication refers to the context in which interaction between a set of participants rests on agreement between them as to which of their diverse statuses forms the basis for their particular interaction. That which confirms the relevant relationship is then *over*-communicated and that which is not relevant is *under*-communicated (see Barth 1966:3).

3. According to Havelock's interpretation, Plato's attack on poets and poetics bespeaks his objection to losing (combining or compressing) the original within

the existing performance. Plato prefers to keep the original separate and then to copy it: i.e. to Plato, "me thinking about Achilles" is preferable to "me identifying with Achilles" (Havelock 1963:159, 209).

4. See also Eliade (1962:57–60) re smelting symbolized as a form of male-female creativity, and Forge (1967:82) regarding the power of painted designs on the façades of ceremonial houses to stimulate the growth of yams.

5. In a comparable manner, according to Fagg, "there is strong reason to believe that in tribal society all dancing, whether sacred or profane, is held to increase the life force of the participants, that a person in stylized movement is *ipso facto* generating force, which can, moreover, be physically passed on to others by a laying on of hands" (Fagg 1973:166). See also Thompson (1974:74) regarding the craft of horseback riding as a transformation of speed and elevation into power.

6. As with any power-filled object, tools can be used for supernaturally induced harm as well as good. See Horridge (1979:13) regarding the magical capabilities of chisels used in the laying of the keels of new ships among the Konjo of South Sulawesi, Indonesia.

7. Bloch (1974:78) notes that formal oratory by learned elders can achieve a comparable conjunction and dissolution of present and future into past, as the elder is himself transformed into an ancestor speaking eternal truth. Similarly, among the Quiché Maya, designs woven in textiles give contemporary form to the past, particularly to ancient Words: "Textile designs are considered to be ancient, which makes their continuing use something like the quotation of an ancient text" (Tedlock and Tedlock 1985:126; see also Klein 1982).

8. Alternatively, if the community rejects the new art as aesthetically unacceptable, the dissident group has failed in its political attempt. See Chapters 4 and 5. In comparable fashion, in northern New Ireland all those who remember select images for the Malangan carvings that are crafted during funerals call themselves "one skin" and can make claims to land and residency (Küchler 1988:632).

9. See Fernandez (1973:207–209) and the discussion in Chapter 5 regarding Fang judges' skillful efforts to shape a new social whole from shattered patterns of behavior through artful and aesthetic use of words and oratory in deciding court cases. Greene reminds us, however, that the socially constructive powers of speech in the hands of a skilled and supernaturally influenced artisan can be transmuted into destructive powers when the poet or seer expresses or releases the damaging power of words by satirizing (1954:24).

10. Strong singles out dance as a particularly important part of such court fêtes. Dance imitated the movement of stars and planets and thus reflected celestial order and harmony. In addition, dance provided visual means by which to express theories of absolute monarchy. "By bringing spectators into the chain by the introduction of general dancing after the main ballet, it became the ideal vehicle, in both France and England, for drawing the onlookers into the ideological theme of the spectacle. In this audience participation they 'renewed' themselves and outwardly

demonstrated their adherence to the ideal principles of government expounded in the court fête" (Strong 1973:140).

CHAPTER 3

1. Regarding first dancers see Griaule (1965:186, 188, 189); Goodale and Koss (1967:183). First musicians, minstrels, and poets Griaule, (1965:45, 187); Foote and Wilson (1970:331–332); Brown (1947:21); Holy Bible: Genesis 4:21; Tedlock and Tedlock (1985:123). First potters, painters and carvers, Lévi-Strauss (1988:21, 150–151, 177–178 and 1973:348); Chipp (1971:155); Buck (1966:308–309); Best (1924, vol 2:559); Goodale and Koss (1967:183). First tattooers, Oliver (1974, vol 1:433); Best (1924, vol 1:169 and vol 2:546). First ship builders, O'Rahilly (1964:526); Horridge (1979:10). First weavers, Griaule (1965:29). First jewelers, Tedlock and Tedlock (1985:123); Soustelle (1961:66–67). First workers in metal, Clive (1937:23); Herbert (1984:42); Eliade (1962:93–96, 53); Rogers (1979:6). These references are far from exhaustive. They are meant to be exemplative of the numerous ethnographic illustrations of traditional beliefs in the ancient origins of skilled crafting.

2. One rationale behind the extraordinary nature accorded such tools is expressed by the Ilahita Arapesh, who attach a special significance to a particularly ingenious style of post-hole digging used in the construction of spirit houses. As Tuzin explains, the digging technique is considered special and remarkable because it operates in a context outside ordinary daily life. It also presupposes a measure of creative inspiration that is felt to be superior to that which the Arapesh feel capable of today. It holds a wonderment because it is a type of technology invented in the forgotten past (1980:132).

3. "We know from Mesopotamian and Egyptian sources that images were fashioned [of precious wood plated with gold with eyes of precious stones, clad with sumptuous garments, crowned with tiaras and adorned with pectorals] and repaired in special workshops in the temples; they had to undergo an elaborate and highly secret ritual of consecration to transform the lifeless matter into a receptacle of the divine presence. During these nocturnal ceremonies they were endowed with life. . . ." (Oppenheim 1977:185–186, 184).

4. Inalienable wealth and skills are things or abilities that are thought to always inherently belong to their original owners even when possessed by others; that is, they relate present possessors to earlier owners or ancestors. See Weiner (1985).

5. The presence of artisans from outside does not obviate the permanent presence of indigenous artisans, though the two categories of crafters may be differentiated in terms of the relative quality of their respective products.

6. The preparation of shamans' esoteric paraphernalia may require comparable journeys on the part of shamanic artisans. See Wilbert (1979:146, 147) for an account of the travels and travails of Warao shaman-crafters.

7. Artisans' travels during the Middle Ages were certainly not limited to journeymen's apprenticeships, but, following ancient precedent, were more generalized: "as in Homeric times when one had to send abroad for 'craftsmen, prophets, physicians, carpenters, and minstrels', so throughout the classical period—and for that matter right on into the Middle Ages—merchants and craftsmen of all types wandered from one city to another as opportunity called them, and refused to make any place their permanent home" (Hasebroek 1933:42–43; Austin and Vidal-Naquet 1977:46, 201). The Homeric reference is to *The Odyssey* (xvii:382).

8. The metalworkers in question were the powerful primordial Telchines, artisans with great supernatural powers who were derived from the sea and whose adventures take place on islands, such as Rhodes and Crete. They could also metamorphose into various sea-related animal forms (Detienne and Vernant 1978:260, 268, 273).

9. Literacy and the ability to consult written books may be counted as one of the skilled crafts of the Dyula and Hausa, who were also excellent weavers, blacksmiths, musicians, and royal praise singers, as well as religious experts and merchants.

10. Healey's general point receives additional support from an observation by Geertz, who notes that the Javanese word for itinerant trader also means "foreigner," "wanderer," or "tramp" (Geertz 1963:43–44). This comment casts no light on which dimension of itinerant trading came first or is the more important—the travel or the trade, but it does strongly suggest that travel and outside associations are equally important variables associated with such trade; that foreigners and wanderers are traders as much as traders are foreigners and wanderers.

11. In the Mayan context, both ancient and modern, such travel is frequently in the form of pilgrimage to sacred places, though traveling merchants are also well documented. Such merchants may also have been skilled artisans of a sort, since there are references to those who could read the painted codices and play musical instruments (Carmack 1976:8).

12. The qualitative significance of roads and pathways as ritually or qualitatively safe passageways through or across otherwise uncultured, wild, or dangerous expanses of land or sea and as delineating the form of the cultural landscape is worthy of a separate study. Both people and objects are seen to pass along such roads that are delineated not only in physical terms but also as socially and ideologically significant pathways originally opened by earlier ancestors and spirits as they traveled the earth as creative culture heroes. Such pathways convey temporal as well as spatial qualities of distance. See, for example, Ingold (1987:151–153); Biernoff (1978); Kahn (1990); Reichel-Dolmatoff (1978:262); see also note 14 below.

13. "In prayers that prepare the way for a long trip, one asks not only that there be no robbers in the road, but that policemen, soldiers, and customs officials look the other way" (Tedlock 1985:260).

14. The pathways marked by foreign goods can be overtly expressed, as in the

complex concept of the *keda* or road that kula valuables travel along (Appadurai 1986:18–19) or in the pathway made of foreign-associated barkcloth along which the ruler of Lau (in Fiji) is led during his investiture to signify the foreign derivation of the original ancestral title holder. Barkcloth in Fiji also serves as the path of the god in the vertical sense, too, for when hung from rafters at the sacred end of the temple, it becomes "the avenue by which the god descends to enter the priest" (Sahlins 1981:118, 117).

Also, acquisition of knowledge of the means to produce or reproduce skillfully crafted materials may be comparable to acquisition of a finished good; thus acquisition of a new song or dance from outside is as relevant as acquisition of an exquisitely woven textile or delicately fashioned piece of metalwork.

15. Relics themselves were not crafted objects, though the reliquaries containing them were frequently artistic masterpieces. The relics themselves had no need of further workmanship to provide or transform mystical potency since they themselves were believed literally to be pieces of sacred ecclesiastical ancestors.

16. Discussing the values accorded Turkmen carpets by Western collectors and connoisseurs, Spooner also concludes that attributes of authenticity have to do with distance, "especially the interpretation of cultural distance over space and time from one social situation to another. Any reduction in that distance threatens authenticity" (1987:222). He further notes that authenticity may be considered 1) to be a measure of quality; 2) to require special knowledge to recognize; 3) to reside not in the carpet itself but in the relationship between carpet and weaver; and 4) is likely to become rarer as time goes on (ibid.:223). All of these points fit well with the model suggested in this volume.

CHAPTER 4

1. Not all skilled artisans in the Greek pantheon were portrayed as physically deformed; Apollo, god of music, was ideally handsome.

2. Note the discussion by Detienne and Vernant concerning the meaning of Hephaistos' curved limbs (1978: Chapter 9) as well as comments by Dasen (1988:264) regarding "curving processes" in the human form.

3. This point is also illustrated in the Popol Vuh when the creator-Makers and Modelers realized that their final human creations were too perfect, having complete and god-like knowledge and vision of everything. Thus the creator-gods weakened the eyes of the first true humans, blurring their absolute vision to see only things at hand; reducing their means of understanding and thus their knowledge (Tedlock 1985:47, 166–167).

4. See Detienne and Vernant (1978) for extended discussion of the particular type of intelligence, *metis,* recognized in ancient Greek culture as the basis for success in all types of skilled performance.

5. It is essential to emphasize that aesthetics considered in an elitist context is

applicable to societies that are institutionally non-centralized as well as those that are centralized since reference is to qualities and values rather than to political structure. Similarly, master artisans may figure as epitomes of humanness in non-centralized as well as centralized societies.

6. This statement derives from a medieval Indian treatise on statecraft, the Śukranītisāra of Śukrācārya. When sculptures of rulers or other pieces of art are destroyed or damaged intentionally, as the archaeological record sometimes shows, one intent may be to destroy the aesthetics and perfection, that is, the good or the morality, and therefore the status and the power of the elite to whom the art refers.

CHAPTER 5

1. Rabineau notes that shamans, who are distinctively separate from other village leaders in Cashinahua society, make aesthetically deviant headdresses considered to be either poorly made or unconventional in design. Such deviance is attributed to shamans' far closer and more direct contact with the spirit world, for shamans are under the influence of spirits rather than controlling them. Alleged inability to craft feathers in an orderly manner signifies the power that spirits have over shamans (Rabineau 1975:97, 106).

2. Additional examples of political leaders who were also practicing artisans can be found in Firth (1925:280, 281–282); Holm (1983:23, 27); Forge (1962:10); Oswalt (1979:262); Maduro (1976:236); and Lucie-Smith (1981:80).

3. A selection of pertinent references to chiefly association with smithing in traditional African societies includes Rogers (1979:6); Crowley (1972:37); Cline (1937:124, 126–127); Balandier (1968:36, 41); Herbert (1984:34); Himmelheber (1963:88); Eliade (1962:85, 92); Alpers (1975:21). See also Kinross (1977:151); Addison (1908:4, 16–17, 25, 110–111); Helms (1979:147); Stone (1977:127–128).

4. Schneider and Schneider offer a fine discussion of the qualitative criteria associated with elites using the elite landowners of rural Sicily as example. They point out that "even selfish sumptuary indulgence takes on a positive valence insofar as it can be shown to add grace, charm, and aesthetic value to the places where elite families live. . . . an elite contributes to its community and is awarded high status for doing so" (1983:160).

5. Similarly, in traditional Chinese political thought lords at the dawn of history were credited with teaching divination and mathematics, with composing the calendar, inventing musical instruments of bamboo, and teaching the use of money, boats, and carriages and the arts of working in clay, metal, and wood. The first emperor also built the first temple and the first palace in addition to establishing religious rituals and teaching medicine. Likewise in African oral histories chiefly culture heroes, who are often identified as newcomers originally derived from outside, frequently introduce new crops or new techniques and new political

organization, all of which ushers in a new and "ideal" social and political order (Kopytoff 1987:50).

6. There are other comparable ways of literally or physically shaping or fashioning a polity, as seen, for example, in the characteristics of royal progresses in which, when kings journey around the countryside making appearances, "they mark it, like some wolf or tiger spreading his scent through his territory, as almost physically part of them" (Geertz 1977:153 and passim). With respect to kings as builders of cities or public works, though much can be gained by such activity, much can also be lost if the demands on laborers are too great or are misdirected. See Duncan (1990:162–163, 176–179).

7. Goldman further notes that "a changeover in the headmanship comes with the building of a new maloca . . . [for any one of a variety of reasons]. On those occasions, the man who feels confident of his support undertakes to put up the main beams of the new house, with the help of his own brothers and of his sons. . . . The building of a maloca constitutes an election . . ." (1963:155).

8. This latter comment refers to the practice of sanctifying stone quarries with shrines and making offerings so that the stone might not give out and the buildings constructed from it might not fall. The name of Viracocha, the creator-deity, was also given to one such quarry.

9. See also Mary Douglas (1966:51–52) regarding the symbolism of physical perfection and purity of all things and beings associated with that which is in any way "holy."

10. Compare the concept of the *halach uinic* or "real man," indicative of head chiefs among the lowland Maya (Clendinnen 1987:25).

11. To the Kwakiutl, trees are deemed to be alive, to have spirits and be a source of power in their own right. Thus trees do not merely constitute useful materials, but "forms of life that undergo transformations, becoming all other forms," that is, are changed into canoes, boxes, and houses that are alive, too (Goldman 1975:192, 193). Houses, in fact, are conceived of symbolically as boxes or containers composed of lineage members (Seguin 1986:483).

12. Association of Jupiter with places of worship, travelers' rest stops, and teachers' homes would also seem to relate the planet to outside-related phenomena in general, including deities, esoteric knowledge, foreign goods (probably) and persons specialized therein. Compare Hermes (Chapter 1, note 1).

13. Hocart speaks here of Homer's views of the ideal king. The word "justice," as used here, has the wider Greek meaning of custom and propriety, that is, all that is just, lawful, virtuous, and pious, including the fear of the gods.

CHAPTER 6

1. Basic discussion of appropriation as a distinctly human activity can be found in Ingold (1987). However, whereas Ingold is concerned with differentiating

between human perceptions and environmental uses and the perceptions and environmental uses made by other types of living things, I am concerned with further differentiations within categories of human perceptions and environmental uses. I believe these differentiations are accorded contrastive qualities within human society as significant as those Ingold recognizes as separating the human from the non-human realms.

2. In taking this position I accept the argument that in non-industrial societies most basic appropriation, especially production and consumption of domestic items and subsistence goods, is conducted locally or domestically.

3. Tchernia continues, "The presence of millions of amphorae for Italian wine in Gaul does not result from an effort to step up the market for wine. Rather the amphorae of wine were an advantageous exchange currency for the metals and slaves of which Italy was in need" (1983:99–100).

4. The full implication of this statement rests on the Dogon belief that cowries tangibly represent and actually contain the Word, meaning ancestral truth, which should be spread about and accumulated as much as possible. Cowries are also a means to effect exchange, a process which also involves truthful words of agreement between the parties involved (Griaule 1965:202, 204).

5. This differentiation between cosmological and sociological is not intended to deny a cosmological context for sociologically significant values and qualities, particularly as emically expressed, but to emphasize areas of relative importance that are pertinent to distinguishing between exchange and acquisition.

6. Just what constitutes qualitatively different kinds of beings can be a difficult question, especially when, as in some societies, the same type or kind of beings may be believed to assume different manifestations of formal or outward appearance. But in general, human beings living in a given home society may be considered qualitatively distinctive from whatever manifestations of existence are out there, including various types of spirits or ancestors or other super- or sub-human beings. Some humans, of course, may make extreme efforts to approximate the more positively valued of such beings, and especially in the case of shamans may be thought to have achieved that approximation, just as various spirit beings may assume anthropomorphic qualities. See Ingold (1987:257) regarding concepts about the shaman and the bear among northern hunters.

7. See Sahlins (1981a) for an informative case study that does take this view.

8. A way other than raids or war, although these, too, as well as marriage, can be usefully interpreted within contexts of cosmology and the acquisition of supernatural treasures from outside. See, for example, Goldman (1975:71).

9. Consider Sahlins' discussion of Hawaiian approaches to early trade with the West. "The Hawaiians had at first conceived of their practical transactions with Captain Cook on the model of sacrifice. Their initial gifts were small pigs, presented as offerings together with the banana plants, sugar cane and ritual formulas suitable on such occasions. Priests took the lead in these prestations at

Kauai in 1778. The episode in which the first Hawaiian on board the *Resolution* nonchalantly appropriated what came to hand had been preceded by the proper 'orations' chanted at the ship's side. . . . later Hawaiian traditions continued to picture their exchange with Cook as offerings of men to god" (Sahlins 1981a: 37–38).

10. It should be noted that the inalienable quality of goods associated with their circumstances of production is by no means limited to long-distance acquisition but can also be a highly important factor in some circumstances of exchange, including gift exchange and some usages of so-called primitive money (Csikszentmihalyi and Rochberg-Halton 1981:37–38; Griaule 1965:202).

11. It must be understood that from the perspective of northern hunters, bears are not ordinary wild food animals but are regarded as special emissaries from the outside spirit world with strong anthropomorphic qualities in their physical form and behavior; in fact, as shamanic humans masquerading as bears. Although ordinary hunting expresses appropriation of necessary outside resources, bear hunting, in my terms, constitutes acquisition of a uniquely valued good with inalienable qualities deriving from its origins as a very special animal spirit. See Ingold (1987:257–261).

12. "In practice," Ingold continues, "what happens at the end of the feast is that there are placed before the bear's head offerings of cooked food which are conceived as provisions for its journey. . . . Various objects, regarded as gifts, may also be placed on the head, carcass or skin: this presentation is sometimes known as 'dressing' the bear. Then, after a suitable time has elapsed, the head with its associated paraphernalia is carried out into the forest, perhaps in a specifically auspicious direction, and deposited on a raised platform or in the cleft trunk of a tree, safe from the depradations [*sic*] of dogs. And there it remains for posterity" (1987:259). See also the description of the Ainu bear ceremony by Ohnuki-Tierney (1974:90–96).

13. For this statement to hold it is also necessary to distinguish the concept of qualitatively neutral commoditized goods from the broader class of appropriated goods as understood by Ingold. Appropriated goods are not qualitatively neutral either. Ingold recognizes appropriation as a uniquely human behavior characterized by the fact that humans by definition cognize their environment in a manner unique to the species. (Other species in Ingold's terms do not appropriate but extract things from their environments.) Thus all goods obtained from such cognized environments would presumably partake of some of the qualities accorded that environment. The widespread application of ritual to appropriative activities in traditional society would seem to support the point.

14. Acquisition must precede distribution or exchange (see Chapter 8). Acquisition can also be effected within a given society in situations where the ultimate goal of a putative exchange transaction involves access to desired goods rather than recognition of social relations per se or when ostensible social relations are ma-

nipulated or exploited to acquire certain goods or serve the dual purpose of goods acquisition and expression of social relations at the same time, as Oliver points out for traditional Tahiti (1974:1088). The latter may be particularly characteristic of exchange activities at the inter-group or regional level (Gregory 1982:43).

15. Viewed historically, anthropological interest in acquisition has by no means been lacking, but in recent years acquisition per se seems to have been accorded less general interest than has been given to exchange and other forms of distribution as well as to production and consumption. Interest in acquisition has also varied according to ethnographic region. Areas where goods are traditionally accumulated for elaborate display have required that more scholarly attention be given to questions of how and why such displays are developed. But even here, interest in accumulation for display at home may be analytically somewhat separate from interest in acquisition of things from afar.

16. Compare the origins of conus shells among the Nyamwezi of East Africa as discussed in Chapter 7, note 6.

17. That the foreign trade and traders and access to their benefits were accorded cosmological significance is further evidenced by the fact that the Midewiwin Society had its own creation narratives, in one of which "the arrival of megis [cowie] 'looked as if a white man was loading a great big ship' . . . It was perhaps no coincidence that Mides constructed some of their special rattles from Hudson's Bay Company tobacco cans. . . ." (Vecsey 1983:183).

18. The argument has been made, again using New Guinea data, that trade in aesthetically valued (art-related) goods, for which there is constant demand, assures continued access to utilitarian goods whose demand may be more variable. Functional connections of this sort between art and economics are not necessarily challenged by the perspective developed here in which the aesthetics of acquired goods are valued for their own qualitative significance. However, interpretations arguing that traffic in art-related items exists primarily or entirely to facilitate access to utilitarian goods are challenged. See Anderson (1979:33–35) for further discussion.

19. An example of such readmission rituals is given in Gregory (1982:185, from Salisbury) in which Siane (New Guinea) laborers, who have been working on coastal plantations outside and who have accumulated goods to take home with them at the end of their work contract, are ritually readmitted and transformed, along with their goods, so as to fit once again into the properly socialized framework of the world within.

20. That is, specific goods are required for a given ceremony, or to complete a specific set of regalia, or to effect an exchange with a given partner at a given time and place.

21. Commercial trade being generalized, nonpersonalistic, secular, dealing with things (commodities) that are thoroughly self-contained, meaning thoroughly alienable, with profits as a goal and involving the ordinary people of the less-real

world to the extent that the concept of honor in the sense of *noblesse oblige* is not relevant to the undertaking (see Chapter 8).

CHAPTER 7

1. Shamanic trances also are believed to effect passages through sacralized space and time but in a state of pure spirituality that generally renders the physical manifestations of space and time static (while in trance the shaman lies in his hammock or sits motionless in the ceremonial house).

2. The sun itself may be regarded as simply taking the form of a horse. "The sun is not only the giver of light and warmth, but also the speedy and unwearied traveller who circles the world each day. . . . As the horse was the swiftest of terrestrial travellers, the sun was fittingly regarded as the courser of the heavens. Sometimes the sun-god was imagined as having the form of a horse" (O'Rahilly 1964:290–291).

3. It might be noted, too, that in myth, like early Irish lore, magical horses, like canoes or chariots or even shoes, can also be "crafted" by divine smiths or artificers (O'Rahilly 1964:525–526).

4. When heroes are credited with crafting the first animal-powered travel conveyances, they are also frequently credited with the creation of the animal itself, as seen in the magical horse mentioned above and the giant white sled dog mentioned here. These heroic creations can also be compared with the human skills of domestication that have provided ("transformed") horses, camels, dogs, and the like for travel and for other human uses.

5. See also Brown (1986:227) regarding the associations of the East Wind with the sun, travel conveyances, and the acquisition of desirable foreign goods in an Algonkian tale. Also Errington and Gewertz (1986:105) regarding a peripatetic Chambri ancestor who established fish-for-sago (see Gewertz 1980) barter markets throughout the Sepik region of New Guinea and traveled far and wide teaching the virtues of cultural interdependence among groups and the importance of importing outside power for the benefit of those at home.

6. Conus shells were an important part of Tanzanian chiefly regalia especially when making offerings to beneficent rain-making ancestors. Though obtained from the geographically distant east, conus shells, which carried solar associations, were said to derive from above, another example of a qualitative conjunction of horizontal with vertical distance. See Shorter (1972:99, 101–102, 129, 189).

7. See Lévi-Strauss (1978:135, 157–158, 182, 188–192, 456) and Campbell (1949: 134–136) regarding the catastrophic disorder that once occurred when the driver of the sun's chariot lost that vital control.

8. Alternatively, the magical services of less dangerous hippopotami could be engaged. "A hippo, it was said, would not only swim alongside the owner's boat on a trip to give him protection, but would also carry him on its back through

high waves and storms and even across whirlpools. Hippos were thought to be rather benign and did not have the frightening associations of crocodiles" (Harms 1981:202, 204).

9. Magical assistance or the protection and aid of ancestors and deities for good sailing is "deemed as essential as the purely technical side" of navigation and travel, and is common on water voyages, which hold many physical and spiritual perils. See also Harding (1967:25); Cochrane (1970:31); Williams (1932:146, 147). Tannenbaum (1987:696) discusses the magical protective powers of tattoos for travelers and traders.

10. See Helms (1988:111–113) and Brown (1947) regarding Hermes as god of distant things and experiences in general and as patron of those who delve into distance.

11. For examples see Benet (1957:196, 201); Revere (1957:52); Arnold (1957:166); Hasebroek (1933:128); Wilks (1975:287, 297); Henderson (1972:271); Shaw (1979:95). See also Brown (1947:34).

12. It is noteworthy, too, that Hermes was the god not only of trade and craftsmanship but also of the "boundary point" where transactions occurred, while the Celtic Mercury was patron not only of all arts and of journeys but also of "commercial affairs" (Brown 1947:38, 41; Rees and Rees 1961:143).

13. *Bori* dancers were definitely flawed creators, being prostitutes and unattached divorcees "who fell short of the Islamic ideal" (Spencer 1985:18).

14. See also Clendinnen (1987:149) for a graphic description of huge trade-related dances in Yucatan. Also consider in this context the Siassi dance-trade festivals discussed in Chapter 3.

15. A comparable expression of the moral necessity for order and control in potentially difficult situations of long-distance acquisition may also be seen in the formal presentations and sometimes delicate negotiation processes that officially transpire between traveler/traders and elites (or their representatives) as preliminaries to mutually agreeable acquisition; negotiations and formalities that again frequently irked and bemused impatient and businesslike European traders at the courts or compounds of traditional native rulers. See Roth (1968:135–136, 139); Toby (1984:185–193); Franke (1983:129–130); Hevia (1990). A more informal but just as delicately and gracefully (aesthetically) maneuvered exercise in foreign acquisition is described by Thomson in East Africa in the late nineteenth century (1881:236–237).

16. For the same reason flattery, essentially praising the aesthetic qualities of the other, may work comparable wonders (Munn 1983:284–285; Scoditti 1983:270).

17. There may be more to these circumstances than immediately meets the eye when correspondence is made between outside qualities of the bush and European foreigners as equally suitable final resting places for basically inalienable objects. See Küchler (1988:633 and 1987:240) for some further details.

18. The same pressure also caused tremendous intensification of the skills of

war and of slaving as means of tapping outside resources. See Feierman (1974:172, 177–179).

19. Stealth contrasts here with the boldness of open robbery with which Hermes, with his emphasis on mental skill and cunning, has little or nothing to do (Brown 1947:6–12).

20. Jane and Peter Schneider speak of the *casa civile* or "great house" of the large landowners and bosses of nineteenth-century rural Sicily: "The *casa civile* was distinctive in many ways. Made wholly or partially from cut stone, rather than rough stone and stucco, it was richly decorated and furnished with imports as well as the products of specially trained local craftsmen. In addition, it fulfilled what were considered to be requirements of civilized living, notwithstanding its location in a rural town. This meant that its many rooms were set off from one another according to function: separate sleeping quarters for male and female children, hosts and guests; and specialized rooms for toiletries, dining, ceremonial occasions, and managing the family's estate. The largest houses in Villamaura had ballrooms for dancing furnished with imported grand pianos, and one *palazzo* also contained a chapel" (1983:161–162).

21. See Chapter 3 and Helms (1988:94–110).

CHAPTER 8

1. See Kopytoff (1987:3–86 and passim) for detailed discussion of this phenomenon in Africa, where it has been particularly widespread; also Traube (1986:52–58); Sahlins (1981b).

2. In traditional society the infamy of retailing contrasts with the honorable act of large-scale wholesaling. As wholesalers, honorable persons are acting as mediators and transformers expressing the ideal of long-distance acquisition by standing at a critical junction between the outside and the social heartland where they may oversee the acquisition of beneficial things from afar for the greater good at home (Perimbam 1973:427; Konetzke 1953–1954:117–119; Pike 1972:21–34; Wheatley 1971:283–284).

3. See Gunther (1972:102, 126) regarding Haida chiefs who refused to trade with Europeans before the proper ceremonial formalities were conducted or who tried to change the preferred European system of trade because "They were too proud to become commercial."

4. Actually, foreign traders, like foreign artisans, can expect to be treated either with honor or with low esteem at royal courts. European traders of the Age of Discovery and succeeding centuries, for example, report both kinds of treatment at the hands of native elites. Sometimes they were received with honorable alacrity while at other times they had to wait a long while before presenting their credentials. They might be given very good living quarters or very bad accommodations. They might be treated with honor and courtesy or be regarded as exotic low status

curiosities and commanded to perform for the amusement of the court and royal family (Toby 1984:190, 193–195).

5. In addition to whatever other relational ties and qualities may be involved, distribution of acquired wealth within society also becomes a microcosm of the wider universe in which supernatural distributors (masters of the animals, beneficent deities) or powerful distant rulers distribute goods to society's acquisitional specialists, who in turn distribute things locally.

6. Similarly, those members of society who receive distributed goods and who may be perceived as indirect acquirers frequently receive (acquire) such rewards in recognition of notable activity and achievement.

7. Distribution may also be seen as a necessary precondition that opens the way for further acquisition by emptying the coffers of the acquirer and thereby making room for additional acquisition to occur. See Seguin (1986:483–484, 491 and passim).

8. Lévi-Strauss also notes, with reference to various myths, that distribution may be regarded as a necessary evil. "To this very day, mankind has always dreamed of seizing and fixing that fleeting moment when it was possible to believe that the law of exchange could be evaded, that one could gain without losing, enjoy without sharing. . . . [Paradise means] removing to an equally unattainable past or future the joys, eternally denied to social man, of a world in which one might keep to oneself (Lévi-Strauss 1969b:496–497; see also Taylor and Aragon 1991:116).

9. See Smith (1962:313); Snyder (1975, esp. 153–161).

10. Development of large-scale agricultural enterprises with slaves was also evidence of personal achievement due to one's hand (Bradbury 1973:140).

11. See Beattie (1971:142); Bushnell and Bushnell (1977:131); Balandier (1968: 54); Goldman (1940:353–354, 366); Vaughan (1970:151, 163).

12. The well-being indicated took the form of long life and success, especially in the "conceptually related activities of courtship, hunting, and warfare" (Hamell 1986–1987:77).

13. To house the collection of European artifacts the Asantehene Osei Tutu Kwame (1804–1823) built a large stone house (the *aban*) purportedly inspired by learning of the British Museum. See Stanley (1874 [reprinted 1971]:232–235) for a partial inventory of the Asantehene's treasure palace; also Wilks (1975:200–201). See also Sahlins (1990:49) and Bayly (1986:305) regarding the profusion of novelties in a court as a mark of great kingship.

14. Following death and burial, portions of the deceased's appropriated estate might be redistributed by the Asantehene to the heirs or to other personages in order to achieve still greater accumulation. "Thus the ethics of the cultural system were reinforced and replicated through successive generations" (McCaskie 1983:34).

15. See also Ogilvie (1969:42) for a particularly vivid discussion of the common practice of sacrifice or presenting offerings as a means of nourishing and sustaining godly or ancestral vitality.

16. In addition to burial or confiscation there are instances when accumulated wealth is simply allowed to rot. This process probably conceptually parallels burial (for example, Sahlins 1981a:31). Some forms of acquisition and distribution among the living, such as the Northwest Coast potlatch, are also conceptualized as involving ancestors (Kan 1986:198–200; also note 17).

17. Death is not always necessary to put this process into motion. The grandiose acquisition that preceded Northwest Coast potlatching also connoted ancestral connections and ancestor-like identification. The fame of the acquirer, which itself conveyed supernatural power, was equated with the quantity (mass and weight) of things accumulated. These were best represented after European contact by immense quantities of blankets or prior to European contact by animal skins that are described as constituting a veritable mountain of goods. Mountains, in turn, constituted a traditional access point to the heavens. In short, acquisition literally provided a way of reaching towards, contacting, and becoming like the ancestors (Goldman 1975:60).

18. Concern with appropriate type of goods can be paralleled with concern for appropriate type of behavior. Weeks, discussing the interpretation of art depicted in Old Kingdom Egyptian tombs, argues that attributes associated with the deceased (as depicted, for example, on relief scenes painted on tomb walls) related to the social or personal role that the deceased was expected to perform in the afterlife. Consequently, such qualities or behaviors were carefully selected from the range of attributes associated with his earthly, individual existence, some of which would have been excluded as irrelevant to his new task (1979:71–72).

19. Comments by Hall, speaking of early Cambodian states, are appropriate in this context: "Personal achievements in an individual's lifetime earned him ancestor status. Those who became prosperous thereby demonstrated that their contact with the ancestors was greater than that of others of their generation. Achievements and meritorious deeds were normally associated with superior spiritual prowess. Those with prowess were able to influence their fellow man's stature in this life as well as their hopes for recognition after death" (Hall 1985:305, note 12).

20. See Weiner (1985:223–234) regarding acquisition and accumulation as symbolic of group immortality.

21. Such wealth included slaves, who were often buried with an important chief or other man of wealth.

22. Another description of burial with vast amounts of cloth, similar to the observation mentioned by Harms, is given by Quiggin (1949:58). The association of quantities of cloth with ancestral deities themselves is also found among the Inka, where cloth also held tremendous political-ideological significance, being virtually synonymous with cosmic wealth and treasure. Golden statues of the Sun or Thunder, when publically displayed, were "smothered in feather blankets." In addition, "some representations of the Sun and Thunder were actually made of thick blankets, so tightly packed that the image could stand by itself" (Murra 1980:77). A comparable situation in which vast amounts of gold were buried with

kings in order that "the land will not be lacking in gold that will attract the [European] traders to come and trade with them" is discussed in Bhila (1982:137).

23. Following the same logic, offerings may be buried in the fields to ensure the soil's fertility. See, for example, Sutlive (1978:70–71).

24. Davenport, speaking of the great memorial celebrations of the Eastern Solomon Islands (Chapter 4), notes that the individuals for whose spirits these feasts are held were "notable achievers" during their lifetimes. By this celebration "These select few are elevated to the company of those spirits who control the destinies of the living" (1986:104).

CHAPTER 9

1. The ceremonial and political use and significance accorded long yams also seem to suit skillfully crafted goods rather than naturally endowed ones. See Roscoe (1989).

2. This means "the capacity to signal fairly complex social messages (as do pepper in cuisine, silk in dress, jewels in adornment, and relics in worship)" (Appadurai 1986:38).

3. Harding cautions, however, that ideas about wealth vary and no one criterion of wealth is considered more important than another by the Sio. For example, woven net bags, which require much labor and are used in social obligations but wear out quickly, are not considered wealth, but red ochre, which is consumed and doesn't require much labor to initially acquire, is considered wealth because it is highly valued (1967:73).

4. In considering all that labor—crafting—implies in traditional societies, in addition to the qualities of skilled crafting mentioned earlier, there is the related perspective that things are better if another person makes them, in which the inalienable qualities of human-made goods, the personal magical potency imputed by artisans to the things they make, are expressed in a sociological as well as political-ideological sense (McCarthy 1939:172). See, for example, note 20. See also Labby (1976) regarding the concept of ancestors' labor as a valued quality in human endeavors.

5. Slaves were products of the sea since they arrived, as war captives, by canoe. Concerning tree bark as skin and skins in general, "The skin is the animal's essential attribute from which, however, it is separable, in the way in which soul separates from body. When in myth, animals give their skins to humans they offer with them their characteristic animal qualities" (Goldman 1975:125, 4).

6. Navel-city refers to the political center or capital of the state as the ultimate focus of the polity's activities (Errington 1983:200; 1989:33).

7. The fact that skilled hunting shares characteristics of both skilled crafting and long-distance acquisition and may be seen as comparable to both these activities further supports the validity of attempting to seek commonalities between long-distance acquisition and skilled crafting, as this essay tries to do.

8. See also Goldman 1975:43; Ingold 1987:248–249; Ridington 1988:99;

McNaughton 1982:54–56; Lévi-Strauss 1978:296–297; Segal 1982:33; Adkins 1985:286.

9. See Ingold 1987:152–153; Glaze 1981:43; Gubser 1965:29; Gregory 1982:45; Anderson 1985:22.

10. See Walens 1982:183; McNaughton 1982:54–56; Godelier 1986:97, 176; Roberts 1970:68; Hendricks 1988:221.

11. See Feit 1986:178–180; Anderson 1985:22, 30, 80; Goldman 1940:370; Rosengren 1987:27, 33; Hanaway 1971:27; Goldman 1975:52; Errington 1984:155–156; Heusch 1982:22.

12. For example, flawed hunters may become royal executioners (Maquet 1970:95–96, 113; Lewis 1970:183–184; Lewis 1962:381). Skilled hunters who are highly regarded also may be associated with rulership as prestigeful agents of the king (Roth 1968:144, 145).

13. *Dalilu* is described as a "program of action" for achieving a given goal, often involving ritual and supernaturally potent ingredients (McNaughton 1982:56).

14. See also Maquet (1970:95–96) regarding the Twa first as hunters and then, as game became scarce, potters; Stenning (1960:150–151) regarding the Iru as royal artisans (carvers, smiths, musicians), hunters, diviners and "doctors" among the Nyankole; Finnegan (1970:112) regarding the Yoruba deity Ogun, "god of iron," "worshipped particularly by warriors, hunters, and blacksmiths."

15. Another important area of conjunction between hunting and skilled crafting is found in those situations where successful mastery of the supernatural aspect of hunting "technology" requires knowledge and production of select crafted items, such as songs, dances, and paraphernalia (Hendricks 1988:221; Walens 1982:183). Consider, too, the link between the hunter and the smith who crafts his spears (Himmelheber 1963:97–98).

16. In Northwest Coast society, after European contact, Hudson's Bay blankets came to tangibly express the wealth that now was centered on the world of Europeans rather than on the traditional world of animals. Europeans now provided provisions as animals had before; consequently, blankets came to represent the unconsumed and durable manifestation of the consumable material goods that Europeans provided for people. Blankets as a kind of covering (Gunther 1972:9, 14, 29, 104) could constitute an outer "skin" of the Europeans that was separable from them as animal skins were separable from animals or tree bark from trees. As such, blankets may have been thought to contain the essential attributes or qualities of Europeans as animal skins did for animals. As the elite hunter with a mountain goat skin had power to catch other mountain goats, so those chiefs who had acquired Hudson's Bay blankets evidenced power to continue to acquire goods from Europeans.

17. See also Kuper (1973) for an example of continued emphasis on traditional use of leather and naturally endowed things even after foreign textiles became available.

18. In such societies ranking may be expressed by gradations of type of fabric

or mode of costume construction such that the king may wear fine sewn or tailored cloth, elites wear costumes of fine fabrics (silk, brocade) but made of only one piece of cloth, and commoners wear cotton or skins. Alternatively the king may be distinguished from other great lords by wearing fine mantles of cotton embroidered with multi-colored design and featherwork, while the common soldier wears only the simplest mantle without special designs and commoners, on pain of death, wear garments of maguey fiber (Bray 1978: 389–390; Hunwick 1980: 425; Anon. 1981: 147; Levtzion 1973: 109; Bayly 1986: 296; Kuper 1973: 351).

19. Concerning investment of labor as imbuing with aesthetic quality, Clark relates that academic robes worn by H.R.H. Prince Philip as Chancellor of the University of Cambridge took about 120 working hours to cut and hand sew. The elaborate gold ornamentation and designs worked into the robes required 320–350 working hours to complete (Clark 1986: 109).

20. "Nor do they Call any thing a present which Nature produces, except accompanied by something which is procured by the Assistance of labour or the Art of Man; for which reason they always give Cloth or some thing else with their Gifts, Provisions being held of No value being produced by Nature . . ." (Morrison quoted in Oliver 1974: 587 and 346 regarding Tahiti). The distinction here is between crafted goods and subsistence items.

21. See Appadurai (1986: 52) regarding foreign European goods as seemingly magically produced; also Guy (n.d.: 3) regarding kingly attire that was believed to be magically woven by beings in a jar in the middle of the ocean.

22. Red cloth and red harness were also very appropriate to the traditional color-coding of the Indian warrior classes (Bayly 1986: 304).

23. Similarly, "Certain trade goods were selected and valued because they were a visible demonstration of the power of ancestral order to incorporate an alien and potentially hostile world and subvert it to serve its own purpose" (Rowlands 1987: 61 regarding chiefdoms of Cameroon, west-central Africa).

CHAPTER 10

1. Other tangible expressions of such creative transformation include curing illness, controlling weather, and enhancing agricultural and human fertility.

2. For examples see Lamphear (1970: 84); Alpers (1969: 409); Oswalt (1979: 213); Goldman (1940: 383 and 1975: 52–53).

3. Ethnographic examples are particularly numerous for Africa. For a selection see Shorter (1972: 243–244); Heusch (1982: 165); Bhila (1982: 11–12); Fairley (1987: 95–96); Feierman (1974: Chapter 2); Thompson (1974: 49); Gilbert (1987: 325); Rowlands (1987: 57).

4. Salomon (1986: 83); d'Azevedo (1975: 12); Tosh (1970: 117); Balandier (1968: 101); Roscoe (1911: 412); Hartwig (1976: 69). The benefits to be gained from trading ivory in some of these examples should not be allowed to obscure the symbolic significance of hunting per se.

5. Cieza de León (1959:104–105); Hillenbrand (1988:25 and previous pages); Hanaway (1969:22); Anderson (1985:63–67); Oppenheim (1977:193); Nelson (1987: 169–170).

6. "Far" in geographical terms may vary greatly cross-culturally. Such distances are always culturally defined and culturally specific. Not infrequently, distances are measured by length of time taken by a particular type of traveler traveling in a particular manner to traverse a particular distance rather than by standardized measures of distance. See Hastrup (1985:58) for an illustrative description of how distance was measured in medieval Scandinavia.

7. "The ruling elite in India and elsewhere, who were accustomed to derive their main income from an agrarian base, saw the sea as a object of diversion and a highway through which travelled the good things of life" such as delicacies from the Middle East. When the seventeenth-century Mughal emperor, Jahangir, visited the maritime province of Gujarat, "it was to hunt wild elephants and to 'look on the salt sea'" (Chandhuri 1985:123). The significance of the diversionary nature of the sea may be considered comparable to the symbolism contained in hunting as kingly sport.

8. A Kwakiutl chief stands to speak, takes up his chief's mask, and holds the dark mask over his head. "Then he becomes Dzunukwa, shouting . . . the paralyzing cry of the wealth-and-power-giver, dark monster of the forest" (Holm 1983:157). Other transformative masks linked their human owners with the chief of the undersea world, source of copper and other treasures and wealth (ibid.:162).

9. See Northrup 1978:144; Oswalt 1979:213–214; Alpers 1969:409–410; Lamphear 1970:89–90; Harms 1981:145–146.

10. See Whittaker 1983:163, 167; Duby 1974:60, 100, 105, 151, 243.

11. See Hartwig 1976:71, 82; Perinbam 1973:427–428; Mouser 1980:501; Hall 1985:54; Oberg 1973:87; Goldman 1940:353; Hartwig 1976:167; Sundström 1974:64.

12. See Salomon 1986:105, 115, 141–142; Wilks 1975:436, 469, 691; Dumett 1979: 58; Sundström 1974:64–65.

13. See Pearson 1976:17; Jablow 1966:35; Levtzion 1973:163; Adamu 1978:45; Cunnison 1961:71; Northrup 1978:96–97; Hartwig 1976:82.

14. As Duby notes, this preoccupation in itself might lead the historian or anthropologist to attribute a disproportionate royal role to economic trade per se.

15. See Bhila 1982:75, 81, 134–135, 209; Harms 1981:73; Duby 1974:251; Rowlands 1987:62; Hall 1985:99; Geertz 1980:87.

16. See Roberts 1970:70; Law 1978:45–48, 255; Hilbert 1982:58, 62–63; Bhila 1982:203; Abrahams 1967:38; Stein 1965:51; Hastrup 1985:226.

17. *Sharifs* were persons claiming descent from the Prophet Muhammad. See Sundman (n.d.:12); Duby (1974:52); McCaskie (1983:28); Bayly (1986:300–301, 305–306); Appadurai (1986:44); Csikszentmihalyi and Rochberg-Halton (1981:48).

18. The search for goods from afar and the accumulation of wealth that will

perpetuate the temporal era of a ruler and assure the continued social reproduction of society are paralleled both in myth and in real life by spatial travels in search of wives "with the aim of perpetuating the species, that is, of ensuring the periodicity of the generations which, in the final analysis, is measured by the *span* of human life" (Lévi-Strauss 1978:171).

19. "'Big men' were credited with the ability to control the dead. . . . Assistance was obtained from the dead as a result of the 'big man's' exclusive knowledge. . . . In this way the 'big men' were able to ensure garden fertility and successful trading voyages'" (Cochrane 1970:15–16).

20. Rich regalia also can establish the identity and thus the effectiveness of images of deities: "The identity of the image, which alone guaranteed its functioning as adequate manifestation of the deity, seems to have been established less by means of facial expression than by the details of paraphernalia and divine attire" (Oppenheim 1977:185).

21. The "sheer ideal" is reflected in the effect that costume has upon us all. As Bell notes: "Clothes generalize the shape of the body, reduce it to a more geometrical form and suggest a classical perfection of outline which is rare in nature, and this is eminently a property of many forms of sumptuous dress" (1949:33).

CHAPTER II

1. For additional examples and discussion see Balandier (1970:106 and Chapter 5); Gilbert (1989:66–68); Beidelman (1983:33).

2. I prefer for the moment not to associate either political-cosmological format with particular levels of sociocultural complexity since the data suggest that both models are found, or at least clearly prefigured, in both centralized and noncentralized polities. See Tambiah (1977:69).

3. Tambiah's concept of the "galactic polity" (1977) is comparable in many respects to perspectives considered here. Tambiah also makes the point with regard to these political structures that "there are no *prima facie* grounds for explaining their manifestation as immediate and *direct* projections of ecological considerations or the logistical constraints of sociopolitical organization. The logic of their use cannot be reduced to a simple causal explanation" (1977:70–71). Rather, the organizational pattern elucidated "certain key indigenous concepts" in a number of economically, socially, and politically significant structural and spatial arrangements (ibid.:73–74, 91).

4. This identification is commonly found in the literature, usually in descriptions of so-called raw materials received from afar being exchanged for crafted or manufactured goods.

5. Cecelia Klein has documented that in post-classic Mexican cosmography the direction of south (frequently associated with west), which would also be the main direction taken by pochteca leaving the Aztec heartland, was symbolically associ-

ated with the earth, with midnight and darkness, with death and the underworld. In contrast, north (frequently allied with east), which would correspond to the direction by which returning pochteca re-entered the Mexican heartland, was associated with high noon, with the sky, with life and light, and with wisdom (Klein 1975:72, 79, 80, 82; Brotherston 1976; León-Portilla 1963:31).

6. Compare the collecting passions of Asante and of Mughal Indian monarchs described in Chapters 8 and 9, respectively. See also Schafer (1963).

7. As many authors have pointed out, this ideological perspective also usefully legitimizes more overt political controls. But it is misleading to view the ideological component entirely as a cover for subjugation. The moralistic and epitomizing principles and precepts involved in traditional political worlds were regarded as valuable and legitimate, as well as legitimating, goals in their own right. They stood as one of several possible means for dealing with "international relations" (Jing-shen 1983:81).

8. This thought was clearly expressed by the Asante monarch, Osei Bonsu, explaining why visiting traders to his capital should not be taxed as a revenue source. "I cannot tell them to give me gold, when they buy and sell the goods . . . but I must give them gold and provisions, and send them home happy and rich, that it may be known in other countries that I am great king, and know what is right" (Dupuis, quoted in Wilks 1971:133).

9. Some of which, to be sure, could be used for further purposes of trade within and without the empire (e.g. Farquhar 1957:64–65). The significance and value of these gifts to the foreign recipients, which is frequently interpreted in terms of the apparent assimilation of these peripheral groups into the orbit of the center, must be understood within the context of their own cosmological views concerning the meaning of valued goods acquired from a powerful outside realm. Discussion of this perspective falls within the purview of the second type of acquisitional system under discussion in the following chapter.

10. See Schafer 1963 and 1967; also Helms (1988:124–126) for summary of the exotic qualities attributed to imports from the far frontiers of the Chinese world-order and for additional references.

11. See also Schafer (1967:95–99) regarding ancient Chinese conqueror-heroes and benefactors of the southern frontier who after death were both deified and gradually correlated with local tribal hero-gods and group ancestors. This practice indicates a similar conjunction and common identification from the barbaric point of view between ancestral deities of the center (the Chinese) and those of the native or outside realms. See Chapter 12.

12. "A structural analysis of the Tlingit model of the world . . . revealed the centrality of the 'inside'/'outside' opposition. The 'inside' was usually positively marked and associated with the Tlingit people, the village, the warmth of the fire, dryness, abundance of food, and so forth. The 'outside' was associated with the non-Tlingit, the dangerous domains of the forest and the sea, cold, wetness, fam-

ine, and so on. The Tlingit had to venture into the 'outside' to obtain wealth and superhuman power, but preferred to return to the safety of the 'inside' (Kan 1986:209 note 13).

13. See also the Eskimo ceremony for the dead summarized in Chapter 10.

14. Generally comparable relationships between outsiders and the ancestral line of the home group may have also underwritten the seemingly curious fact that in the traditional Chinese bureaucracy the important Hung-lu Office "was responsible both for the funerals of members of the imperial family and for the reception and entertainment of foreign guests" (Schafer 1963:26).

15. See Hammell (1986–1987) concerning European goods as naturally endowed and for discussion of correlations between European goods and certain native expressions of natural powers.

16. Also significant here is evidence that, if Huron men married Algonkian wives, the couple lived in Huron country. Nor would any Huron woman consent to live among the Algonkians (Trigger 1976:65). Some of these marriages may have resulted from the practice of trading partners exchanging children as a gesture of good will-cum-hostage (Trigger 1969:39–40).

17. The Huron were also busily engaged with Iroquoian tribes to the south and west and obtained a range of items from their outside contacts overall. Included were tobacco, black squirrel skins, raccoon skin robes, various shells, native copper, buffalo robes. Though these items are generally termed luxury goods in the literature, it is my supposition that the Huron regarded most of them as primarily naturally endowed items (see Trigger 1976: Chapter 2).

18. When they attended Algonkian feasts the Huron also brought their own food, seemingly a tribal form of Lévi-Straussian comment on the uncultured state of the Algonkians.

19. See also Harding (1967) regarding the Siassi. Other New Guinea "centers of cultural florescence—centers whose cultural and symbolic productions appear to be considered intrinsically superior, resulting in their export to a culturally dependent periphery" are the Iatmul and the Abelam (Roscoe 1989:227).

20. See also Turnbull (1965:Chapters 3 and 6) regarding Bantu villagers incorporation of forest pygmies into villagers' boys' initiation ceremonies in order to extend the sanctions of village ancestors to pygmy providers.

21. The essential question in this and similar cases asks whether the Murik are exchanging goods to express relationships with Islanders or whether they are acquiring goods desired for their own qualities via the mechanism of kinship symbols. The former perspective views the Murik and the Islanders as comparable forms of humanness within the same cultural system, while the latter recognizes that significant qualitative distinctions may be felt at least by the Murik between themselves and Islanders as outsiders.

22. In New Guinea the symbolism of pigs as ultimate wealth items and as major ceremonial items acquired from the outside could be pursued along this line, par-

ticularly in the sense that pigs may constitute substitutes for outside "people" in attendance at the important initiation feasts that constitute legitimation of the moral ancestral order and modes of social reproduction at the center. See Roscoe (1989:223–225); Healey (1985).

23. Yapese ritual specialists have power to "increase food crops and fish, stop epidemics, ward off typhoons, make rain, promote the fertility of women, and kill off pestilences of ants" (Lessa 1950:46).

24. See Harrison (1987) for description of a comparable chain of superordinate centers and outer realms in New Guinea.

CHAPTER 12

1. For example, Rassers identifies the Javanese smithy, a point of creative crafting, as conceptually constituting a type of primitive temple or a "sky-tree" (kayon), all of which are places of contact between cosmological realms (1959: 223–224, 244).

2. For example, Wilbert (1979:145–146), Turner (1972:226, 229–230).

3. This regalia probably is symbolically comparable to the splendor of the sun and full moon obtained by mythical ancestors on an earlier excursion to the east.

4. "Alternatively, he said, people thought that perhaps people in distant places obtained them, like stone axes, from quarries" (ibid.). The first Europeans in the area were thought initially to be sky people.

5. Since building is one of the major expressions of such crafting, note also the Yao imitation of coastal Arab village forms and customs, including dress, mannerisms, architectural style, boats, and coastal flora, described in Chapter 2.

6. In considering the significance of things acquired from a distance, whether they be naturally endowed or skillfully crafted, it is quite possible that the distinctive qualitative characteristics of the acquisitional endeavor are evidenced by a relatively few categories of selected items—by fine textiles, for example, or carved stools or shells or slender piglets or long yams; items that constitute symbolically key resources identifying the overall nature of the outside-inside association. Other products may also be obtained that are not valued quite as highly or in quite the same manner, though they may be expected to convey the general sense of the association (see Schneider 1978; Roscoe 1989).

7. The difficulty here, of course, lies in the probability that the earthly leadership of the superordinate center-out-there has its own interpretation of the significance and usefulness of the acquisitional frontier polity which constitutes part of its own cosmographical outside realm.

8. It is noteworthy that, in traditional Africa, as elsewhere, military strength and success are frequently interpreted as evidence of spiritual superiority, too.

9. The stool was in Asante appreciation of the assistance in war of spiritually powerful Banda charms.

10. Another example of the overwhelming importance for political legitimacy at home of association with symbols and encapsulations of temporally/spatially distant places and personages is found in the conflicts and controversies among descent groups of middle Sepik River polities over who "owned" such things as the river, the sun, the east wind, lightning, and architectural components of certain cult houses (Harrison 1987:495). Harrison then notes that "This highly disputatious concern with symbolic privileges has continued well into the modern period. Some years ago, for instance, one of the subclans in the Manambu village of Avatip laid claim to European clothes as a totem, on the basis of a purported mythological link with their colonial administrators; and this bid for prestige provoked its main political rival, the subclan Sarak, to claim totemic ownership of the Queen" (ibid.).

11. The acquisitive activities of groups like the Manam, who appear to obtain created paraphernalia from a symbolically significant region rather than from a designated central place, may well prefigure more sharply delineated acquisitional situations.

12. See Fairbank (1968); Farquhar (1957); Rossabi (1983); Hevia (1990); Toby (1984); Lopez (1945) for excellent accounts of such maneuverings among the diverse polities involved in various world orders of the traditional Far East and of the Byzantine empire; also Schafer (1967:61–69) regarding more forceful insurrections by groups on the southern frontier of China. On a smaller scale, Turnbull provides an insightful discussion of comparable relationships between Mbuti pygmies and Bantu agricultural villagers (1965, esp. 63–70; see also Grinker 1990). The role of Egypt vis-à-vis outlying peoples in the ancient Mediterranean world as discussed by Bernal (1987) may have been comparable.

13. A system-wide functional unity may appear to be strongly evidenced in such associations by the fact that shared languages, pseudo kinship terms, and even occasional intermarriages may be found between superordinate centers and adjacent polities. Full consideration of this point warrants separate study in itself. Suffice it to say here that, as we have seen, acceptance of a superordinate center's language by an acquiring heartland is usually in the form of a second language, not a replacement of mother tongue. Similarly, extension of kin terms or initiation rites, like second languages, signifies modes or methods of conducting particular acquisitive activities and intents that are separate and distinct from the operation of the indigenous kinship systems of both groups (see Grinker 1990:112–113). Intermarriage in particular would seem to support a mutually understood system, but it is necessary to separate the personal acts and intents of specific individuals from the alliances of entire groups. Marriage in such circumstances, like language or pseudo kin terms, provides channels for attainment of desired personal goals more than it creates ties between groups. In the case of the Bella Coola and Carrier, for example, intermarriage between a few Bella Coola women and a few Carrier men basically provided a few Bella Coola fathers-in-law with means to acquire valued furs and a few unusually successful Carrier men with enhanced political status and influential outside ties (Goldman 1940:342–344).

14. Net hammocks may well have been regarded as natural products in the same sense as reed mats in the Inca world order (Chapter 9).

CHAPTER 13

1. The particulars of each case, of course, are further shaped by economic, social, and political history.

2. Though not considered here, raid and warfare may be added to this list.

References

ABIR, M.
  1970   Southern Ethiopia. In *Pre-Colonial African Trade,* edited by Richard
          Gray and David Birmingham, pp. 119–138. London: Oxford University
          Press.

ABRAHAMS, R. G.
  1967   *The Political Organization of Unyamwezi.* London: Cambridge Univer-
          sity Press.

ABRAMSON, J. A.
  1976   Style Change in an Upper Sepik Contact Situation. In *Ethnic and Tourist
          Arts: Cultural Expressions from the Fourth World,* edited by Nelson H. H.
          Graburn, pp. 249–265. Berkeley: University of California Press.

ADAMU, MAHDI
  1978   *The Hausa Factor in West African History.* Ibadan: Oxford University
          Press Nigeria.

ADDISON, JULIA DE WOLF
  1908   *Arts and Crafts in the Middle Ages.* Boston: Page Co.

ADKINS, ARTHUR W. H.
  1985   Ethics and the Breakdown of the Cosmogony in Ancient Greece. In
          Comogony and Ethical Order, edited by Robin W. Lovin and Frank E.
          Reynolds, pp. 279–309. Chicago: University of Chicago Press.

AIJMER, GÖRAN
  1979   Reconciling Power with Authority: An Aspect of Statecraft in Tradi-
          tional Laos. *Man* n.s. 14:734–749.
  1984a   Ostentation: I, Dominance Represented by Inspectable, Indexical Ac-
          tion. Department of Social Anthropology, University of Gothenburg.
          Semantics of Political Processes, Interim Report No. 23.

1984b   Ostentation: II, Objects. Department of Social Anthropology, University of Gothenburg. Semantics of Political Processes, Interim Report No. 24.

n.d.   Musings on Distribution. Department of Social Anthropology, University of Gothenburg. Semantics of Political Processes, Interim Report No. 4.

ALKIRE, WILLIAM H.

1965   *Lamotrek Atoll and Inter-Island Socioeconomic Ties*. Urbana: University of Illinois Press.

ALPERS, EDWARD A.

1969   Trade, State, and Society among the Yao in the Nineteenth Century. *Journal of African History* 10:405–420.

1975   *Ivory and Slaves*. Berkeley: University of California Press.

AMES, DAVID W.

1973   A Sociocultural View of Hausa Musical Activity. In *The Traditional Artist in African Societies,* edited by Warren L. d'Azevedo, pp. 128–161. Bloomington: Indiana University Press.

1973   Igbo and Hausa Musicians: A Comparative Examination. *Ethnomusicology* 17:250–278.

ANDERSON, BENEDICT R. O'G.

1972   The Idea of Power in Javanese Culture. In *Culture and Politics in Indonesia,* edited by Claire Holt, pp. 1–69. Ithaca: Cornell University Press.

ANDERSON, J. K.

1985   *Hunting in the Ancient World*. Berkeley: University of California Press.

ANDERSON, LOIS ANN

1971   The Interrelation of African and Arab Musics: Some Preliminary Considerations. In *Essays on Music and History in Africa,* edited by Klaus P. Wachsmann, pp. 143–170. Evanston: Northwestern University Press.

ANDERSON, RICHARD L.

1979   *Art in Primitive Societies*. Englewood Cliffs, N.J.: Prentice-Hall, Inc.

1990   *Calliope's Sisters*. Englewood Cliffs, N.J.: Prentice-Hall, Inc.

ANDREWS, ANTHONY P.

1983   *Maya Salt Production and Trade*. Tucson: The University of Arizona Press.

ANONYMOUS

1981   Kitab al-Istibsar fi ajaib al-amsar. In *Corpus of Early Arabic Sources for West African History,* edited by N. Levtzion and J. F. P. Hopkins, pp. 138–151. Cambridge: Cambridge University Press.

APPADURAI, ARJUN

1986   Introduction: Commodities and the Politics of Value. In *The Secret Life of Things,* edited by Arjun Appadurai, pp. 3–63. Cambridge: Cambridge University Press.

ARHIN, KWAME
1970   Aspects of the Ashanti Northern Trade in the Nineteenth Century. *Africa* 40:363–373.

ARISTOTLE
1962   *The Politics of Aristotle.* Translated by Ernest Barker. New York: Oxford University Press.

ARMSTRONG, ROBERT G.
1980   The Dynamics and Symbolism of Idoma Kingship. In *West African Culture Dynamics,* edited by B. K. Swartz, Jr. and Raymond Dumett, pp. 393–412. The Hague: Mouton Publishers.

ARNOLD, ROSEMARY
1957   A Port of Trade: Whydah on the Guinea Coast. In *Trade and Market in the Early Empires,* edited by Karl Polanyi, Conrad Arensberg, Harry Pearson, pp. 154–176. Glencoe, Ill.: The Free Press.

ATTENBOROUGH, DAVID
1976   *The Tribal Eye.* New York: W. W. Norton & Co.

AUSTIN, M. M., AND P. VIDAL-NAQUET
1977   *Economic and Social History of Ancient Greece: An Introduction.* Berkeley: University of California Press.

AYRTON, MICHAEL
1967   *The Maze Maker.* New York: Holt, Rinehart & Winston.

BALANDIER, GEORGES
1968   *Daily Life in the Kingdom of the Kongo.* George Allen & Unwin. New York: Pantheon Books, Random House.
1970   *Political Anthropology.* New York: Pantheon Books, Random House.

BANKOLE, AYO, JUDITH BUSH, AND SADEK H. SAMAAN
1975   The Yoruba Master Drummer. *African Arts* 8:48–56, 77–78.

BARNES, GINA L.
1987   The Role of the *be* in the Formation of the Yamato State. In *Specialization, Exchange, and Complex Societies,* edited by Elizabeth M. Brumfiel and Timothy K. Earle, pp. 86–101. Cambridge: Cambridge University Press.

BARTH, FREDRICK
1966   *Models of Social Organization.* Royal Anthropological Institute of Great Britain and Ireland.

BASSO, ELLEN B.
1973   *The Kalapalo Indians of Central Brazil.* New York: Holt, Rinehart & Winston.

BAYLY, C. A.
1986   The Origins of Swadeshi (Home Industry): Cloth and Indian Society, 1700–1930. In *The Social Life of Things,* edited by Arjun Appadurai, pp. 285–322. Cambridge: Cambridge University Press.

BEATTIE, JOHN

1971   *The Nyoro State.* Oxford: Clarendon Press.

BEIDELMAN, THOMAS O.

1983   *The Kaguru: A Matrilineal People of East Africa.* Prospect Heights, Ill.: Waveland Press (Reissue of 1971 edition).

BELL, QUENTIN

1949   *On Human Finery.* New York: A. A. Wyn, Inc.

BEN-AMOS, PAULA

1975   Professionals and Amateurs in Benin Court Carving. In *African Images,* edited by Daniel McCall and Edna Bay, pp. 170–189. New York: Africana Publishing Co.

1976   "A La Recherche du Temps Perdu": On Being an Ebony-Carver in Benin. In *Ethnic and Tourist Arts,* edited by Nelson H. H. Graburn, pp. 320–333. Berkeley: University of California Press.

BENET, FRANCISCO

1957   Explosive Markets: The Berber Highlands. In *Trade and Market in the Early Empires,* edited by Karl Polanyi, Conrad Arensberg, Harry Pearson, pp. 188–217. Glencoe, Ill.: The Free Press.

BERNAL, IGNACIO

1969   Individual Artistic Creativity in Pre-Columbian Mexico. In *Tradition and Creativity in Tribal Art,* edited by Daniel P. Biebuyck, pp. 71–83. Berkeley: University of California Press.

BERNAL, MARTIN

1987   *Black Athena: The Afroasiatic Roots of Classical Civilization.* vol. 1: *The Fabrication of Ancient Greece 1785–1985.* New Brunswick, N.J.: Rutgers University Press.

BERNDT, RONALD M.

1952   A Cargo Movement in the Eastern Central Highlands of New Guinea. *Oceania* 23:40–65.

1971   Some Methodological Considerations in the Study of Australian Aboriginal Art. In *Art and Aesthetics in Primitive Societies,* edited by Carol F. Jopling, pp. 99–126. New York: E. P. Dutton & Co.

BEST, ELSDON

1924   *The Maori.* vols. 1 and 2. Memoirs of the Polynesian Society, vol. 5. Wellington, New Zealand: Printed by Harry H. Tombs.

BHILA, H. H. K.

1982   *Trade and Politics in a Shona Kingdom.* Burnt Mill, Harlow, Essex: Longman.

BIEBUYCK, DANIEL

1969   Introduction. In *Tradition and Creativity in Tribal Art,* edited by Daniel P. Biebuyck, pp. 1–23. Berkeley: University of California Press.

1972   The *Kindi* Aristocrats and their Art among the Lega. In *African Art and*

Leadership, edited by Douglas Fraser and Herbert Cole, pp. 7–20. Madison: The University of Wisconsin Press.

BIERNOFF, DAVID

1978   Safe and Dangerous Places. In *Australian Aboriginal Concepts,* edited by L. R. Hiatt, pp. 93–105. New Jersey: Humanities Press.

BIRD, CHARLES S., AND MARTHA B. KENDALL

1980   The Mande Hero. In *Explorations in African Systems of Thought,* edited by Ivan Karp and Charles S. Bird, pp. 13–26. Bloomington: Indiana University Press.

BLOCH, MAURICE

1974   Symbols, Song, Dance and Features of Articulation *or* Is Religion an Extreme Form of Traditional Authority? *Archives Européennes de Sociologie* 15:55–81.

BOVILL, E. W.

1970   *The Golden Trade of the Moors.* 2nd ed. London: Oxford University Press.

BRADBURY, R. E.

1973   *Benin Studies.* London: Oxford University Press.

BRAVMANN, RENÉ A.

1972   The Diffusion of Ashanti Political Art. In *African Art and Leadership,* edited by D. Fraser and H. M. Cole, pp. 153–172. Madison: University of Wisconsin Press.

BRAY, WARWICK

1978   Civilizing the Aztecs. In *The Evolution of Social Systems,* edited by J. Friedman and M. J. Rowlands, pp. 373–400. Pittsburgh: University of Pittsburgh Press.

BROTHERSTON, GORDON

1976   Mesoamerican Description of Space II: Signs for Direction. *Ibero-Amerikanisches Archiv* n.s. 2:39–62.

BROWN, JENNIFER S. H.

1986   Northern Algonquians from Lake Superior and Hudson Bay to Manitoba in the Historical Period. In *Native Peoples: The Canadian Experience,* edited by R. Bruce Morrison and C. Roderick Wilson, pp. 208–236. Toronto: McClelland & Stewart Ltd.

BROWN, NORMAN O.

1947   *Hermes the Thief: The Evolution of a Myth.* New York: Vintage Books.

BRUMFIEL, ELIZABETH M.

1987   Elite and Utilitarian Crafts in the Aztec State. In *Specialization, Exchange, and Complex Societies,* edited by Elizabeth Brumfiel and Timothy Earle, pp. 102–118. Cambridge: Cambridge University Press.

BRUMFIEL, ELIZABETH M., AND TIMOTHY K. EARLE

1987   Specialization, Exchange, and Complex Societies: An Introduction. In *Specialization, Exchange, and Complex Societies,* edited by Elizabeth Brumfiel and Timothy Earle, pp. 1–9. Cambridge: Cambridge University Press.

BUCK, PETER H. (TE RANGI HIROA)

1934   *Mangaian Society.* Bernice P. Bishop Museum, Bull. 122. Honolulu: Bernice P. Bishop Museum.

1966   *The Coming of the Maori.* Wellington: Whitcombe and Tombs, Ltd.

BURCKHARDT, TITUS

1987   *Mirror of the Intellect.* Translated and edited by William Stoddart. Albany: State University of New York Press.

BUSHNELL, JOHN, AND DONNA BUSHNELL

1977   Wealth, Work, and World View in Native Northwest California: Sacred Significance and Psychoanalytic Symbolism. In *Flowers of the Wind,* edited by Thomas Blackburn, pp. 120–182. Socorro, New Mexico: Ballena Press.

CAMPBELL, ALAN T.

1989   *To Square with Genesis.* Iowa City: University of Iowa Press.

CAMPBELL, JOSEPH

1949   *The Hero with a Thousand Faces.* New York: Pantheon Books.

CANNADINE, DAVID

1987   Introduction: Divine Rites of Kings. In *Rituals of Royalty,* edited by David Cannadine and Simon Price, pp. 1–19. Cambridge: Cambridge University Press.

CARMACK, ROBERT M.

1976   Ethnohistory of the Central Quiché: The Community of Utatlan. In *Archaeology and Ethnohistory of the Central Quiché,* edited by Dwight T. Wallace and Robert M. Carmack, pp. 1–19. Institute for Mesoamerican Studies, State University of New York at Albany, Publication No. 1.

CARPENTER, EDMUND

1971   The Eskimo Artist. In *Anthropology and Art,* edited by Charlotte M. Otten, pp. 163–171. Garden City, New York: The Natural History Press.

CARTIER, MICHEL

1982   Barbarians Through Chinese Eyes: The Emergence of an Anthropological Approach to Ethnic Differences. *The Comparative Civilizations Review* 6:1–14.

CASSON, LIONEL

1984   *Ancient Trade and Society.* Detroit: Wayne State University Press.

CELLINI, BENVENUTO

1927   *The Life of Benvenuto Cellini.* Translated by John A. Symonds. New York: Charles Scribner's Sons.

CHANG, K. C.

1974   Urbanism and the King in Ancient China. *World Archaeology* 6:1–14.

CHAPMAN, ANNE C.

1957   Port of Trade Enclaves in Aztec and Maya Civilizations. In *Trade and Market in the Early Empires,* edited by Karl Polanyi, Conrad Arensberg, Harry Pearson, pp. 114–153. Glencoe, Ill.: The Free Press.

CHAUDHURI, K. N.

1985   *Trade and Civilization in the Indian Ocean.* Cambridge: Cambridge University Press.

CHERNOFF, JOHN MILLER

1979   *African Rhythm and African Sensibility.* Chicago: University of Chicago Press.

CHILDE, V. GORDON

1951   *Man Makes Himself.* New York: New American Library.

CHIPP, HERSCHEL B.

1971   Formal and Symbolic Factors in the Art Styles of Primitive Cultures. In *Art and Aesthetics in Primitive Societies,* edited by Carol F. Jopling, pp. 146–170. New York: E. P. Dutton & Co.

CIEZA DE LEÓN, PEDRO DE

1959   *The Incas.* Norman: University of Oklahoma Press.

CLARK, GRAHAME

1986   *Symbols of Excellence.* Cambridge: Cambridge University Press.

CLENDINNEN, INGA

1987   *Ambivalent Conquests.* Cambridge: Cambridge University Press.

CLINE, WALTER

1937   *Mining and Metallurgy in Negro Africa.* General Series in Anthropology, No. 5. Menasha, Wis.: George Banta Publishing Co.

COCHRANE, GLYNN

1970   *Big Men and Cargo Cults.* Oxford: Clarendon Press.

COLE, HERBERT M.

1972   Ibo Art and Authority. In *African Art and Leadership,* edited by Douglas Fraser and Herbert M. Cole, pp. 79–98. Madison: University of Wisconsin Press.

COLSON, ELIZABETH

1962   Trade and Wealth Among the Tonga. In *Markets in Africa,* edited by Paul Bohannan and George Dalton, pp. 601–616. Northwestern, Ill.: Northwestern University Press.

COOMARASWAMY, ANANDA K.

1935   *The Transformation of Nature in Art.* Cambridge: Harvard University Press.

CORDWELL, JUSTINE M.

1979   The Very Human Arts of Transformation. In *The Fabrics of Culture,* edited by Justine M. Cordwell and Ronald A. Schwarz, pp. 47–76. Mouton: The Hague.

COURT, ARTELIA

1985   *Puck of the Droms.* Berkeley: University of California Press.

COVARRUBIAS, MIGUEL

1938   *Island of Bali.* New York: Alfred A. Knopf.

CROWLEY, DANIEL J.

1972   Chokwe: Political Art in a Plebian Society. In *African Art & Leadership,* edited by Douglas Fraser and Herbert M. Cole, pp. 21–40. Madison: University of Wisconsin Press.

1973   Aesthetic Value and Professionalism in African Art: Three Cases from the Katanga Chokwe. In *The Traditional Artist in African Societies,* edited by Warren L. d'Azevedo, pp. 221–249. Bloomington: Indiana University Press.

CSIKSZENTMIHALYI, MIHALY, AND EUGENE ROCHBERG-HALTON

1981   *The Meaning of Things: Domestic Symbols and the Self.* Cambridge: Cambridge University Press.

CUNNISON, IAN

1961   Kazembe and the Portuguese 1798–1832. *Journal of African History* 11:61–76.

DASEN, VÉRONIQUE

1988   Dwarfism in Egypt and Classical Antiquity: Iconography and Medical History. *Medical History* 32:253–276.

DAVENPORT, WILLIAM H.

1986   Two Kinds of Value in the Eastern Solomon Islands. In *The Social Life of Things,* edited by Arjun Appadurai, pp. 95–109. Cambridge: Cambridge University Press.

D'AZEVEDO, WARREN L.

1973a   Mask Makers and Myth in Western Liberia. In *Primitive Art and Society,* edited by Anthony Forge, pp. 126–150. London: Oxford University Press.

1973b   Sources of Gola Artistry. In *The Traditional Artist in African Societies,* edited by W. L. d'Azevedo, pp. 282–339. Bloomington: Indiana University Press.

1975   *The Artist Archetype in Gola Culture.* Desert Research Institute, University of Nevada. Preprint no. 14. Distributed by Liberian Studies, University of Delaware.

DETIENNE, MARCEL, AND JEAN-PIERRE VERNANT

1978   *Cunning Intelligence in Greek Culture and Society.* New Jersey: Humanities Press (Sussex: Harvester Press).

DIAMOND, STANLEY

1960   Plato and the Definition of the Primitive. In *Culture in History: Essays in Honor of Paul Radin,* edited by S. Diamond, pp. 118–141. New York: Columbia University Press.

DODDS, E. R.

1951   *The Greeks and the Irrational*. Berkeley: University of California Press.

DOUGLAS, MARY

1966   *Purity and Danger*. London: Routledge and Kegan Paul.

DUBY, GEORGES

1974   *The Early Growth of the European Economy*. Ithaca: Cornell University Press.

DUMETT, RAYMOND E.

1979   Precolonial Gold Mining and the State in the Akan Region: With a Critique of the Terray Hypothesis. *Research in Economic Anthropology* 2:37–68.

DUMONT, JEAN-PAUL

1977   Musical Politics: On Some Symbolic Aspects of the Musical Instruments of the Panare Indians. In *Anthropology and the Climate of Opinion*, edited by Stanley A. Freed, pp. 206–214. Annals of the New York Academy of Sciences, vol. 293. New York: The New York Academy of Sciences.

DUNCAN, JAMES S.

1990   *The City as Text: The Politics of Landscape Interpretation in the Kandyan Kingdom*. Cambridge: Cambridge University Press.

EARLE, TIMOTHY

1978   *Economics and Social Organization of a Complex Chiefdom: The Halelea District, Kaua'i, Hawaii*. Anthropological Papers, no. 63. Museum of Anthropology. Ann Arbor: University of Michigan.

1982   The Ecology and Politics of Primitive Valuables. In *Culture and Ecology: Eclectic Perspectives*, edited by John G. Kennedy and Robert B. Edgerton, pp. 65–83. Papers of the American Anthropological Association. Washington, D.C.

1987   Specialization and the Production of Wealth: Hawaiian Chiefdoms and the Inka Empire. In *Specialization, Exchange, and Complex Societies*, edited by Elizabeth Brumfiel and Timothy Earle, pp. 64–75. London: Cambridge University Press.

EBERHARD, WOLFRAM

1965   *Conquerors and Rulers*. 2nd, revised ed. Leiden: E. J. Brill.

ELIADE, MIRCEA

1958   *Patterns in Comparative Religion*. New York: Sheed and Ward.

1959   *Cosmos and History: The Myth of the Eternal Return*. New York: Harper & Brothers.

1962   *The Forge and the Crucible*. New York: Harper & Row.

ELISOFON, ELIOT

1958   *The Sculpture of Africa*. Text by William Fagg. New York: Frederick A. Praeger.

ERRINGTON, FREDERICK K.

1984   *Manners and Meaning in West Sumatra.* New Haven: Yale University Press.

ERRINGTON, FREDERICK, AND DEBORAH GEWERTZ

1985   The Chief of the Chambri: Social Change and Cultural Permeability among a New Guinea People. *American Ethnologist* 12 : 442–454.

1986   The Confluence of Powers: Entropy and Importation among the Chambri. *Oceania* 57 : 99–113.

ERRINGTON, SHELLY

1983   The Place of Regalia in Luwu. In *Centers, Symbols, and Hierarchies: Essays on the Classical States of Southeast Asia,* edited by Lorraine Gesick, pp. 194–230. Yale University Southeast Asia Studies, Monograph Series no. 26. New Haven, Conn.

1989   *Meaning and Power in a Southeast Asian Realm.* Princeton, New Jersey: Princeton University Press.

EVANS, JOAN

1976   *Magical Jewels of the Middle Ages and the Renaissance.* New York: Dover Publications, Inc.

FAGG, WILLIAM

1969   The African Artist. In *Tradition and Creativity in Tribal Art,* edited by Daniel Biebuyck, pp. 42–57. Berkeley: University of California Press.

1973   In Search of Meaning in African Art. In *Primitive Art and Society,* edited by Anthony Forge, pp. 151–168. London: Oxford University Press.

FAIRBANK, JOHN K., ED.

1968   *The Chinese World Order.* Cambridge: Harvard University Press.

FAIRLEY, NANCY J.

1987   Ideology and State Formation: The Ekie of Southern Zaire. In *The African Frontier,* edited by Igor Kopytoff, pp. 89–100. Bloomington: Indiana University Press.

FALLERS, LLOYD A., WITH F. K. KAMOGA AND S. B. K. MUSOKE

1964   Social Stratification in Traditional Buganda. In *The King's Men,* edited by L. A. Fallers, pp. 64–116. London: Oxford University Press.

FARQUHAR, DAVID M.

1957   Oirat-Chinese Trade Relations, 1408–1446. *Festschrift für Nikolaus Poppe zum 60. Geburtstag am 8. August 1957,* pp. 61–68. [no editor given]. Studia Altaica V. Wiesbaden: Otto Harrassowitz.

FEIERMAN, STEVEN

1974   *The Shambaa Kingdom.* Madison: University of Wisconsin Press.

FEIT, HARVEY A.

1986   Hunting and the Quest for Power: The James Bay Cree and Whitemen in the Twentieth Century. In *Native Peoples,* edited by R. Bruce Morrison and C. Roderick Wilson, pp. 171–207. Toronto: McClelland and Stewart.

FELDMAN, LAWRENCE H.
1985   *A Tumpline Economy.* Culver City, Calif.: Labyrinthos.

FERNANDEZ, JAMES W.
1973   The Exposition and Imposition of Order: Artistic Expression in Fang Culture. In *The Traditional Artist in African Societies,* edited by Warren L. d'Azevedo, pp. 194–220. Bloomington: Indiana University Press.
1982   *Bwiti.* Princeton, New Jersey: Princeton University Press.

FINNEGAN, RUTH
1970   *Oral Literature in Africa.* Oxford: The Clarendon Press.

FIRTH, RAYMOND
1925   The Maori Carver. *Journal of the Polynesian Society* 34:277–291.
1936   Tattooing in Tikopia. *Man* no. 236:173–177.

FISHER, JAMES F.
1986   *Trans-Himalayan Traders.* Berkeley: University of California Press.

FISHER, ROBIN
1977   *Contact and Conflict.* Vancouver: University of British Columbia Press.

FOOTE, PETER G., AND DAVID M. WILSON
1970   *The Viking Achievement.* New York: Praeger Publishers.

FORGE, ANTHONY
1962   Paint—A Magical Substance. *Palette* 9:9–17.
1967   The Abelam Artist. In *Social Organization: Essays Presented to Raymond Firth,* edited by Maurice Freedman, pp. 65–84. Chicago: Aldine Publishing Co.

FORTES, MEYER
1962   Ritual and Office in Tribal Society. In *Essays on the Ritual of Social Relations,* edited by Max Gluckman, pp. 53–88. Manchester: Manchester University Press.

FRANKE, HERBERT
1983   Sung Embassies: Some General Observations. In *China Among Equals,* edited by Morris Rossabi, pp. 116–148. Berkeley: University of California Press.

FRANKFORT, HENRI
1948   *Kingship and the Gods.* Chicago: University of Chicago Press.

FRASER, DOUGLAS
1972   The Fish-legged Figure in Benin and Yoruba Art. In *African Art and Leadership,* edited by D. Fraser and H. M. Cole, pp. 261–294. Madison: University of Wisconsin Press.

FRASER, DOUGLAS, AND HERBERT M. COLE
1972   Art and Leadership: An Overview. In *African Art and Leadership,* edited by D. Fraser and H. M. Cole, pp. 295–328. Madison: University of Wisconsin Press.

GEARY, PATRICK
1986   Sacred Commodities: The Circulation of Medieval Relics. In *The Social*

Life of Things, edited by Arjun Appadurai, pp. 169–194. Cambridge: Cambridge University Press.

GEERTZ, CLIFFORD

1977   Centers, Kings, and Charisma: Reflections on the Symbolics of Power. In *Culture and Its Creators,* edited by Joseph Ben-David and Terry Nichols Clark, pp. 150–171. Chicago: University of Chicago Press.

1980   *Negara.* Princeton: Princeton University Press.

1983   *Local Knowledge.* New York: Basic Books, Inc.

GERBRANDS, ADRIAN A.

1957   *Art as an Element of Culture, Especially in Negro-Africa.* Mededelingen van het Rijksmuseum voor Volkenkunde, Leiden, no. 12. Leiden: E. J. Brill.

1967   *Wow-Ipits. Eight Asmat Woodcarvers of New Guinea.* The Hague: Mouton & Co.

1971   Art as an Element of Culture in Africa. In *Anthropology and Art,* edited by Charlotte M. Otten, pp. 366–382. Garden City, New York: The Natural History Press.

GESICK, LORRAINE

1983   Introduction. In *Centers, Symbols, and Hierarchies: Essays on the Classical States of Southeast Asia,* edited by Lorraine Gesick, pp. 1–8. Monograph series no. 26. New Haven, Conn.: Yale University Southeast Asia Studies.

GEWERTZ, DEBORAH

1980   Of Symbolic Anchors and Sago Soup: The Rhetoric of Exchange among the Chambri of Papua New Guinea. *Journal of the Polynesian Society* 89:309–328.

GIDDENS, ANTHONY

1984   *The Constitution of Society.* Berkeley: University of California Press.

GILBERT, MICHELLE

1987   The Person of the King: Ritual and Power in a Ghanaian State. In *Rituals of Royalty,* edited by David Cannadine and Simon Price, pp. 298–330. Cambridge: Cambridge University Press.

1989   Sources of Power in Akuropon-Akuapem: Ambiguity in Classification. In *Creativity of Power,* edited by W. Arens and Ivan Karp, pp. 59–90. Washington: Smithsonian Institution Press.

GILLESPIE, SUSAN D.

1989   *The Aztec Kings.* Tucson: University of Arizona Press.

GLACKEN, CLARENCE J.

1967   *Traces on the Rhodian Shore.* Berkeley: University of CaliforniaPress.

GLADWIN, THOMAS

1970   *East is a Big Bird.* Cambridge: Harvard University Press.

GLAZE, ANITA J.

1981   *Art and Death in a Senufo Village.* Bloomington: Indiana University Press.

GLUCKMAN, MAX
1965   *Politics, Law and Ritual in Tribal Society.* New York: The New American Library.
1965a   *The Ideas in Barotse Jurisprudence.* New Haven: Yale University Press.

GODELIER, MAURICE
1977   *Perspectives in Marxist Anthropology.* Cambridge: Cambridge University Press.
1986   *The Making of Great Men.* Cambridge: Cambridge University Press.

GOLDMAN, IRVING
1940   The Alkatcho Carrier of British Columbia. In *Acculturation in Seven American Indian Tribes,* edited by Ralph Linton, pp. 333–389. New York: D. Appleton-Century Co.
1963   *The Cubeo: Indians of the Northwest Amazon.* Urbana: University of Illinois Press.
1970   *Ancient Polynesian Society.* Chicago: University of Chicago Press.
1975   *The Mouth of Heaven.* New York: John Wiley & Sons.

GOODALE, JANE C., AND JOAN D. KOSS
1967   The Cultural Context of Creativity Among Tiwi. In *Essays on the Verbal and Visual Arts,* edited by June Helm, pp. 175–191. Proceedings of the 1966 Annual Spring Meeting of the American Ethnological Society. Seattle: University of Washington Press.

GOODENOUGH, WARD H.
1986   Sky World and This World: The Place of Kachaw in Micronesian Cosmology. *American Anthropologist* 88:551–568.

GOODRICH, NORMA L.
1960   *The Ancient Myths.* New York: Mentor Books.

GOODY, JACK
1971   *Technology, Tradition, and the State in Africa.* London: Oxford University Press.

GOSSEN, GARY H.
1974   *Chamulas in the World of the Sun.* Cambridge: Harvard University Press.
1975   Animal Souls and Human Destiny in Chamula. *Man* 10:448–461.

GRABURN, NELSON H. H.
1976   Eskimo Art: The Eastern Canadian Arctic. In *Ethnic and Tourist Arts,* edited by Nelson H. H. Graburn, pp. 39–55. Berkeley: University of California Press.

GREENE, DAVID
1954   Early Irish Literature. In *Early Irish Society,* edited by Myles Dillon, pp. 22–35. Cork: The Mercier Press.
1954b   Early Irish Society. In *Early Irish Society,* edited by Myles Dillon, pp. 79–89. Cork: The Mercier Press.

GREGORY, C. A.
1982   *Gifts and Commodities.* London: Academic Press.

GRIAULE, MARCEL

1965   *Conversations with Ogotemmeli.* London: Oxford University Press (for the International African Institute).

GRINKER, ROY R.

1990   Images of Denigration: Structuring Inequality between Foragers and Farmers in the Ituri Forest, Zaire. *American Ethnologist* 17:111–130.

GUBSER, NICHOLAS J.

1965   *The Nunamiut Eskimos, Hunters of Caribou.* New Haven: Yale University Press.

GUNTHER, ERNA

1972   *Indian Life on the Northwest Coast of North America as Seen by the Early Explorers and Fur Traders during the Last Decades of the Eighteenth Century.* Chicago: University of Chicago Press.

GUSS, DAVID M.

1989   *To Weave and Sing.* Berkeley: University of California Press.

GUY, JOHN

n.d.   *Symbolism in Robes, Mantles, and Cloaks.* University of St. Andrews, Dept. of Spanish Folklore Seminar, Working Papers no. 1 (no publisher given)

HALL, KENNETH R.

1985   *Maritime Trade and State Development in Early Southeast Asia.* Honolulu: University of Hawaii Press.

HAMELL, GEORGE R.

1986–   Strawberries, Floating Islands, and Rabbit Captains: Mythical Realities
1987   and European Contact in the Northeast During the Sixteenth and Seventeenth Centuries. *Journal of Canadian Studies* 21 (Winter):72–94.

HANAWAY, WILLIAM L., JR.

1971   The Concept of the Hunt in Persian Literature. *Boston Museum Bulletin* 69:21–33.

HANSON, F. ALLAN, AND LOUISE HANSON

1983   *Counterpoint in Maori Culture.* London: Routledge & Kegan Paul.

HARDING, THOMAS G.

1967   *Voyagers of the Vitiaz Straits.* Seattle: University of Washington Press.

HARMS, ROBERT W.

1981   *River of Wealth, River of Sorrow.* New Haven: Yale University Press.

HARRISON, SIMON

1987   Cultural Efflorescence and Political Evolution on the Sepik River. *American Ethnologist* 14:491–507.

HARTWIG, GERALD W.

1976   *The Art of Survival in East Africa.* London: Holmes & Meier Publisher.

HASEBROEK, JOHANNES

1933   *Trade and Politics in Ancient Greece.* London: G. Bell and Sons, Ltd.

HASTRUP, KIRSTEN
1985   *Culture and History in Medieval Iceland.* Oxford: Clarendon Press.
HATCHER, EVELYN PAYNE
1985   *Art as Culture.* Lanham: University Press of America.
HAVELOCK, ERIC A.
1963   *Preface to Plato.* Cambridge: Belknap Press of Harvard University Press.
HEALEY, CHRISTOPHER J.
1984   Trade and Sociability: Balanced Reciprocity as Generosity in the New Guinea Highlands. *American Ethnologist* 11:42–60.
1985   Pigs, Cassowaries, and the Gift of the Flesh: A Symbolic Triad in Maring Cosmology. *Ethnology* 24:153–165.
1990   *Maring Hunters and Traders.* Berkeley: University of California Press.
HELMS, MARY W.
1969   The Cultural Ecology of a Colonial Tribe. *Ethnology* 8:76–84.
1979   *Ancient Panama: Chiefs in Search of Power.* Austin: University of Texas Press.
1983   Miskito Slaving and Culture Contact: Ethnicity and Opportunity in an Expanding Population. *Journal of Anthropological Research* 39:179–197.
1987   The "Hermes Factor" and Long-Distance Trade. *Shadow* 4(2):40–49.
1988   *Ulysses' Sail: An Ethnographic Odyssey of Power, Knowledge and Geographical Distance.* Princeton, New Jersey: Princeton University Press.
n.d.   Native Cosmology and European Trade. Paper prepared for the 46th International Congress of Americanists. Amsterdam, 1988.
HENDERSON, RICHARD N.
1972   *The King In Every Man.* New Haven: Yale University Press.
HENDRICKS, JANET WALL
1988   Power and Knowledge: Discourse and Ideological Transformation among the Shuar. *American Ethnologist* 15:216–238.
HERBERT, EUGENIA W.
1984   *Red Gold of Africa.* Madison: University of Wisconsin Press.
HEUSCH, LUC DE
1982   *The Drunken King or The Origin of the State.* Bloomington: Indiana University Press.
HEVIA, JAMES L.
1990   Disposing Bodies and Configuring Space in Manchu Imperial Ritual. Paper read at the annual meeting of the American Ethnological Society, Atlanta, Ga.
HILLENBRAND, ROBERT
1988   The Symbolism of the Rayed Nimbus in Early Islamic Art. In *Kingship,* edited by Emily Lyle, pp. 1–52. Cosmos, vol. 2 (1986). Edinburgh: The Traditional Cosmology Society.

HIMMELHEBER, HANS

1963   Personality and Technique of African Sculptors. In *Technique and Personality*, edited by Margaret Mead, Junius Bird, Hans Himmelheber, pp. 79–110. New York: The Museum of Primitive Art.

HO, PING-TI

1959   Aspects of Social Mobility in China, 1368–1911. *Comparative Studies in Society and History* 1:330–359.

HOCART, A. M.

1969   *Kingship*. London: Oxford University Press.

HODDER, IAN

1982   Toward a Contextual Approach to Prehistoric Exchange. In *Contexts for Prehistoric Exchange*, edited by Jonathan E. Ericson and Timothy K. Earle, pp. 199–212. New York: Academic Press.

HOLM, BILL

1983   *Smoky-Top. The Art and Times of Willie Seaweed*. Seattle: University of Washington Press.

HOLY BIBLE

1977   *The New Oxford Annotated Bible with the Apocrypha*. Revised Standard Version. Edited by Herbert May and Bruce Metzger. New York: Oxford University Press.

HORRIDGE, G. ADRIAN

1979   *The Konjo Boatbuilders and the Bugis Prahus of South Sulawesi*. Maritime Monographs and Reports no. 40. Greenwich, London: National Maritime Museum.

HUGH-JONES, STEPHEN

1979   *The Palm and the Pleiades*. Cambridge: Cambridge University Press.

HUNWICK, J. O.

1980   Gao and the Almoravids: A Hypothesis. In *West African Culture Dynamics*, edited by B. K. Swartz, Jr. and Raymond E. Dumett, pp. 413–430. The Hague: Mouton Publishers.

INGOLD, TIM

1987   *The Appropriation of Nature*. Iowa City: University of Iowa Press.

JABLOW, JOSEPH

1966   *The Cheyenne in Plains Indian Trade Relations 1795–1840*. Seattle: University of Washington Press.

JACOBSEN, THORKILD

1965   Enuma Elish—"The Babylonian Genesis." In *Theories of the Universe*, edited by Milton Munitz, pp. 8–20. New York: The Free Press.

JING-SHEN, TAO

1983   Barbarians or Northerners: Northern Sung Images of the Khitans. In *China Among Equals*, edited by Morris Rossabi, pp. 66–86. Berkeley: University of California Press.

JOHNSON, NORRIS BROCK

1989   Anthropology and the Spirit of Art. Paper presented at the annual meeting of the American Anthropological Association, Washington, D.C. 1989.

KAEPPLER, ADRIENNE L.

1985   Structured Movement Systems in Tonga. In *Society and the Dance,* edited by Paul Spencer, pp. 92–118. Cambridge: Cambridge University Press.

KAHN, MIRIAM

1990   Stone-faced Ancestors: The Spatial Anchoring of Myth in Wamira, Papua New Guinea. *Ethnology* 29:51–66.

KAN, SERGEI

1986   The 19th-century Tlingit Potlatch: A New Perspective. *American Ethnologist* 13:191–212.

KANTOROWICZ, ERNST H.

1957   *The King's Two Bodies.* Princeton: Princeton University Press.

KEIM, CURTIS A.

1983   Long-Distance Trade and the Mangbetu. *Journal of African History* 24:1–22.

KINROSS, LORD

1977   *The Ottoman Centuries.* New York: William Morrow and Co.

KLEIN, CECELIA F.

1975   Post-classic Mexican Death Imagery as a Sign of Cyclic Completion. In *Death and the Afterlife in Pre-Columbian America,* edited by Elizabeth P. Benson, pp. 69–86. Dumbarton Oaks Research Library and Collections. Washington, D.C.

1982   Woven Heaven, Tangled Earth. In *Ethnoastronomy and Archaeoastronomy in the American Tropics,* edited by Anthony Aveni and Gary Urton, pp. 1–35. Annals of the New York Academy of Sciences, vol. 385. New York: The New York Academy of Sciences.

KOLFF, D. H. A.

1971   Sannyasi Trader-Soldiers. *The Indian Economic and Social History Review* 8:213–218.

KONETZKE, RICHARD

1953–   Entrepreneurial Activities of Spanish and Portuguese Noblemen in Me-
1954   dieval Times. *Explorations in Entrepreneurial History* 6:115–120.

KOOIJMAN, S.

1959   *The Art of Lake Sentani.* New York: Museum of Primitive Art.

KOPYTOFF, IGOR

1987   The Internal African Frontier: The Making of African Political Culture. In *The African Frontier,* edited by Igor Kopytoff, pp. 3–86. Bloomington: Indiana University Press.

KOPYTOFF, IGOR, ED.
1987   *The African Frontier.* Bloomington: Indiana University Press.
KRAUSE, AUREL
1956   *The Tlingit Indians.* Translated by Erna Gunther. Seattle: University of Washington Press.
KÜCHLER, SUSANNE
1987   Malangan: Art and Memory in a Melanesian Society. *Man* 22:238–255.
1988   Malangan: Objects, Sacrifice and the Production of Memory. *American Ethnologist* 15:625–637.
KUPER, HILDA
1973   Costume and Cosmology: The Animal Symbolism of the *Ncwala. Man* 8:613–630.
KUS, SUSAN
1986   Sensuous Human Activity and the State. In *Comparative Studies in the Development of Complex Societies: Modes of Domination.* vol. 1. Organized by Tim Champion and Michael Rowlands, pp. 1–11. World Archaeological Congress. Department of Archaeology, University of Southampton.
LABBY, DAVID
1976   *The Demystification of Yap.* Chicago: University of Chicago Press.
LAMPHEAR, JOHN
1970   The Kamba and the Northern Mrima Coast. In *Pre-Colonial African Trade,* edited by Richard Gray and David Birmingham, pp. 75–102. London: Oxford University Press.
LAUNAY, ROBERT
1982   *Traders Without Trade.* London: Cambridge University Press.
LAW, ROBIN
1978   Slave, Trade, and Taxes: The Material Basis of Political Power in Precolonial West Africa. *Research in Economic Anthropology* 1:37–52.
LEACH, JERRY W.
1983a   Trobriand Territorial Categories and the Problem of Who is Not in the Kula. In *The Kula: New Perspectives on Massim Exchange,* edited by Jerry W. Leach and Edmund Leach, pp. 121–146. Cambridge: Cambridge University Press.
1983b   Introduction. In *The Kula: New Perspectives on Massim Exchange,* edited by Jerry W. Leach and Edmund Leach, pp. 1–26. Cambridge: Cambridge University Press.
LEÓN-PORTILLA, MIGUEL
1963   *Aztec Thought and Culture.* Norman: University of Oklahoma Press.
LESSA, WILLIAM A.
1950   Ulithi and the Outer Native World. *American Anthropologist* 52:27–52.
LÉVI-STRAUSS, CLAUDE
1963   The Bear and the Barber. *Journal of the Royal Anthropological Institute* 93:1–11.

1969a   *The Raw and the Cooked.* New York: Harper & Row.
1969b   *The Elementary Structures of Kinship and Marriage.* London: Eyre and Spottiswoode.
1973   *From Honey to Ashes.* New York: Harper & Row.
1978   *The Origin of Table Manners.* New York: Harper & Row.
1988   *The Jealous Potter.* Chicago: University of Chicago Press.

LEVTZION, NEHEMIA
1968   *Muslims and Chiefs in West Africa.* Oxford: The Clarendon Press.
1973   *Ancient Ghana and Mali.* London: Methuen & Co.

LEWIS, HERBERT S.
1970   Wealth, Influence, and Prestige among the Shoa Galla. In *Social Stratification in Africa,* edited by Arthur Tuden and Leonard Plotnikov, pp. 163–186. New York: The Free Press.

LEWIS, I. M.
1962   Trade and Markets in Northern Somaliland. In *Markets in Africa,* edited by Paul Bohannan and George Dalton, pp. 365–385. Evanston, Ill.: Northwestern University Press.

LEWIS, PHILLIP H.
1961   The Artist in New Ireland Society. In *The Artist in Tribal Society,* edited by Marian W. Smith, pp. 71–79. New York: The Free Press of Glencoe.

LINDSTROM, LAMONT
1984   Doctor, Lawyer, Wise Man, Priest: Big-men and Knowledge in Melanesia. *Man* 19:291–309.

LINGENFELTER, SHERWOOD G.
1975   *Yap: Political Leadership and Culture Change in an Island Society.* Honolulu: University Press of Hawaii.

LINTON, RALPH
1939   Marquesan Culture. In *The Individual and His Society,* edited by Abram Kardiner, pp. 137–196. New York: Columbia University Press.

LIPSET, DAVID M.
1985   Seafaring Sepiks: Ecology, Warfare, and Prestige in Murik Trade. *Research in Economic Anthropology* 7:67–94.

LOPEZ, ROBERT SABATINO
1945   Silk Industry in the Byzantine Empire. *Speculum* 20:1–42.

LORD, ALBERT B.
1960   *The Singer of Tales.* Cambridge: Harvard University Press.

LUCIE-SMITH, EDWARD
1981   *The Story of Craft: The Craftsman's Role in Society.* Ithaca: Cornell University Press (Cornell/Phaidon Books)

LUTKEHAUS, NANCY
1985   Pigs, Politics, and Pleasure: Manam Perspectives on Trade and Regional Integration. *Research in Economic Anthropology* 7:123–141.

MADURO, RENALDO
1974   Artistic Creativity and Aging in India. *International Journal of Aging and Human Development* 5:303–329.
1976   The Brahmin Painters of Nathdwara, Rajasthan. In *Ethnic and Tourist Arts*, edited by Nelson H. Graburn, pp. 227–244. Berkeley: University of California Press.

MANN, MICHAEL
1986   *The Sources of Social Power*, vol. 1. Cambridge: Cambridge University Press.

MAQUET, JACQUES
1970   Rwanda Castes. In *Social Stratification in Africa*, edited by Arthur Tuden and Leonard Plotnicov, pp. 93–124. New York: The Free Press.

MAURER, EVAN M.
1979   Symbol and Identification in North American Indian Clothing. In *The Fabrics of Culture*, edited by Justine M. Cordwell and Ronald A. Schwarz, pp. 119–142. The Hague: Mouton Publishers.

MBITI, JOHN S.
1969   *African Religions & Philosophy*. New York: Praeger Publishers.

MCCARTHY, F. D.
1939   "Trade" in Aboriginal Australia and "Trade" Relationships with Torres Strait, New Guinea and Malaya. *Oceania* 9:405–438 and 10:80–105, 171–195.

MCCASKIE, T. C.
1983   Accumulation, Wealth and Belief in Asante History. *Africa* 53:23–43.

MCKINLEY, ROBERT
1979   Zaman Dan Masa, Eras and Periods: Religious Evolution and the Permanence of Epistemological Ages in Malay Cultures. In *The Imagination of Reality*, edited by A. L. Becker and Aram Yengoyan, pp. 303–324. Norwood, N.J.: ABLEX Publishing Co.

MCMULLEN, DAVID
1987   Bureaucrats and Cosmology: The Ritual Code of T'ang China. In *Rituals of Royalty*, edited by David Cannadine and Simon Price, pp. 181–236. Cambridge: Cambridge University Press.

MCNAUGHTON, PATRICK R.
1982   The Shirts That Mande Hunters Wear. *African Arts* 15:54–58, 91.

MEILLASSOUX, CLAUDE
1971   Introduction. In *The Development of Indigenous Trade and Markets in West Africa*, edited by Claude Meillassoux, pp. 3–90. London: Oxford University Press.

MENESES, ELOISE HIEBERT
1987   Traders and Marginality in a Complex Social System. *Ethnology* 26:231–244.

MESSENGER, JOHN C.

1973   The Role of the Carver in Anang Society. In *The Traditional Artist in African Societies,* edited by Warren L. d'Azevedo, pp. 101–127. Bloomington: Indiana University Press.

MESSING, SIMON D.

1962   The Abyssinian Market Trade. In *Markets in Africa,* edited by Paul Bohannan and George Dalton, pp. 386–408. Evanston: Northwestern University Press.

METRAUX, RHODA

1978   Aristocracy and Meritocracy: Leadership among the Eastern Iatmul. *Anthropological Quarterly* 5:47–58.

MILLS, GEORGE

1973   Art and the Anthropological Lens. In *The Traditional Artist in African Societies,* edited by Warren d'Azevedo, pp. 379–416. Bloomington: Indiana University Press.

MINES, MATTISON

1984   *The Warrior Merchants: Textiles, Trade, and Territory in South India.* Cambridge: Cambridge University Press.

MOMIGLIANO, ARNALDO

1944   Sea Power in Greek Thought. *The Classical Review* 58:1–7.

MORPHY, H.

1989   From Dull to Brilliant: The Aesthetics of Spiritual Power among the Yolngu. *Man* 24:21–40.

MOSCATI, SABATINO

1968   *The World of the Phoenicians.* New York: Frederick A. Praeger.

MOUNTFORD, CHARLES P.

1961   The Artist and his Art in an Australian Aboriginal Society. In *The Artist in Tribal Society,* edited by Marian W. Smith, pp. 1–13. New York: The Free Press of Glencoe.

MOUSER, BRUCE L.

1980   Accommodation and Assimilation in the Landlord-Stranger Relationship. In *West African Culture Dynamics,* edited by B. K. Swartz, Jr., and Raymond Dumett, pp. 495–514. The Hague: Mouton Publishers.

MOZIÑO, JOSÉ MARIANO

1970   *Noticias de Nutka.* Seattle: University of Washington Press.

MUNN, NANCY

1977   The Spatiotemporal Transformations of Gawa Canoes. *Journal de la Société de Océanistes* 33:39–54.

1983   Gawan Kula: Spatiotemporal Control and the Symbolism of Influence. In *The Kula: New Perspectives on Massim Exchange,* edited by Jerry W. Leach & Edmund Leach, pp. 277–308. Cambridge: Cambridge University Press.

1986   *The Fame of Gawa.* Cambridge: Cambridge University Press.

MURIE, JAMES R.
1981   *Ceremonies of the Pawnee.* Part I: *The Skiri.* Edited by Douglas R. Parks. Washington, D.C.: Smithsonian Institution Press.

MURRA, JOHN V.
1980   *The Economic Organization of the Inka State.* Research in Economic Anthropology, Supplement 1. Greenwich, Conn.: JAI Press, Inc.

NELSON, JANET L.
1987   The Lord's Anointed and the People's Choice: Carolingian Royal Ritual. In *Rituals of Royalty,* edited by David Cannadine and Simon Price, pp. 137–180. Cambridge: Cambridge University Press.

NETTING, ROBERT
1972   Sacred Power and Centralization: Aspects of Political Adaptation in Africa. In *Population Growth,* edited by Brian Spooner, pp. 219–244. Cambridge, Mass.: MIT Press.

NILES, SUSAN A.
1987   *Callachaca.* Iowa City: University of Iowa Press.

NKETIA, J. H. KWABENA
1971   History and the Organization of Music in West Africa. In *Essays on Music and History in Africa,* edited by Klaus P. Wachsmann, pp. 3–25. Evanston, Ill.: Northwestern University Press.

NORTHRUP, DAVID
1972   The Growth of Trade Among the Igbo Before 1800. *Journal of African History* 13:217–236.
1978   *Trade Without Rulers.* Oxford: Clarendon Press.

OBERG, KALERVO
1973   *The Social Economy of the Tlingit Indians.* Seattle: University of Washington Press.

OGILVIE, R. M.
1969   *The Romans and Their Gods in the Age of Augustus.* London: Chatto and Windus.

OHNUKI-TIERNEY, EMIKO
1974   *The Ainu of the Northwest Coast of Southern Sakhalin.* Prospect Heights, Ill.: Waveland Press.

OLIVER, DOUGLAS L.
1974   *Ancient Tahitian Society.* vols. 1 and 2. Honolulu: University Press of Hawaii.

OPPENHEIM, A. LEO
1977   *Ancient Mesopotamia.* Revised edition. Chicago: University of Chicago Press.

O'RAHILLY, THOMAS F.
1964   *Early Irish History and Mythology.* Dublin: Dublin Institute for Advanced Studies.

ORTNER, SHERRY B.
  1973   On Key Symbols. *American Anthropologist* 75:1338–1346.
OSWALT, WENDELL H.
  1979   *Eskimos and Explorers*. Novato, Calif.: Chandler & Sharp, Pub.
OTTENBERG, SIMON, AND PHOEBE OTTENBERG
  1962   Afikpo Markets: 1900–1960. In *Markets in Africa*, edited by Paul Bohan-
          nan and George Dalton, pp. 118–169. Evanston: Northwestern Univer-
          sity Press.
PACKARD, RANDALL M.
  1981   *Chiefship and Cosmology*. Bloomington: Indiana University Press.
PADEN, JOHN N.
  1970   Aspects of Emirship in Kano. In *West African Chiefs*, edited by Michael
          Crowder and Obaro Ikime, pp. 162–186. New York: Africana Publishing
          Corp.
PASZTORY, ESTHER
  1983   *Aztec Art*. New York: Harry N. Abrams, Inc.
PEARSON, M. N.
  1976   *Merchants and Rulers in Gujarat*. Berkeley: University of California
          Press.
PERINBAM, B. MARIE
  1973   Social Relations in the Trans-Saharan and Western Sudanese Trade: An
          Overview. *Comparative Studies in Society and History* 15:416–436.
PIKE, RUTH
  1972   *Aristocrats and Traders*. Ithaca: Cornell University Press.
POLANYI, KARL
  1957a   The Economy as Instituted Process. In *Trade and Market in the Early
          Empires*, edited by Karl Polanyi, Conrad Arensberg, and Harry Pearson,
          pp. 243–270. Glencoe, Ill.: The Free Press.
  1957b   Marketless Trading in Hammurabi's Time. In *Trade and Market in the
          Early Empires*, edited by Karl Polanyi, Conrad Arensberg, and Harry
          Pearson, pp. 12–26. Glencoe, Ill.: The Free Press.
  1966   *Dahomey and the Slave Trade*. Seattle: University of Washington Press.
POOLE, FITZ JOHN PORTER
  1982   The Ritual Forging of Identity: Aspects of Person and Self in Bimin-
          Kuskusmin Male Initiation. In *Rituals of Manhood*, edited by Gilbert
          Herdt, pp. 99–154. Berkeley: University of California Press.
PRICE, DAVID
  1981   Nambiquara Leadership. *American Ethnologist* 8:686–708.
PRICE, SALLY, AND RICHARD PRICE
  1980   *Afro-American Arts of the Suriname Rain Forest*. Berkeley: University of
          California Press.
QUIGGIN, A. HINGSTON
  1949   *A Survey of Primitive Money*. London: Methuen & Co.

RABINEAU, PHYLLIS
  1975   Artists and Leaders: The Social Context of Creativity in a Tropical For-
          est Culture. In *The Cashinahua of Eastern Peru*, vol. l, edited by Jane
          Dwyer, pp. 87–109. Haffenreffer Museum of Anthropology, Studies in
          Anthropology and Material Culture, Brown University.
RAMSEYER, URS
  1977   *The Art and Culture of Bali*. Oxford: Oxford University Press.
RASSERS, W. H.
  1959   *Pañji, The Culture Hero*. Koninklijk Instituut voor Taat-, Land- en Volk-
          enkunde. Translation Series 3. The Hague: Martinus Nijhoff.
RATTRAY, R. S.
  1927   *Religion and Art in Ashanti*. Oxford: The Clarendon Press.
READ, HERBERT
  1963   *To Hell with Culture*. New York: Schocken Books.
REES, ALWYN, AND BRINLEY REES
  1961   *Celtic Heritage*. London: Thames and Hudson.
REICHEL-DOLMATOFF, GERARDO
  1976   Cosmology as Ecological Analysis: A View from the Rain Forest. *Man*
          n.s. 11:307–318.
  1978   Desana Animal Categories, Food Restrictions, and the Concept of
          Color Energies. *Journal of Latin American Lore* 4:243–291.
REINA, RUBEN E., AND ROBERT M. HILL, II
  1978   *The Traditional Pottery of Guatemala*. Austin: University of Texas Press.
REVERE, ROBERT B.
  1957   'No Man's Coast': Ports of Trade in the Eastern Mediterranean. In *Trade
          and Market in the Early Empires*, edited by Karl Polanyi, Conrad Arens-
          berg, Harry Pearson, pp. 38–63. Glencoe, Ill.: The Free Press.
RICHARDS, AUDREY I., ED.
  1960   *East African Chiefs*. New York: Frederick A. Praeger.
RIDINGTON, ROBIN
  1988   Knowledge, Power, and the Individual in Subarctic Hunting Societies.
          American Anthropologist 90:98–110.
ROBERTS, ANDREW
  1970   Nyamwezi Trade. In *Pre-Colonial African Trade*, edited by Richard Gray
          and David Birmingham, pp. 39–74. New York: Oxford University
          Press.
ROGERS, DONNA COATES
  1979   *Royal Art of the Kuba*. Austin: University of Texas Press.
ROGERS, MICHAEL C.
  1983   National Consciousness in Medieval Korea: The Impact of Liao and
          Chin on Koryo. In *China Among Equals*, edited by Morris Rossabi,
          pp. 151–172. Berkeley: University of California Press.

ROSCOE, PAUL B.

1988   The Far Side of Hurun: The Management of Melanesian Millenarian Movements. *American Ethnologist* 15:515–529.

1989   The Pig and the Long Yam: The Expansion of a Sepik Cultural Complex. *Ethnology* 28:219–232.

ROSENGREN, DAN

1987   Hunting and Gender Complementarity among the Matsigenka of Southeastern Peru. Ethnographical Museum, Göteborg, Sweden. Annual Reports for 1985/1986, pp. 25–34.

ROSSABI, MORRIS, ED.

1983   *China Among Equals.* Berkeley: University of California Press.

ROTH, H. LING

1968   *Great Benin.* New York: Barnes & Noble, Inc.

ROTHENBERG, JEROME

1985   *Technicians of the Sacred.* Berkeley: University of California Press.

ROWLANDS, MICHAEL

1987   Power and Moral Order in Precolonial West-Central Africa. In *Specialization, Exchange, and Complex Societies,* edited by Elizabeth Brumfiel and Timothy Earle, pp. 52–63. Cambridge: Cambridge University Press.

SAHAGÚN, FRAY BERNARDINO DE

1963   *General History of the Things of New Spain.* Book 11: *Earthly Things.* Translated by Charles E. Dibble and Arthur J. O. Anderson. Santa Fe: The School of American Research and the University of Utah.

SAHLINS, MARSHALL

1972   *Stone Age Economics.* Chicago: Aldine-Atherton, Inc.

1981a   *Historical Metaphors and Mythical Realities.* Ann Arbor: The University of Michigan Press.

1981   The Stranger-King. *Journal of Pacific History* 26:107–132.

1990   The Political Economy of Grandeur in Hawaii from 1810 to 1830. In *Culture Through Time: Anthropological Approaches,* edited by Emiko Ohnuki-Tierney, pp. 26–56. Stanford: Stanford University Press.

SALOMON, FRANK

1986   *Native Lords of Quito in the Age of the Incas.* Cambridge: Cambridge University Press.

SANDARS, N. K.

1964   *The Epic of Gilgamesh.* Baltimore: Penguin Books.

SCHAEFER, STACY B.

1991   The Loom as a Sacred Power Object in Huichol Culture. In *Art in Small Scale Societies: Contemporary Readings,* edited by Richard Anderson and Karen Field. Englewood Cliffs, N.J.: Prentice-Hall (in press).

1989–   The Loom and Time in the Huichol World. *Journal of Latin American*
1990   *Lore* (in press).

SCHAFER, EDWARD H.
1963   *The Golden Peaches of Samarkand.* Berkeley: University of California Press.
1967   *The Vermilion Bird.* Berkeley: University of California Press.

SCHELE, LINDA, AND DAVID FREIDEL
1990   *A Forest of Kings.* New York: William Morrow and Co.

SCHELE, LINDA, AND MARY ELLEN MILLER
1986   *The Blood of Kings: Dynasty and Ritual in Maya Art.* New York: George Braziller, Inc.

SCHMITZ, CARL A.
1963   *Wantoat.* The Hague: Mouton & Co.

SCHNEIDER, HAROLD K.
1971   The Interpretation of Pakot Visual Art. In *Art and Aesthetics in Primitive Societies,* edited by Carol Jopling, pp. 55–63. New York: E. P. Dutton & Co.
1973   The Subsistence Role of Cattle Among the Pakot and in East Africa. In *Peoples and Cultures of Africa,* edited by Elliott Skinner, pp. 159–187. Garden City, New York: Doubleday/Natural History Press.

SCHNEIDER, JANE
1978   Peacocks and Penguins: The Political Economy of European Cloth and Colors. *American Ethnologist* 5 : 413–447.

SCHNEIDER, JANE, AND PETER SCHNEIDER
1983   The Reproduction of the Ruling Class in Latifundist Sicily, 1860–1920. In *Elites: Ethnographic Issues,* edited by George Marcus, pp. 141–168. Albuquerque: University of New Mexico Press.

SCODITTI, GIANCARLO M. G., WITH JERRY W. LEACH
1983   Kula on Kitava. In *The Kula: New Perspectives on Massim Exchange,* edited by Jerry W. Leach and Edmund Leach, pp. 249–276. Cambridge: Cambridge University Press.

SEEGER, ANTHONY
1987   *Why Suyá Sing.* Cambridge: Cambridge University Press.
n.d.   Sing Their Songs, Take their Power: Musical Responses To Powerful Strangers among the Suyá of Brazil. Paper presented at the 1985 annual meeting of the American Anthropological Association. Washington, D.C.

SEGAL, CHARLES
1982   *Dionysiac Poetics and Euripides' Bacchae.* Princeton, New Jersey: Princeton University Press.

SEGUIN, MARGARET
1986   Understanding Tsimshian Potlatch. In *Native Peoples: The Canadian Experience,* edited by R. Bruce Morrison and C. Roderick Wilson, pp. 473–500. Toronto: McClelland and Stewart, Ltd.

SHAW, BRENT D.

1979   Rural Periodic Markets in Roman North Africa as Mechanisms of Social Integration and Control. *Research in Economic Anthropology* 2:91–117.

SHORTER, AYLWARD

1972   *Chiefship in Western Tanzania.* Oxford: Clarendon Press.

SILVERMAN-PROUST, GAIL P.

1988   Weaving Technique and the Registration of Knowledge in the Cuzco Area of Peru. *Journal of Latin American Lore* 14:207–241.

SKINNER, ELLIOTT P.

1962   Trade and Markets among the Mossi People. In *Markets in Africa,* edited by Paul Bohannan and George Dalton, pp. 237–278. Evanston: Northwestern University Press.

SMITH, MICHAEL G.

1962   Exchange and Marketing Among the Hausa. In *Markets in Africa,* edited by Paul Bohannan and George Dalton, pp. 299–334. Evanston, Ill.: Northwestern University Press.

SNODGRASS, A. M.

1983   Heavy Freight in Archaic Greece. In *Trade in the Ancient Economy,* edited by Peter Garnsey, Keith Hopkins, C. R. Whittaker, pp. 16–26. Berkeley: University of California Press.

SNYDER, SALLY

1975   Quest for the Sacred in Northern Puget Sound: An Interpretation of Potlatch. *Ethnology* 14:149–161.

SOUSTELLE, JACQUES

1961   *Daily Life of the Aztecs.* Stanford: Stanford University Press.

SPAULDING, JAY

1984   The Management of Exchange in Sinnar, c. 1700. In *Trade and Traders in the Sudan,* edited by Leif O. Manger, pp. 25–48. Occasional Paper no. 32, African Savannah Studies. Department of Social Anthropology, University of Bergen.

SPENCER, CHARLES S.

1987   Rethinking the Chiefdom. In *Chiefdoms in the Americas,* edited by Robert D. Drennan and Carlos A. Uribe, pp. 369–389. Lanham: University Press of America.

SPENCER, PAUL

1985   Introduction: Interpretations of the Dance in Anthropology. In *Society and the Dance,* edited by Paul Spencer, pp. 1–46. Cambridge: Cambridge University Press.

SPENCER, ROBERT F.

1959   *The North Alaskan Eskimo.* Smithsonian Institution, Bureau of American Ethnology Bulletin 171. Washington, D.C.: United States Government Printing Office.

SPOONER, BRIAN

1986   Weavers and Dealers: The Authenticity of an Oriental Carpet. In *The Social Life of Things,* edited by Arjun Appadurai, pp. 195–235. Cambridge: Cambridge University Press.

ST. JOHN, CHRISTOPHER

1970   Kazembe and the Tanganyika-Nyasa Corridor, 1800–1890. In *Pre-Colonial African Trade,* edited by Richard Gray and David Birmingham, pp. 202–227. London: Oxford University Press.

STEIN, BURTON

1965   Coromandel Trade in Medieval India. In *Merchants and Scholars,* edited by John Parker, pp. 49–62. Minneapolis: The University of Minnesota Press.

STENNING, D. J.

1960   The Nyankole. In *East African Chiefs,* edited by Audrey I. Richards, pp. 146–173. New York: Frederick A. Praeger.

STEPHEN, MICHELE

1979   An Honourable Man: Mekeo Views of the Village Constable. *The Journal of Pacific History* 14 (part 2): 85–99.

STONE, DORIS

1977   *Pre-Columbian Man in Costa Rica.* Cambridge: Peabody Museum Press, Harvard University.

STRATHERN, ANDREW

1971   *The Rope of Moka.* Cambridge: Cambridge University Press.

1983   The Kula in Comparative Perspective. In *The Kula: New Perspectives on Massim Exchange,* edited by Jerry Leach and Edmund Leach, pp. 73–88. Cambridge: Cambridge University Press.

STRONG, ROY

1973   *Splendor at Court.* Boston: Houghton Mifflin Co.

SUNDMAN, KERSTIN

n.d.   Some Theoretical Suggestions regarding the Anthropological Study of Political Speeches. Semantics of Political Processes, Interim Report No. 50. Department of Social Anthropology, University of Gothenburg. Gothenburg, Sweden.

SUNDSTRÖM, LARS

1974   *The Exchange Economy of Pre-Colonial Tropical Africa.* New York: St. Martin's Press.

SUTHERLAND-HARRIS, NICOLA

1970   Trade and the Rozwi Mambo. In *Pre-Colonial African Trade,* edited by Richard Gray and David Birmingham, pp. 243–266. London: Oxford University Press.

SUTLIVE, JR., VINSON H.

1978   *The Iban of Sarawak.* Arlington Heights, Ill.: AHM Publishing Corp.

TADMOR, HAYIM

1986   Monarchy and the Elite in Assyria and Babylonia: The Question of Royal Accountability. In *The Origins and Diversity of Axial Age Civilizations,* edited by S. N. Eisenstadt, pp. 203–224. The State University of New York Press.

TAMBIAH, STEPHEN

1976   *World Conqueror and World Renouncer.* Cambridge: Cambridge University Press.

1977   The Galactic Polity: The Structure of Traditional Kingdoms in Southeast Asia. In *Anthropology and the Climate of Opinion,* edited by Stanley Freed, pp. 69–97. Annals of the New York Academy of Sciences, vol. 293. New York: The New York Academy of Sciences.

1983   On Flying Witches and Flying Canoes: The Coding of Male and Female Values. In *The Kula: New Perspectives on Massim Exchange,* edited by Jerry W. Leach and Edmund Leach, pp. 171–200. London: Cambridge University Press.

TANNENBAUM, NICOLA

1987   Tattoos: Invulnerability and Power in Shan Cosmology. *American Ethnologist* 14:693–711.

TAYLOR, ANNE-CHRISTINE

1981   God-Wealth: The Achuar and the Missions. In *Cultural Transformations and Ethnicity in Modern Ecuador,* edited by Norman E. Whitten, Jr., pp. 647–676. Urbana: University of Illinois Press.

TAYLOR, PAUL M., AND LORRAINE V. ARAGON, WITH ASSISTANCE FROM ANNAMARIE L. RICE

1991   *Beyond the Java Sea: Art of Indonesia's Outer Islands.* Washington, D.C.: The National Museum of Natural History, Smithsonian Institution.

TCHERNIA, ANDRÉ

1983   Italian Wine in Gaul at the End of the Republic. In *Trade in the Ancient Economy,* edited by Peter Garnsey, Keith Hopkins, and C. R. Whittaker, pp. 87–104. Berkeley: University of California Press.

TEDLOCK, BARBARA, AND DENNIS TEDLOCK

1985   Text and Textile: Language and Technology in the Arts of the Quiché Maya. *Journal of Anthropological Research* 41:121–146.

TEDLOCK, DENNIS, TRANS. AND COMMENTARY

1985   *Popol Vuh.* New York: Simon and Schuster.

THOMPSON, ROBERT FARRIS

1974   *African Art in Motion: Icon and Act.* Los Angeles: University of California Press.

THOMSON, JOSEPH

1881   *To The Central African Lakes and Back.* vol. I. London: Sampson Low, Marston, Searle, and Rivington.

TOBY, RONALD
1984   *State and Diplomacy in Early Modern Japan*. Princeton: Princeton University Press.
TOSH, JOHN
1970   The Northern Interlacustrine Region. In *Pre-Colonial African Trade*, edited by Richard Gray and David Birmingham, pp. 103–118. London: Oxford University Press.
TRAUBE, ELIZABETH G.
1986   *Cosmology and Social Life*. Chicago: University of Chicago Press.
TRIGGER, BRUCE G.
1969   *The Huron, Farmers of the North*. New York: Holt, Rinehart and Winston.
1976   *The Children of Aataentsic I*. Montreal: McGill-Queens University Press.
TURNBULL, COLIN M.
1965   *Wayward Servants*. Garden City, New York: The Natural History Press.
TURNER, TERENCE S.
1971   Cosmetics: The Language of Bodily Adornment. In *Conformity and Conflict*, edited by James P. Spradley and David W. McCurdy, pp. 96–105. Little, Brown, and Co.
TURNER, VICTOR
1972   The Center Out There: Pilgrim's Goal. *History of Religions* 12:191–230.
TUZIN, DONALD F.
1978   Politics, Power, and Divine Artistry in Ilahita. *Anthropological Quarterly* 51:61–67.
1980   *The Voice of the Tambaran*. Berkeley: University of California Press.
VAN BEEK, WALTER E. A.
1987   *The Kapsiki of the Mandara Hills*. Prospect Heights, Ill.: Waveland Press.
VAUGHAN, RICHARD
1970   *Philip the Good: The Apogee of Burgundy*. London: Longmans.
VECSEY, CHRISTOPHER
1983   *Traditional Ojibwa Religion*. Philadelphia: The American Philosophical Society.
WACHSMANN, KLAUS P.
1971   Musical Instruments in Kiganda Tradition and Their Place in the East African Scene. In *Essays on Music and History in Africa*, edited by Klaus Wachsmann, pp. 93–134. Evanston, Ill.: Northwestern University Press.
WALENS, STANLEY
1982   The Weight of My Name is a Mountain of Blankets: Potlatch Ceremonies. In *Celebration*, edited by Victor Turner, pp. 178–189. Washington, D.C.: Smithsonian Institution Press.
WECHSLER, HOWARD J.
1985   *Offerings of Jade and Silk*. New Haven: Yale University Press.

WEEKS, KENT R.

1979   Art, Word, and the Egyptian World View. In *Egyptology and the Social Sciences,* edited by Kent Weeks, pp. 57–81. Cairo: American University in Cairo Press.

WEINER, ANNETTE B.

1983   'A World of Made is Not a World of Born': Doing Kula on Kiriwina. In *The Kula: New Perspectives on Massim Exchange,* edited by Jerry W. Leach and Edmund Leach, pp. 147–170. Cambridge: Cambridge University Press.

1985   Inalienable Wealth. *American Ethnologist* 12:210–227.

WELLENKAMP, JANE C.

1988   Order and Disorder in Toraja Thought and Ritual. *Ethnology* 27:311–326.

WENDELL, CHARLES

1971   Baghdad: *Imago Mundi,* and other Foundation-Lore. *International Journal of Middle East Studies* 2:99–128.

WERNER, DENNIS

1981   Are Some People More Equal than Others? Status Inequality among the Mekranoti Indians of Central Brazil. *Journal of Anthropological Research* 37:360–373.

WHEATLEY, PAUL

1971   *The Pivot of the Four Quarters.* Chicago: Aldine.

WHITTAKER, C. R.

1983   Late Roman Trade and Traders. In *Trade in the Ancient Economy,* edited by Peter Garnsey, Keith Hopkins, and C. R. Whittaker, pp. 163–180. Berkeley: University of California Press.

WILBERT, JOHANNES

1979   Geography and Telluric Lore of the Orinoco Delta. *Journal of Latin American Lore* 5:129–150.

WILKS, IVOR

1971   Asante Policy Towards the Hausa Trade in the Nineteenth Century. In *The Development of Indigenous Trade and Markets in West Africa,* edited by Claude Meillassoux, pp. 124–144. London: Oxford University Press.

1975   *Asante in the Nineteenth Century.* Cambridge: Cambridge University Press.

1979   The Golden Stool and the Elephant Tail: An Essay on Wealth in Asante. *Research in Economic Anthropology* 2:1–36.

WILLIAMS, F. E.

1932   Trading Voyages from the Gulf of Papua. *Oceania* 3:139–166.

WILLIAMS, NANCY

1976   Australian Aboriginal Art at Yirrkala: The Introduction and Development of Marketing. In *Ethnic and Tourist Arts,* edited by Nelson H. H. Graburn, pp. 266–284. Berkeley: University of California Press.

WRIGHT, BONNIE L.

1989   The Power of Articulation. In *The Creativity of Power,* edited by W. Arens and Ivan Karp, pp. 39–57. Washington: Smithsonian Institution Press.

WOLF, ERIC R.

1982   *Europe and the People Without History.* Berkeley: University of California Press.

YOSHINOBU, SHIBA

1983   Sung Foreign Trade: Its Scope and Organization. In *China Among Equals,* edited by Morris Rossabi, pp. 89–115. Berkeley: University of California Press.

Index

www.ingramcontent.com/pod-product-compliance
Ingram Content Group UK Ltd.
Pitfield, Milton Keynes, MK11 3LW, UK
UKHW010305240525
458861UK00002B/239